Zion National Park: Summit Routes

Second Edition
Courtney Purcell

ISBN 978-0692436653

Warning

Hiking, scrambling, climbing and canyoneering are outdoor activities where you may be seriously injured or die! **Read this warning before using this book.**

This book describes a wide variety of adventures, some of which involve considerable risk. Those who pursue the activities in this guidebook should be fully cognizant of these risks and take appropriate steps to minimize them. Some of these steps include:

-**Consult** with other information sources about current conditions and to verify the information in this book;

-**Apply** common sense in regard to current, past and likely future weather conditions, and condition of the environment, as well as your own capabilities to deal with emergencies and unforeseen events;

-**Carry proper equipment**, which may include a map and compass, plenty of water, cold-water and cold-weather protective clothing, and technical equipment, as needed.

The objectives outlined in this book are primarily intended for experienced hikers, scramblers, and climbers who will exercise informed judgment and caution. **Still, the dangers should not be minimalized.**

Pursue adventures in and around Zion National Park that are appropriate to your physical conditioning, experience and skill set. Enjoy the easier routes and objectives first, and gradually work your way toward the harder ones.

-**Class 1 & 2** routes will be fun for most hikers;

-**Class 2+ & 3** routes require greater fitness and more advanced skills, such as assessing natural hazards and taking care of oneself in remote and/or topographically complex locations. These routes carry considerably more risk than class 1 & 2 routes;

-**Class 3+ to Class 5** routes typically require steep, loose and exposed climbing (and downclimbing), sometimes of a sustained nature; potential ropework and specific skills in a challenging and sometimes technical environment. You must be proficient at rappelling and setting anchors in an ever-changing natural landscape. Obtain technical expertise via proper training, as well as appropriate equipment, before venturing onto the more advanced routes in the book.

This book is not an instruction manual. Obtain proper instruction before venturing onto any of these potentially dangerous routes in and around Zion National Park.

The information in this guidebook was compiled over many ascents, and was most likely accurate at the time of publication. However, conditions can change rapidly and the wise explorer expects the unexpected, and is prepared to find or create anchors when necessary, and deal with awkward and unexpected challenges as they are encountered. Where reality and this book disagree, make decisions based on reality.

There are no warranties, expressed or implied, that this guidebook is accurate or that the information contained is reliable. By using this book you assume the risk of descriptive errors and sole responsibility for your safety. Proceed entirely at your own risk. **You are responsible for your own safety.** The author and publisher assume no responsibility for accidents, injury or death incurred as a result of the use or misuse of information contained in this book. Hiking, scrambling and climbing in Zion National Park (and the desert at large) includes inherent risks which no amount of care, caution or expertise can eliminate. The information provided in this book is no substitute for quality topographic maps and a compass, excellent route-finding skills, terrific physical conditioning and good judgment.

About canyoneering:

Although parts of this book talk about canyoneering routes around the peaks, please remember this is not a canyoneering guide or instruction manual. For those interested in peaks requiring approaches and/or descents via technical canyons, I highly recommend you obtain proper training, equipment and appropriate canyoneering-specific experience before utilizing these routes. The canyon environment is especially unforgiving of incompetence. Remember that.

In addition to what you find here, consult with the park (and other sources) about current conditions in any canyons you may be tempted to enter. Recognize that canyons are constantly changing environments that have the ability to kill you when you exercise poor judgment, and the beta you find here is **not** entirely accurate. Tom Jones's *Zion: Canyoneering* guidebook, www.CanyoneeringUSA.com and www.climb-utah.com are good resources for detailed beta.

As in hiking and climbing, bring a map and know how to use it. Figure out where the route goes then use your judgment in the field to make certain you are in the right place.

Clothing and warmth recommendations in this book are for the summer season. **Exercise extreme caution** when descending canyons in the spring, fall or winter, and carry more protection from cold water. Even in summer, cold water can be a problem in many canyons. Hypothermia, technical activity and swimming are a bad combination that can quickly lead to death.

Fixed anchors should be treated with suspicion, and backed up whenever possible. Bolts and drilled pitons can have a short life in the soft sandstone of Zion National Park. They can fail with no outward signs of weakness. Additionally, many bolts are placed by people who have little or no idea of how to do it properly. Canyons are a dynamic environment, and even large chockstones and logs can become unstable and dangerous as anchors. **Be prepared for the route to be different than described.**

Essential gear for canyoneering often includes a helmet, a harness, a rope and a rappel device; plus extra rope, slings, food, water, a headlamp and warm layers, like a windbreaker and fleece jacket, and a drybag to keep it all dry.

Canyoneering Ratings:

The **Canyon Rating System** was developed by the American Canyoneering Association (ACA) as something of a cousin to the Yosemite Decimal System used in hiking and climbing. It provides a basic idea of the difficulties you might expect from the canyon. In the back of the book, I provide ratings for the canyoneering routes mentioned in the book. The ratings reflect typical summer conditions.

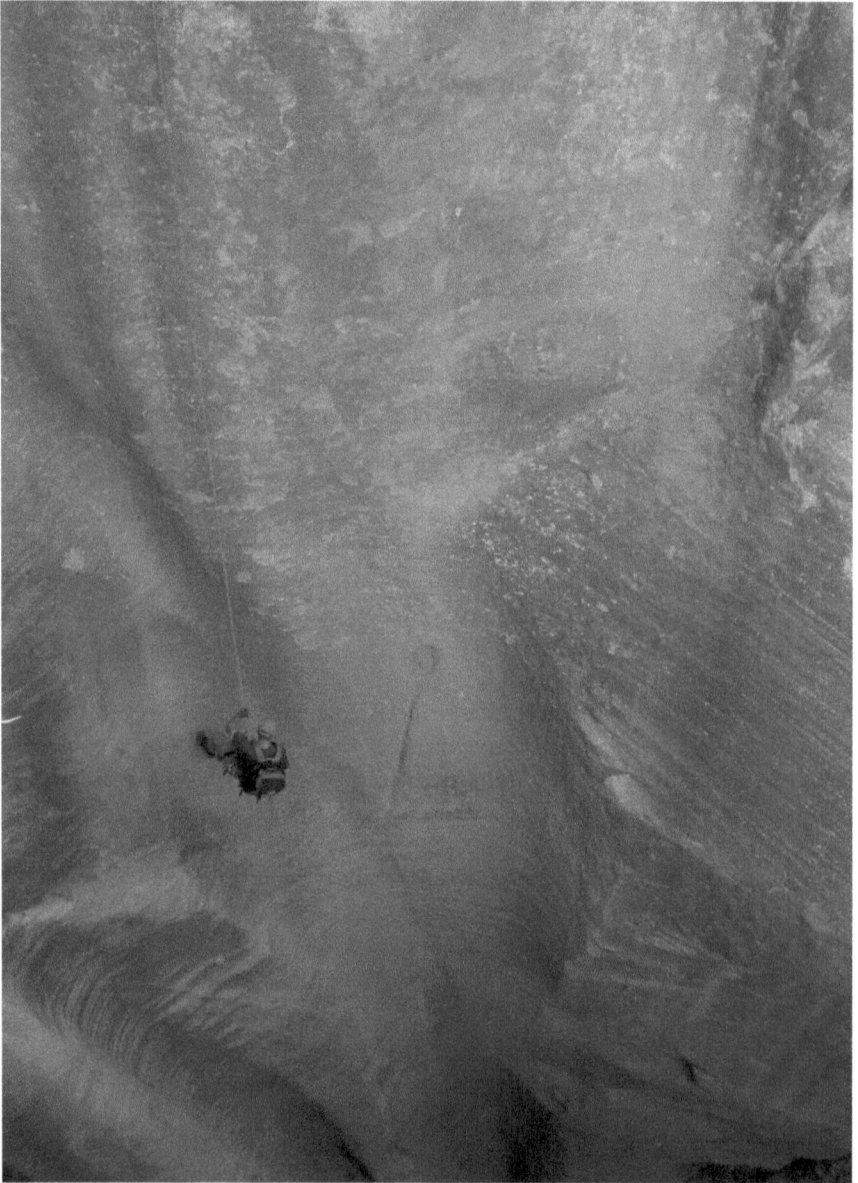

Double-A descending Walker Gulch

-The first part of the rating, such as the "3" in 3BIII, refers to the technicality of the canyon.

-A "1" refers to a non-technical canyon hike. No rope or other technical gear is needed.

-A "2" is a basic canyon, wherein one might need to do some scrambling to work through the occasional obstacle. A rope might be useful for assistance with packs, belays, etc. Up-canyon escape options (without fixed ropes) are available.

-A "3" is an intermediate-level canyon. There may be actual climbing (and/or downclimbing) and/or rappels involved. A rope will be needed and a retreat up-canyon would necessitate fixed ropes.

-A "4" refers to an advanced-level canyon. Multi-pitch rappels, difficult climbing and/or complex rope work can be expected. Natural anchors may be challenging to establish, and unique canyoneering obstacles, such as keeper potholes, may be present.

-The second part the rating, such as the "B" in 3BIII, refers to the water volume and current in the canyon.

-An "A" means that the canyon is typically dry or contains little water. Wading to waist deep may be required.

-A "B" means that there is water in the canyon. The water should have little or no current. Swimming can be expected.

-A "C" means that there is water in the canyon and it moves swiftly. Expect waterfalls…and expect that wet canyon rope techniques will be needed.

-The third part of the rating, such as the "III" in 3BIII, refers to the grade of the canyon, same as the Yosemite Decimal System.

-A "I" means that the canyon should only take a couple hours to do.

-A "II" means that the canyon should take about half a day to complete.

-A "III" means that the canyon can be expected to take most of a day to complete.

-A "IV" means that one should expect a long day. A bivouac may be required.

-A "V" means that the canyon should take about two days to complete.

-A "VI" means that the canyon will take two full days (or more) to complete.

Occasionally, a rating will have an "R" or an "X" as well. The "R" means that the canyon is particularly risky. Beginners, even in the presence of solid leaders, are not appropriate. An "X" means that the canyon is appropriate for experts only. Application of the "R" and "X" vary widely.

As with all hiking, scrambling, climbing and canyoneering, don't bite off more than you can swallow. You have been warned!

Double-A rapping the west cliffs of South Guardian Angel

Contents

Mark Beauchamp on the south ridge of The West Temple

With friends in the backcountry above Stevens Wash

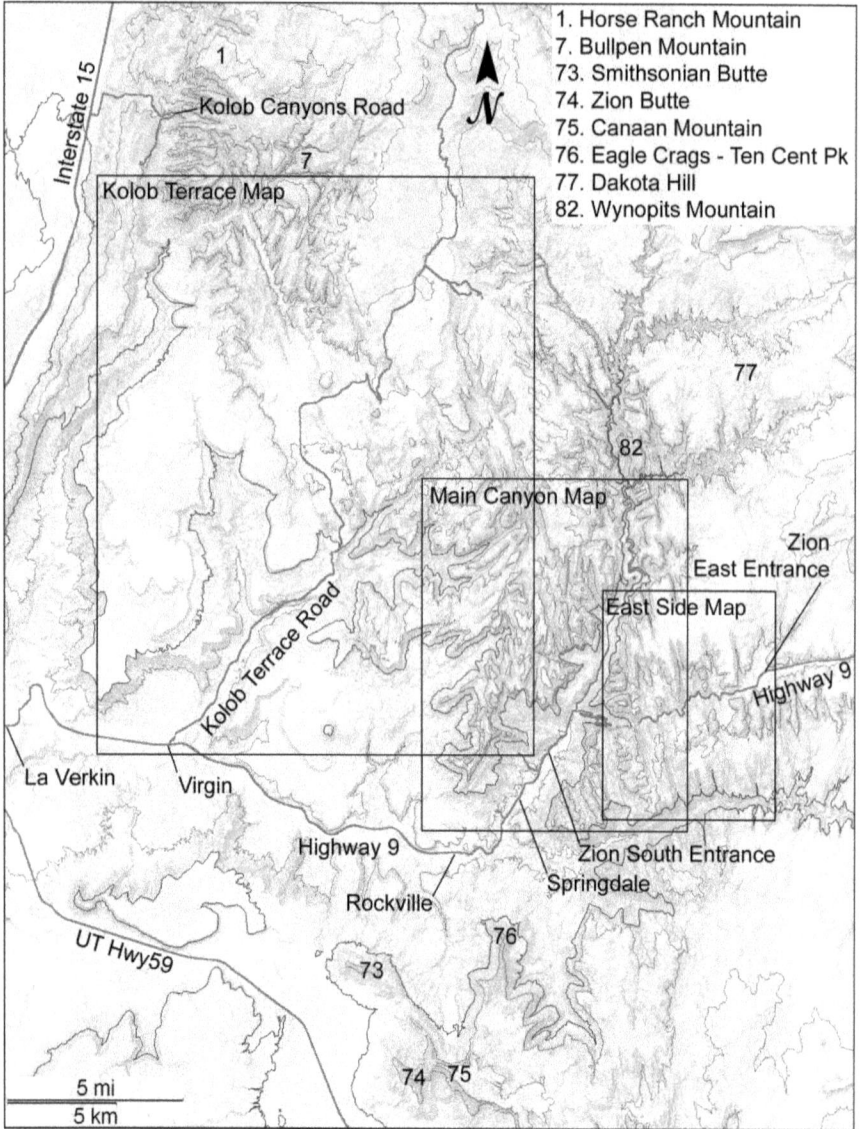

1. Horse Ranch Mountain
7. Bullpen Mountain
73. Smithsonian Butte
74. Zion Butte
75. Canaan Mountain
76. Eagle Crags - Ten Cent Pk
77. Dakota Hill
82. Wynopits Mountain

Overview map of the Zion National Park region. The numbers utilized here are specific only to this map. Note that for the lower portion of Kolob Terrace Road the map depicts the old route from the center of Virgin, prior to the April 2015 opening of the bypass from the east side of Virgin. I recommend the bypass be used.

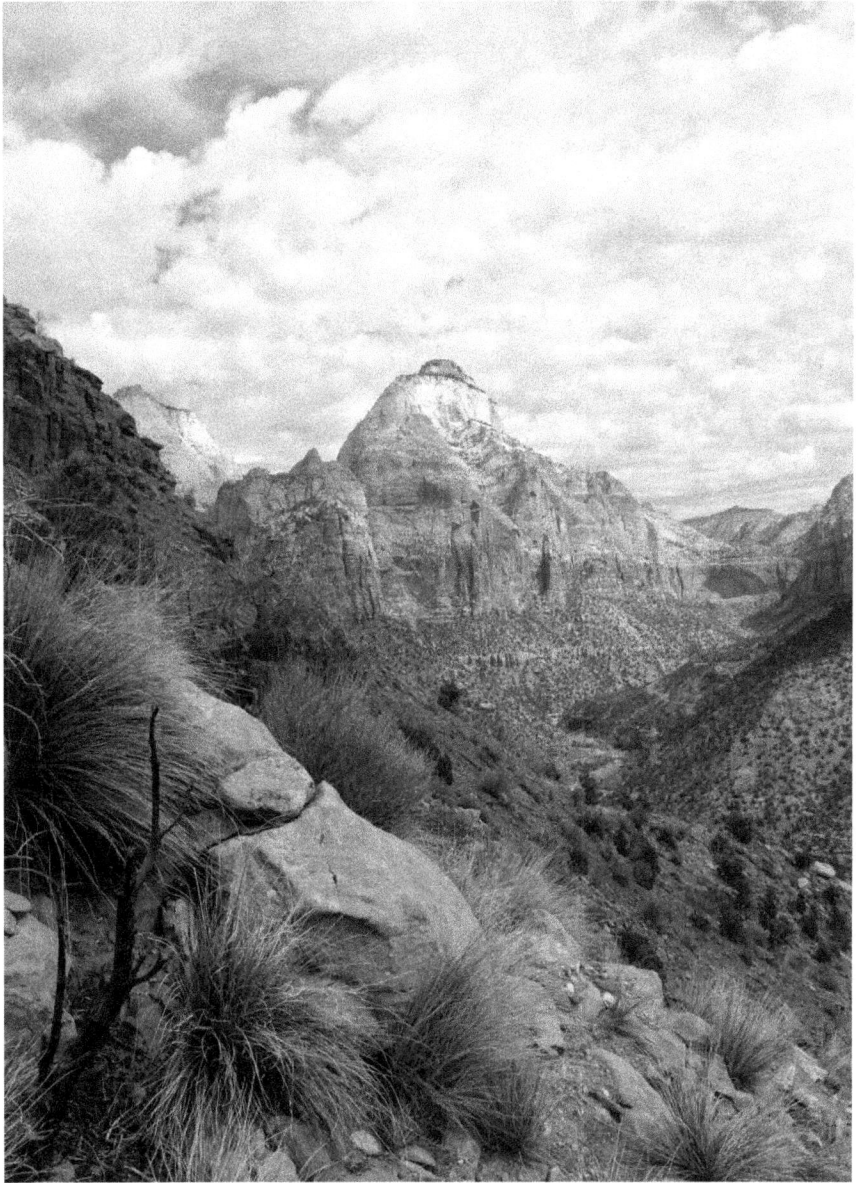
The East Temple from the slopes below Bee Hive Peak

The author and DB approaching the Center of the Universe (Photo by Aron Ralston)

The East Temple, as viewed from the south buttress of Deertrap Mountain

Preface

I love Zion National Park like no other place—it is sacred to me. My explorations here have been vast. The objectives have grown more remote, more obscure, and often more difficult. For the most part, the danger has remained consistent. But my tolerance for risk has diminished. It was nearly five years ago that I climbed what I promised myself was my last "really dangerous" peak in Zion. I promised I would stick to the mellower stuff from here on out. And I have, for the most part. It's hard to justify the risk when you have loved ones at home—and sometimes with you. With no small amount of good fortune, to date I've survived (without even an injury, for that matter) climbs of 182 different summits within the park boundaries. Yet no matter how many I climb, my wishlist of viable (for me) summits only seems to grow longer. More experiences display more opportunities in the mind of a visionary. As of now, eight peaks remain on my to-do list, of which two are among the seven peaks that I've attempted but have thus far been unable to summit.

What does the future hold? I don't know, but I'm excited to find out. For now, I'll focus on the present, and what it holds.

The risk is real. So is the passion.

DB in Langston Canyon

Using This Guide

When to Climb

The prime climbing season in Zion is short, though with appropriate preparation, equipment, knowledge and experience, and cooperative weather and conditions, many of the peaks in this guide can be climbed year-round. But, even with all of those things in your favor, common sense must always prevail.

Let's have a look at the different seasons:

Winter in Zion can be brutally cold, and icy. Higher elevation summits and approaches may be snowed in, such as those approached via the upper Kolob Terrace Road. (The Kolob Terrace Road is typically closed below the Wildcat Trailhead in winter.) Even the bottom of Zion Canyon can see considerable snow and ice during the winter months. And some of the deep, dark canyons that may be used to approach the occasional Zion peak may hold snow and ice patches well into summer.

I've spent very little time climbing the mountains of Zion in winter. It can be dangerous, and it is the worse time of year to climb here. Some low elevation objectives, such as Rockville Bench Peak, are perfectly climbable in winter.

Spring is a fine time to be in Zion, though lingering snow and ice can be problematic in spots. Sandstone slabs covered in snow or ice are not safe. Some canyons may still be choked with snow. The bugs can be annoying, and rattlesnakes become active as the days grow warmer. North faces will likely still hold significant winter snow. I spend March and April of most years here, typically focusing on routes with southern exposures.

Summer in Zion can be brutally hot, often reaching 110 degrees Fahrenheit in lower Zion Canyon. Although the higher summits may be relatively cool in the summer months, expect the lowland desert approaches of many of the peaks to be baking. Water, while easily found in certain parts of the park, can just as easily become impossible to find in others. Carry plenty.

Although it can rain during any season, summer gets a fair amount of the wet stuff. Sandstone should be avoided for 24 to 48 hours after a rain. Wet sandstone is considerably weaker than dry sandstone; it becomes slicker and more easily broken when wet.

Flash floods are also a significant concern in Zion. Rain falling twenty miles away can drain without warning into the wash or canyon you're following toward some mountain peak. Slickrock slabs and faces above washes and canyons can quickly form slippery and treacherous cascades during storms. Check the weather locally, as well as regionally, before heading out. Slot canyons, like those found in Zion National Park, are particularly dangerous during flash flood conditions. Beware of the extent, location and conditions of drainages above where you are visiting.

Like other mountainous places in the region, the summer monsoon season presents other potential problems, such as lightning, heavy rains and wind. High on a mountain, or on a mountain ridge, is not a place to be during a thunderstorm. If you see a storm approaching, retreat. Gambling with lightning is strongly discouraged, and hypothermia associated with cold, windy mountains hit by a storm could result in death.

Although summer is the ideal time to visit the cold, wet canyons of Zion, it is not the ideal season for mountain climbing here. I seldom visit Zion in summer. Higher elevation objectives, such as Horse Ranch Mountain, can be pleasant in summer.

Fall in Zion is perfection, with November being my favorite month for mountaineering in the park. The days are still longish, the weather tends to be stable, the bugs are gone, and the temperatures (super-chilly at night and early in the morning, and gorgeous during the day) are fine.

Ratings

Ratings in this guide are based on the Yosemite Decimal System (YDS). Although YDS ratings are somewhat subjective, your experience should translate to something like this:

Technical Class:

> **Class 1** – a trail or cross-country route that requires nothing more technical than "easy" walking;
>
> **Class 2** – a rough cross-country route that requires the occasional use of hands for balance or simple negotiation;
>
> **Class 3** – scrambling. All four limbs are used, not just for balance, but for regress on the route. The terrain will frequently be steep, though the hand and footholds should be large and apparent. Complex route-finding may be required to find the third class route;
>
> **Class 4** – the ground between scrambling and actual climbing. Expect steep terrain with ample, though possibly small, hand and footholds.
>
> **Class 5** – technical rock climbing. A rope and gear to protect the route in the event of a fall are recommended.
>
> Fifth class is broken down further from 5.0, 5.1, 5.2...5.9, 5.10, etc. to well beyond anything covered in this book. Generally speaking, the higher the number beyond the decimal point, the steeper the climbing and the smaller the holds.

Ram and DB enjoying some hyper-exposed class 2 scrambling
on the southwest ridge route to North Guardian Angel

Risk Rating:

On an occasion or two, you might see a letter, such as PG, R or X, after a 5th class rating. Corresponding to movie ratings, the "higher" the letter, the more "adult" the route: the greater the potential for serious injury or death in the event of a fall due to lack of secure protection possibilities. The nature of the routes in this book is that falls are always a bad idea and almost all routes could be considered R or X.

DB scrambles through a short class 2 stretch on the route to Zion Butte. We brought along a rope, as we didn't know what to expect on the previously un-beta'd route. Smithsonian Butte is in the background.

How YDS is Applied in This Book:

The YDS rating of a route reflects the most technically difficult portion of the route. For example, if a route is essentially a walking trail, but it happens to have a ten-foot section of class 3 scrambling at one point along the way, the route will be rated as being class 3. Routes rated as class 4 might entail only a short section of 4th class scrambling on good rock; while another route of the same rating may be considerably more serious, with sustained, exposed, loose 4th class terrain to be negotiated. Thoroughly read the entire route description to know what you're getting into.

Convoluted, maze-like terrain southeast of North Guardian Angel

If I rate something as, say, class 2+ (or sometimes "class 2-3"), I mean that the route is primarily class 2 with perhaps a spattering of relatively short sections of class 3. Routes with a "+" after them may also suggest that while some may feel the route is "merely" class 4 others may rate the route as "easy" 5th class (5.0 or 5.1). Again, YDS ratings are somewhat subjective.

A rope and protective gear are recommended for 5th class routes in this book. They are also recommended for those folks uncomfortable with routes of a technically "easier" (sub-5th class) nature. While traditional protective gear (such as nuts and cams) is appropriate for some of the routes described in this book, the vast majority of the "technical" terrain I describe is most effectively protected by slinging bushes and trees. Do not mistake some of these smaller bushes and trees for being "bomb-proof" anchors— they can be sketchy...and the only things available.

Most of the class 5 routes herein feature only a short amount of 5th class climbing. I sometimes refer to a short 5th class section of a route as a "scramble," meaning that I did not rope up or protect that section of the route. I do not intend to mislead or "sandbag" – I simply mean that I felt that the section of the route in question was straightforward enough that I could simply "scramble up" it without belaying and protection. YOU, however, may want to protect the same section that I or someone else climbed without protection. Not all fifth class sections have protection available. This is traditional climbing where "the leader shall not fall" has real meaning.

On the flipside, stronger climbers than I may "scramble" a difficult section that I "climbed" with a rope and protection. Factors such as the quality of the rock and the protection available, the length and difficulty of the climbing section, and the exposure (and the climber's experience and abilities), among others, *must* be taken into consideration when deciding whether or not to "rope up." In other words, make your own informed decision of when to use a rope.

Route Descriptions

Some of the mountains have quotation marks around their names. Those peaks do not have official USGS names. In many cases, a local name exists but is not recognized by the USGS; or in some cases, a name me or my partners came up with has been applied. Take 'em or leave 'em. While I certainly find unnamed peaks mysterious and appealing, I also feel naming a peak adds to its character and allows it to stick in the memory a bit more firmly. Next to each peak name I provide the peak's approximate elevation.

The RT (roundtrip) mileage and elevation given for each peak reflects only a rough estimate. Do not expect exact numbers.

The Time Required for each peak suggests the number of hours I would expect the average skilled, small party to take to complete the roundtrip route.

I also provide the latitude and longitude as approximate coordinates for each summit. All coordinates are in WGS 84.

First ascent (FA) and first known ascent (FKA) information is given based on available information. It is not necessarily presuming a peak was previously unclimbed; it is recognized that unrecorded ascents by Native Americans, early explorers, and/or other elusive souls who managed to climb these heinous summits without leaving a trace or record are possible. In an area with so little documented peak climbing history, I've tried to document what little we *do* know. If I failed to give credit to someone who came first, it's not because I intended to steal their thunder—it's because I didn't know about it.

The etymology section for each peak is an attempt to record the history of the peak's name. I am very appreciative of Steve Allen's incredible book, *Utah's Canyon Country Place Names, Volume 1 & 2*, for filling in so many of the blanks in etymology. This book is highly recommended for the canyon country enthusiast.

Like in my other guidebook, *Rambles & Scrambles: A Peakbagging Guide to the Desert Southwest*, I've given a subjective Star Rating for the overall quality of each peak. The Star Ratings go like this:

**** - A classic
*** - Very good
** - Good
* - Eh, 'twas alright

Many of the peaks in this book can be approached via more than one trailhead. Here, I've coupled each peak with the trailhead that would seem to be the most logical.

I have made every reasonable effort to provide detailed and accurate first-hand route information. But I also enjoy the art of route-finding as a part of the joy of mountain climbing. Rather than hold one's hand all the way to the mountaintop, I try to get one started and then point out helpful things one might encounter along the way. I'm trying to share with you what is possible. Those routes that I thought required more-detailed information get it. In keeping with that ethic, I have provided route descriptions only for routes of which I have personal knowledge. In some cases, variations or alternative routes I've not done may be mentioned (and attributed to someone other than me).

Most of the routes described in this book were pieced together, sometimes many years ago, over the course of my explorations of the park. Zion beta was hard to come by during the early years of my explorations, and as such, I did not necessarily find the easiest or most efficient way to climb a peak. Since that time, especially since the publication of the first edition of this book, others have followed, leaving cairns, use trails, and other signs of visitation along paths that may (or may not) have followed mine. This phenomenon may explain why a route I describe may not correspond with visual evidence (such as those cairns, use trails, etc.) a user may see in the backcountry.

Well into the process of writing the first edition of this book, I decided to occasionally incorporate a feature I referred to as *According to Ram…* I've since extended the use of the *According to…* feature to whenever others volunteered useful or alternative information. Found in the beta sections of specific mountains throughout the text, the *According to…* sections feature anecdotes and/or beta that Steve Ramras (the sage-like Zion explorer of decades past and present), Andy Archibald (one of my most reliable and competent Zion partners), Bob Sihler, and others, saw fit to share with me in hopes of providing more information (or at least a good laugh) to the users of this book. Although the first-hand information provided is that person's, the wording is (usually) largely mine. I apologize for any misinterpretation that may have come out of the transition from their mouth to my text. The information is provided to offer ideas to intrepid explorers looking to extend their Zion endeavors, or to give pleasure to those who enjoy simple amusement.

Route lines depicted on some of the photographs are approximate.

I sometimes make mention of "prominence." This is a new-ish area of interest in the peakbagging world. A summit's prominence is the number of feet it rises from the saddle between it and the closest higher neighbor.

Stuff to Bring

Some things should be a standard part of your outdoor packing list. Most of us don't always carry "The 10 Essentials"…but we should.

Things like reliable footwear (good hiking boots and/or approach shoes), an extra layer (such as a windbreaker), sunscreen and a hat, and the like, should always be brought. The colder seasons may require extra layers, and in higher elevations and/or snowy/icy environs, often times snowshoes, crampons, and an ice axe.

Climbing in the desert, bring plenty of water. Though water can occasionally be found in Zion National Park, you can't always count on it. Carry your own water for the day. Water found in the field should be treated or filtered before consumption. Giardia = less time in the mountains.

Topographical maps and a compass (and the knowledge of how to use them) are two important tools of desert and mountain travel. GPS units help, but do not replace a map. Even the most "friendly" of terrains can occasionally have good route-finders scratching their heads in wonder. Zion is not a good place to get lost—the terrain tends to be unforgiving.

Even with a topo map, Zion will frequently surprise the new visitor with troublesome cliffs and impassable canyons. Have a map but be prepared for surprises. The National Geographic *Trails Illustrated #214* Topographic Map (not to be confused with the *Trails Illustrated #214* Outdoor Recreation Map) has worked well for me over the years, though specific maps for the respective areas one is exploring are also recommended. USGS 1:25,000 maps have more detail than the *Trails Illustrated* park maps.

And speaking more of cliffs and canyons: don't climb up, or go down, steep terrain, such as slot canyons, that one cannot retrace steps in…unless you know what lies ahead and are prepared to negotiate it.

Lastly, some basic assumptions have been made. When I speak of ropes, protection, slings, and whatnot, folks should already know what to do with them…and should have (or at minimum, should be with someone who has) appropriate experience with the stuff. An "easy" 5th class (technical) route, such as the southwest face of Twin Brothers (YDS 5.3), is not the appropriate place for a group of newbies to "try using a rope" for the first time. Technical routes are for people with technical skills and experience.

My suggestions for "Stuff to Bring" are not the end-all be-all, but simply suggestions. Make your own decisions on what you will or will not bring.

Native American Artifacts

The Anasazi Indians lived in the area currently known as Zion National Park for about 2,000 years. The Paiute Indians have been in the same area for about 800 years. During this time, both left behind petroglyphs and pictographs. Petroglyphs, which are much more commonly found than pictographs, are designs (often of humans or animals) carved into the soft sandstone found around the park. Pictographs, on the other hand, were painted on the rocks using natural pigments. Unfortunately, time and the elements have washed away most of the pictograph sites in the park, though a few can still be found.

Zion National Park hosts twenty-six known prehistoric sites containing petroglyphs, pictographs, arrowheads, abandoned cliff houses, and pottery. Some of those sites are on and around the mountains I talk about. My hope is that those who love the mountains will also love and appreciate Native American culture and history. Please, if you are fortunate enough to stumble across artifacts, take only pictures. Even a simple touch can damage an ancient site. Leave artifacts for others to enjoy. Besides, it's a crime to take anything.

Other Stuff

-Pack it in/pack it out. In other words, leave nothing in the mountain but footprints. Trash, human waste, etc. should be taken out of the mountains with you. It's not pleasant, but you gotta do it. Carry Restop poop bags and use them. Poop breaks down very slowly in the dry desert environment.

Please practice Leave No Trace ethics.

-When looking for a place to camp, stay well away from desert springs and watering holes. Your presence prevents wildlife from accessing these precious spots.

-Don't harass the critters. Don't feed 'em.

-Hiking in wash bottoms and on durable surfaces (rocks and outcroppings), whenever possible, to minimize impact to soils and vegetation is strongly encouraged. Once the desert crust is broken, soil is exposed to erosive factors. And when sensitive soils (like gypsum and cryptobiotic soils) are trampled, they take a long time to heal.

-Rockfall is an inherent hazard in climbing mountains. I've seen rocks the size of small cars break loose in the mornings and fall hundreds of feet down a mountain slope or face or chute—not something you want to be struck by while climbing through or under that slope or face or chute. You and your partners are another common source of rockfall. Getting struck by even a small rock falling from hundreds of feet above could be disastrous. Helmets are always a good idea, and extreme care should always be taken to prevent knocking rocks down on those climbing below you.

-In addition to my earlier mention of the brittle, slick quality of wet sandstone in Zion, it cannot be overemphasized that, unlike the high quality sandstone of Las Vegas's Red Rock Canyon, Zion's sandstone is typically quite weak, even in the driest of conditions. Brittle, loose, unreliable rock should be anticipated as the norm. For this reason, routes like the largely unprotectable YDS 5.3 southwest face route on Twin Brothers are serious. There's a price to be paid for all of the park's glorious scenery. Treat the terrain with respect. Backcountry rescue in Zion can be a long time coming.

   Test and retest every hold before committing to it…and still don't trust it. Exercise extreme caution.

-The mountains of Zion are not intended for novices—they can be extremely dangerous. With common sense, experience, proper equipment, and the like, hiking, scrambling, climbing and canyoneering with care, caution and respect in Zion can give up a life-changing experience...for the positive. It is one of my favorite places in the world.

The Geographic Breakdown

In this guide, I've broken down the objectives into five areas of the park. They are as follows:

-Kolob Canyons refers to the lesser-visited portion of the park accessed directly off I-15 between St. George and Cedar City, Utah;
-Kolob Terrace refers to that high, spectacular area located off the Kolob Terrace Road outside of Virgin, Utah;
-Zion Canyon refers to, well, Zion Canyon itself;
-East Side refers to the sandstone-laden area of the park between Zion Canyon and Mount Carmel Junction, Utah. It is accessed off of UT-9, the Zion-Mt. Carmel Highway;
-Scattered refers to objectives that don't quite fit into the other areas already described.

Double-A in Goblin Gulch

Zion National Park

From scrub desert to pine forest, baking summer heat to winter snow and ice, Zion National Park is unquestionably one of the most interesting and beautiful places in the United States, if not the world. It reminds one of a Yosemite of sandstone. Utah's most visited park and the eighth most visited national park in the United States, Zion is loaded with slot canyons; high imposing vertical walls (such as on The West Temple, whose 2,200 foot east face might be the highest vertical sandstone wall in the world); lush hanging gardens; quiet, hidden pools of water; waterfalls; the world famous Zion Narrows, through which the Virgin River passes as it drops over its long coarse nine times faster than the Colorado River; and countless other curiosities.

A Brief History

Nineteenth-century Mormon settlers were struck by the awesome beauty of the canyon and named it "Zion" after the "City of God" described in the Old Testament. When Brigham Young traveled to the canyon from Salt Lake City, he agreed with the settlers' assessment of the canyon as a "natural temple of God" but would not permit them to call an earthly place "Zion." Instead, they simply referred to the canyon as "not Zion" or "Little Zion."

In 1908 ranches applied for a survey of land near "Little Zion." The survey resulted in a new monument being proclaimed in 1909. The monument was given the Paiute name Mukuntuweap, which means "straight canyon." In 1917 lodging was built in the canyon and members of the American Civic Association asked President Wilson to change the monument's name to Zion Canyon. The same year, the monument was expanded from 5,840 acres to 76,800 acres, and the name Zion Canyon didn't seem appropriate. Instead, in 1918 the President changed the monument's name to Zion National Monument. Only a year later, the monument became Utah's first national park and the name was changed to Zion National Park.

In 1930 the Zion-Mt. Carmel Highway was completed. A continuation of Utah highway 9, on July 4th of that year the Zion-Mt. Carmel Tunnel was dedicated. The 1.1 mile tunnel, which burrows its way through the park's Navajo sandstone, and its attached highway (both among the most amazing portions of highway to be found in Utah), opened up the park's east side, giving easier access to and from Bryce Canyon and Grand Canyon. It also greatly increased the park's visitation. The highway is open year-round.

Today the park is comprised of more than 147,000 acres and ranges in elevation from 3,700 to 8,726 feet above sea level.

highpoint a short distance away to the southwest. Enjoy the terrific views from the top.

On the summit of Tabernacle Dome

Tabernacle Dome Trailhead

From the UT-9/Kolob Terrace Road junction, follow the paved Kolob Terrace Road for 9.4 miles and park on the shoulder in either of a couple of narrow pull-outs on the west-northwest side of Tabernacle Dome.

The peaks in this subsection are roughly arranged from shortest-hike-from-the-trailhead to longest-hike-from-the-trailhead.

"Tinaja Knoll" (6,360)

Tinaja Knoll is a very nice, relaxing half-day peak with great views of Lee Valley, the Guardian Angels and Cave Knoll, immediately to the north. Views from the summit of the highest hoodoo are sublime.

Of particular interest is the large tinaja just below the top. One warm spring morning, we spent an hour lounging next to the placid waters. It would be hard to do so without nodding off for a quick summit nap—I think I've done just that.

The route-finding on this fun, little crag is one of the joys of time spent with it. Fifty feet of webbing is recommended for the scramble up the exposed highpoint hoodoo.

This sweet tinaja is encountered just below the summit of Tinaja Knoll.

RT Mileage: 2-3
RT Elevation Gain: 800'
Time Required: 2-3 hours
Latitude: +37.3158
Longitude: -113.0969
FA: Unknown; we found no signs of prior visitation on the summit.
Etymology: There's a large tinaja—water-filled on each of our visits—just below the summit hoodoo. The sprawling tinaja was the first I'd come across in Zion. That's an interesting phenomenon when you consider that other slickrock-laden places, like Red Rock Canyon National Conservation Area in nearby Las Vegas, boasts numerous such basins. What a pleasant surprise to encounter one here!
Star Rating: ***

Getting to the Mountain:
Although I included this peak in the Tabernacle Dome Trailhead subsection, it's advantageous to continue north on Kolob Terrace Road for less than one mile, to a point east of Lambs Knoll.

Tinaja Knoll will be the curious slickrock and hoodoo'd feature stretched out along the east side of the road.

Leaving the slickrock and hoodoo wonderland of Tinaja Knoll

Route: From the Southwest (class 3)

From Kolob Terrace Road, hike up a dirt road for a couple hundred yards then cut northeast up a wash to the base of the peak. Sniffing around, locate a shallow class 2-3 gully breaking through the cliffs well south of the summit. Scramble up the gully then exit left near the top and start meandering north toward the final summit hoodoo. This is delightful terrain. The final hoodoo is scrambled on its west side.

Tabernacle Dome (6,451)

While not particularly known for its domes, Zion National Park does hold a striking one—Tabernacle Dome. Rounded and plump on all sides, anyone heading up Kolob Terrace Road toward the Subway or the Guardian Angels has had Tabernacle Dome catch their eye.

With a super-short approach, enjoyable and exposed climbing and scrambling, and incredible scenery, Tabernacle Dome is a worthy objective.

RT Mileage: 1
RT Elevation Gain: 700'
Time required: 2-5 hours
Latitude: +37.2998
Longitude: -113.0933

FA: Unknown
Etymology: Named by early Mormon ranchers for its similar appearance to the dome of the Mormon Tabernacle in Salt Lake City.
Star Rating: ****

Carrie Toelle climbing Tabernacle Dome

Route: Northwest Ridge (YDS 5.2)

From the parking spot just north of the main (north) entrance to True North Villa (a bed & breakfast), cross Grapevine Wash to the east, go over a rise, and hike to the northwestern base of Tabernacle Dome. From the northwesternmost toe of the mountain, continue east up the drainage until it forks. Follow the small right fork about 40 feet and then make a hard right to a cleft in which there is a log on the left wall. This is the start of the route.

Head up this amazing, scrambly weakness until you pick up a use trail and cairns leading toward a small bowl with a saddle at the top. Anticipate a spot of class 4 scrambling down a funky, 7-foot wall shortly before getting to this point. From the saddle, drop down the back side for 20 feet then cut left around a prominent crag and scramble up dirty class 3 slabs to a notch near the base of the northwest ridge.

Scramble up the delightful, slabby northwest ridge (YDS 5.2) for 250 feet to easier terrain. A couple of bushes can be slung for protection, and you'll past an established rappel station (a bush) near the top of the ridge. Class 2-3 scrambling up broken terrain leads to the highpoint.

Two 60m ropes are recommended for the descent.

This is a key chute (just above ground level) needed to access the upper portion of the optimal route up Tabernacle Dome. The chute is commonly accessed through an invisible gap just left of the hoodoo on the right, though it can also be approached from the photographer's position. (Photo by Andy Archibald)

Alternative Descent Route:

Friends of mine pieced together a classic alternative descent route down the southeast face of the dome. With two 60m ropes, one can wander down glorious slickrock southeast from the summit until a class 3 groove is picked up. The groove conveniently allows a reasonable way to descend otherwise steep slabs to a strong tree above the plateau level at the southeastern base of the dome. A 160-foot rappel from the tree leads to the plateau level.

From the plateau level, you can hike south-southwest across highly varied and complex terrain toward a significant number of minor, confusing drainages that eventually breach the western cliffs of the plateau south of Tabernacle Dome. Care must be taken to select an appropriate drainage to descend, as rappel lengths and anchor challenges vary greatly. I have descended two different drainages (each with two 60m ropes being adequate).

This is complex turf, so be careful.

Lambs Knoll Trailhead

From the UT-9/Kolob Terrace Road junction, follow the paved Kolob Terrace Road for about 10.4 miles to a cattle guard at the park boundary, just north of Lambs Knoll. A dirt road veers off to the left and immediately forks. Follow the left fork 0.25 mile to its end at a cul-de-sac.

The peaks in this subsection are roughly arranged from shortest-hike-from-the-trailhead to longest-hike-from-the-trailhead.

"Bobbie Knoll" (6,217)

This small volcanic dome sits closely north-northwest of Lambs Knoll on BLM land near the park boundary. Although it can be hiked from any direction, the west slope, while brushy and not-great, affords a decent (albeit short) wilderness experience.

RT Mileage: 1
RT Elevation Gain: 200'
Time Required: 30-60 minutes
Latitude: +37.3095
Longitude: -113.1134
FA: Unknown
Etymology: This minor peak was named for the recently deceased wife of a longtime friend of mine.
Star Rating: *

Getting to the Mountain:

Follow the driving directions given to the cattle guard at the park boundary. Turn left here onto the dirt road, and immediately take the right fork, which you'll follow around to the west side of the peak to some parking spots amongst a nice pinyon-juniper grove.

Route: West Slope (class 1)

Hike the brushy slope to the treed summit.

Lambs Knoll (6,353)

A delightful, short scramble to a summit with excellent views of this portion of the park, Lambs Knoll offers a lot of bang for the buck.

Lambs Knoll straddles the park boundary. Its 6,310-foot northeast summit hugs the boundary itself, while the higher 6,353-foot southwest summit is just outside the park.

The Lambs Knoll massif is very popular with the many local canyon guiding outfits, who take clients through the several interesting, short slots on the mountain.

Early morning on the summit of Lambs Knoll. (Photo taken by a friend)

RT Mileage: 1
RT Elevation Gain: 500'
Time Required: 2-3 hours
Latitude: +37.3048
Longitude: -113.1107
FA: Unknown
Etymology: According to Steve Allen's *Utah's Canyon Country Place Names, Volume 1*, the peak was named for Edwin Lamb, who came to Virgin in 1862.
Star Rating: **

Route: North Face (class 3)

From the cul-de-sac, follow a well-used trail to the base of the mountain. The trail forks near the base. Follow either fork (class 2-3) about halfway up the mountain, to near the top of a fun and funky mini-slot system. From this area, work generally south through some tedious brush to the base of the main summit crag.

Approach the summit on its east side, where two options present themselves:

1) Scramble up class 3 slabs to gain the south face of the crag then head to the top; or

2) Climb a 15-foot, north-trending crack (class 4) on the east side of the crag that leads to a 7-foot off-width (class 4) on your left. From the top of the off-width, a final class 4 move puts you on the summit.

The south face of Cave Valley Crag

For the descent, you can retrace your steps, or if you're armed with a 60m rope and rappelling equipment, descend one of the north-draining slots mentioned earlier. There are many variations, each of them short and with established anchors. The slots end in a final corridor which dumps you out on the trail. Follow the trail to the right and out to your vehicle.

"North Moqui" (6,042)

This enjoyable little summit has fun scrambling on the summit block and excellent views of Moqui Peak to the southeast and Lambs Knoll to the north-northwest.

While you're in the area, it's worth taking the time to wander out to an excellent viewpoint on the edge of the cliffs at the northwest base of North Moqui. A trail from the nearby True North villa leads to the overlook.

RT Mileage: 1
RT Elevation Gain: 300'
Time Required: 1-2 hours

Latitude: +37.2952
Longitude: -113.1061
FA: Unknown
Etymology: This is the prominent north summit of the Moqui Peak massif.
Star Rating: **

DB traversing Lambs Ledge on the return from North Moqui

Route: North Gully (class 4)

From either the Tabernacle Dome Trailhead or the Lambs Knoll Trailhead, take Kolob Terrace Road to a point east of Lambs Knoll. From here, hike toward an obvious vegetated gully of the north face of North Moqui. Ascend the dirty gully (class 3) to its head then cut left to the highpoint crag, which is climbed (class 4) on its north side.

As an alternative approach to or return for North Moqui, one can follow a wide ledge along the western base of Lambs Knoll to connect North Moqui with the starting point for Bobbie Knoll. Although this is not a great route, there is a way cool, improbable 80' narrow and exposed ledge ("Lambs Ledge") one must traverse along the way.

"Cave Valley Crag" (6,380)

This minor peak (280' of prominence) lies on BLM land west of Kolob Terrace Road and slightly northwest of Cave Knoll.

RT Mileage: 4
RT Elevation Gain: 800'
Time Required: 2-3 hours
Latitude: +37.3253
Longitude: -113.1308
FA: Unknown
Etymology: N/A
Star Rating: **

Getting to the Mountain:

Follow the driving directions given for Bobbie Knoll to the west side of that mountain.

Route: Southeast Slope (class 3)

PRIVATE PROPERTY: There may be private property along the way to or from this peak. Consult a reliable map prior to starting out. I strongly discourage folks from crossing private property without permission from the owners.

Hike generally northwest across sometimes brushy desert toward the base of the peak. Some of the clusters of lesser crags passed along the way are fun to explore, with neat slots and burly summit blocks. Once the base of the peak is reached, hike easy slopes northwest then cut left to reach a gully leading to the final summit block, which is surmounted by a delicate class 3 scramble.

For the return, people have been known to drop east from the mountain to a dirt road that leads directly out to Kolob Terrace Road.

Red Butte Trailhead

From the UT-9/Kolob Terrace Road junction, follow the paved Kolob Terrace Road for 12.0 miles to a dirt road on the left. The dirt road is along a rise on Kolob Terrace Road, on the west side of Spendlove Knoll. Park on the shoulder at the dirt road, or follow the 4WD (sandy) dirt road north and then northwest for a couple of miles (going left at a prominent fork) to near its end below the east face of Red Butte.

The peaks in this subsection are roughly arranged from shortest-hike-from-the-trailhead to longest-hike-from-the-trailhead.

An unusual view of Red Butte

"Burnt Hill" (6,852)

One of the few backcountry peaks of Zion National Park that can be gained via a "trail," Burnt Hill offers a lovely wilderness stroll to a small peak with terrific and seldom seen views of Red Butte, Burnt Mountain, Timber Top Mountain and Langston Mountain.

RT Mileage: 9 (from the pavement)
RT Elevation Gain: 900'
Time required: 2-3 hours
Latitude: +37.3798
Longitude: -113.1455

FA: Unknown
Etymology: Nothing fancy here. It's a hill on the ridge running southeast from Burnt Mountain.
Star Rating: *

Route: South Trail (class 2)

From the eastern base of Red Butte, hike north up the road into the shallow canyon. Near the mellow head of the canyon, hang a left to gain the ridge crest and follow a good game trail north to the summit.

"South Burnt Point" (6,840)

This minor bump of little significance gives one a convenient excuse to visit an easily accessible but seldom-visited portion of the park. There are many cool rock features around here, and the views tend to be righteous.

Burnt Mountain from the summit of Stapley Point

RT Mileage: 10 (from Kolob Terrace Road)
RT Elevation Gain: 900'
Time Required: 3 hours
Latitude: +37.3904
Longitude: -113.1497
FA: Unknown

Etymology: This minor point is just south of Burnt Mountain.
Star Rating: **

Route: South Ridge (class 2)

Follow the directions given for Burnt Hill to the summit of that peak. From there, head down the north slope and meander north to the summit of South Burnt Point. The going is pleasant, mellow, and delightfully scenic.

Stapley Point (6,002)

Stapley Point is slightly northwest of Red Butte and southwest of Burnt Mountain. Although it is easily accessed, it gets little visitation. It's a wonderful spot.

Stapley Point has a 42' of prominence.

RT Mileage: 11 (from Kolob Terrace Road)
RT Elevation Gain: 1,000'
Time Required: 4 hours
Latitude: +37.3841
Longitude: -113.1634
FKA: Courtney Purcell (November 11, 2010)
Etymology: Named for the Stapley family, which moved to Toquerville in the late 1850s
Star Rating: ***

Route: East Ridge (class 2)

Follow the directions given for South Burnt Point to just before the summit of that peak. From there, angle slightly southwest and scramble down to the east ridge of Stapley Point. Follow the ridge, where you'll encounter an awesome collection of weird hoodoos and alcoves and strange rock formations during the final 200 yards leading to the obvious, rounded summit.

Red Butte (7,410)

Located on BLM land just outside of the park, Red Butte is one of the most striking peaks in the vicinity of Zion. A brilliant red, thumb-like spire, the feature is virtually impossible to miss while driving the Kolob Terrace Road toward Kolob Reservoir. Seen by thousands of tourists, Subway hikers and fishermen during the summer, how many have taken the time to wander up the thing? Not many, though the numbers have increased since the publication of the first edition of this guidebook.

Although seldom seen from this vantage point, the peak takes on a very interesting appearance when viewed from peaks to the east and northeast.

RT Mileage: 7 (from the pavement)
RT Elevation Gain: 1,400'
Time Required: 5-7 hours
Latitude: +37.3624
Longitude: -113.1464
FA: Unknown
Etymology: The brilliant red of the thumb-like butte speaks for itself.
Star Rating: ****

Red Butte, as seen from Firepit Knoll to the southeast

Getting to the Mountain:

Before you leave the pavement, take a few minutes to look for possible routes up the mountain. The terrain is more interesting than one might guess. I'll give you a couple of hints:

-Looking at the south and southeast face of the main, thumb-like feature, note a zig-zagging series of vegetated ledges, ramps and chutes. This is the way we took to gain the upper mountain, though other options exist;

-On the upper mountain, make out a crack/chimney system on the southeast face just below the summit. That's the route's crux;

-There's a long ramp (hidden from view on the approach) that can be followed from near the southwest base of the feature directly to the base of the crux;

-Whether by following our approach or finding your own, you'll need to find the hidden ramp (which our approach picks up near its head) and make your way to the base of the crux.

DB climbs the final pitch on Red Butte. Like most of the class 5 peaks in Zion National Park, the vast majority of this route is a hike and scramble, though a small bit—two short pitches, in this case—of technical climbing is required to reach the summit.

Route: South Ramp (YDS 5.6)

Near the southern end of Red Butte, gain the flattish, vegetated ground that comprises the convoluted south ridge of Red Butte. We worked through cliff bands to do so. Fortunately, a number of options are available, such as a weakness found near the southeast face of the feature. Alternatively, it seems you may be able to steer clockwise around the southern tip of the cliffs to gain easier access from the feature's southwest side.

Working through these initial difficulties, head north over brushy but gentle terrain until you reach the steepening terrain of Red Butte proper. Once there, either work your way through the zig-zagging series of vegetated chutes, ramps and ledges mentioned earlier (if you encounter more than three or four class 4-5 moves through the entire thing, you've lost the route we used) to gain the hidden ramp leading to the base of the crux, or find a way to pick up the ramp from its bottom near the southwest base of the mountain. The ramp ends at a notch looking down on the steep east/northeast face of the feature.

Gaining the top of the ramp just before the notch, note a short (10-foot) face leading left past a bush and into a chimney. This is the start of the route's crux pitch (YDS 5.6).

Climb the face, angle left, get into the chimney and climb up about 30 feet to a single bolt belay at a narrow platform. From the belay, step up and left and climb through the last 15 feet of difficulties (YDS 5.2) leading to class 3 terrain just below the summit. You should find an established belay from a large bush just below the top.

For the descent, you may find the top rappel down to the single bolt belay a touch tricky, with the high probability of a pendulum as you approach the bolt. Consider clipping into the bolt as soon as you can before finishing the rappel down to the platform. Rope pull could also be an issue. For the next rappel, head directly down the face rather than down the chimney you climbed up. It is a nice rappel with an easy pull.

A 60m rope, set of cams, and rock shoes are recommended.

"East Neagle" (6,920)

There are certain places in Zion National Park where a sacred, spiritual energy seems to flow more noticeably than elsewhere. One of these places, at the base of the southeast face of Aires Butte, is known as the Center of the Universe. Another of these is at the slickrock saddle of East Neagle and Burnt Mountain, above the head of the main fork of Currant Creek. It is a magical spot.

The peak itself is a nice place with interesting views of an easily accessed yet uncommonly visited part of the park.

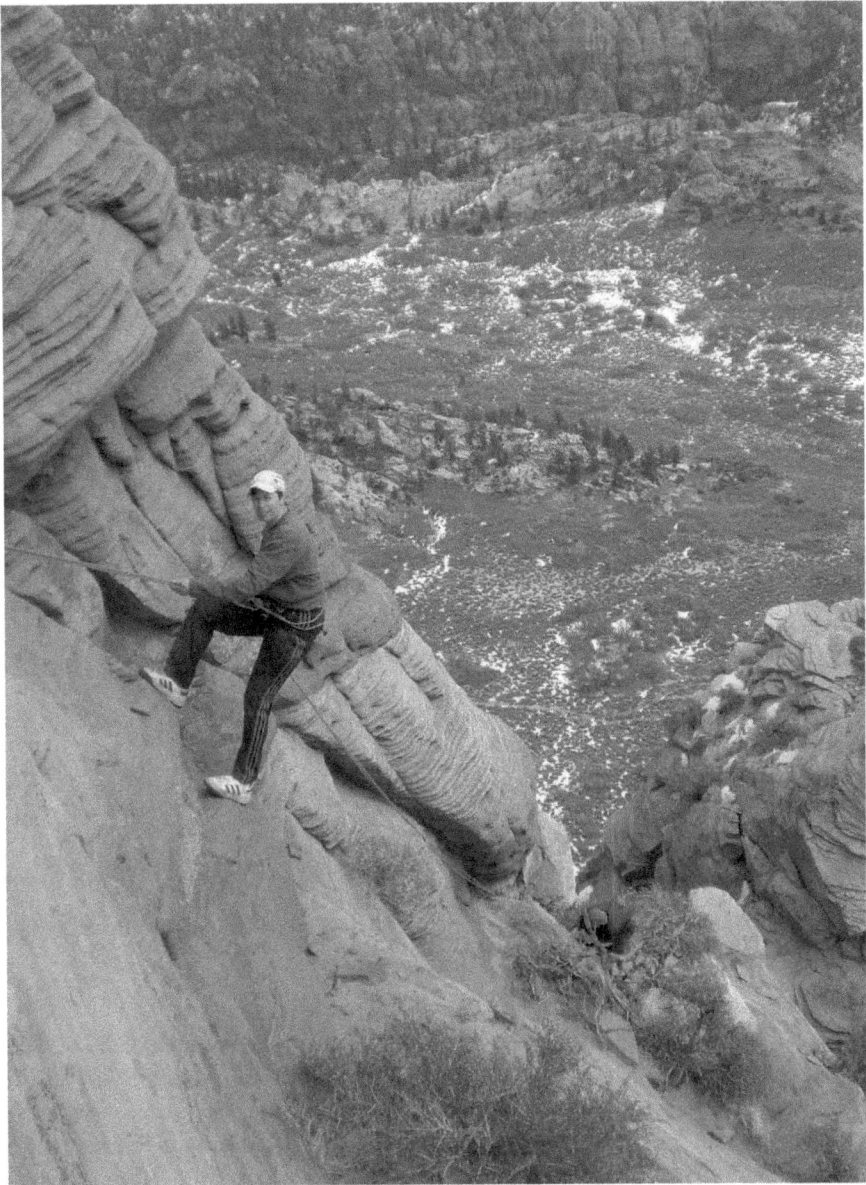

DB rapping the upper pitch on Red Butte

RT Mileage: 12 (from Kolob Terrace Road)
RT Elevation Gain: 1,200'
Time Required: 4-5 hours
Latitude: +37.4008
Longitude: -113.1608

FKA: Courtney Purcell (May 8, 2011)

Etymology: This is the higher, east summit of Neagle Ridge. Interestingly, Steve Allen noted in *Utah's Canyon Country Place Names, Volume 2*, that the correct spelling should be Naegle Ridge, as the feature is named for John Conrad Naegle, a rancher and wine maker who settled in Toquerville and New Harmony but was forced to move to Mexico in 1889 due to anti-polygamy laws.

Star Rating: **

Neagle Ridge (center) and East Neagle (right) from the south

Route: East Ridge (class 2)

Follow the directions given for South Burnt Point to the summit of that peak. Continue down the north face and proceed to the South Burnt Point-Burnt Mountain saddle, where you'll cut left below Burnt Mountain and follow easy, pleasant terrain north-northwest toward the Burnt Mountain-East Neagle saddle. From there, East Neagle is a short scramble away.

Route: Northwest Face (class 3)

As a descent route, simply scramble down the northwest face to gain a charming bowl of sorts northeast of the main summit of Neagle Ridge. From the bowl, it's a straightforward endeavor to wander back to the East Neagle-Burnt Mountain saddle.

Neagle Ridge (6,760)

Before finally pulling the trigger on this isolated peak, which is very impressive and intimidating when viewed from La Verkin Creek Trail south of Gregory Butte, I'd long stared at it from many directions, never quite sure how to approach the summit. Seemingly protected by cliffs on all sides, I often pondered the existence of a reasonable way through. But then I spotted something, a sweeping slab of slickrock, with cliffs above and cliffs below, that seemed to pave a sort of highway of easier ground.

Neagle Ridge from Stapley Point

I'd gone much of the way there before, a few times. So I went for it. With some nice views and plenty of brush, it is a place not unlike many others in the Zion backcountry. After passing through familiar lands and entering that smile-inducing zone of *the new*, I eventually came upon a spot so reminiscent of the Center of the Universe that I suddenly and outrageously proclaimed it 'The NEW Center of the Universe'! This place is magnificent—a slickrock saddle of such charm and ambience that surely the axis of all being rotates around it.

The summit is not far off. We dropped into a tree'd bowl of sorts then approached the final problem from the northeast. The summit, as one might have come to expect, affords wonderful views.

RT Mileage: 12
RT Elevation Gain: 1,200'
Time Required: 5 hours
Latitude: +37.3979
Longitude: -113.1665
FKA: Courtney Purcell & DB (May 8, 2011)
Etymology: See East Neagle
Star Rating: ***

Route: Northeast Face (class 2-3)
Follow the directions given for East Neagle to the East Neagle-Burnt Mountain saddle. From the saddle, head west around the north side of East Neagle to gain the tree'd bowl northeast of Neagle Ridge's summit. Scramble the northeast face to the highpoint.

　　　The summit is a quiet place for introspection and meditation. It's unlikely you'll encounter another soul.

This is the view to the west to Burnt Mountain from the summit of Arch Peak. Charming Hop Valley lies at the foot of both peaks. As much as I've always loved Hop Valley for its subtle beauty and casual strolling opportunities, the tedious and endless deep sand in portions of the valley has limited my number of visits here. *According to DB*...after a long day of hiking through Hop Valley, you never want to visit the beach again.

Burnt Mountain (7,682)

CLOSED TO RECREATIONAL USE—RNA

Burnt Mountain is one of the mighty backcountry peaks of Zion National Park. Resembling a blocky table of sorts, the spacious and flattish, manzanita-covered summit is well guarded by significant, 1,000-foot cliffs on all sides. The gorgeous monolith is readily viewable from Kolob Terrace Road near Hop Valley Trailhead. The mountain has 1,302' of prominence.

According to DB...

More memorable, perhaps, than our ascent of the mountain was the occasion we woke from a nap at the trailhead to find ourselves literally surrounded by dozens of curious cows!

RT Mileage: 11
RT Elevation Gain: 2,500'
Time Required: 6-8 hours
Latitude: +37.4010
Longitude: -113.1535
FA: Unknown
Etymology: Unknown
Star Rating: ***

Wonderful scenery in Hop Valley

Route: South Face (YDS 5.2)

Follow the directions given for South Burnt Point to the summit of that peak. Descend north to the base of Burnt Mountain's impressive south face, noting a convenient S-shaped ledge system on the face. Follow the ledges and ramps of this miraculous break in the huge face and scramble through several short class 5 faces, chimneys and slabs toward the ledge system's end at the upper-right side of the face. Climb into a notch just below the top, drop down the other side, and traverse an exposed, brushy ledge to a final steep face that leads to a steep slab and then the summit plateau. The RNA begins at the mesa-top. As such, the true summit is closed to recreational use.

Hop Valley Trailhead

From the UT-9/Kolob Terrace Road junction, follow the paved Kolob Terrace Road for 12.6 miles to the signed Hop Valley Trailhead on the left. Park along the dirt loop. Although it's obscured by trees and not easily seen from the pavement, there's a bathroom here—one of only three park toilets along Kolob Terrace Road, though there's another at the campground at Lava Point.

The peaks in this subsection are roughly arranged from shortest-hike-from-the-trailhead to longest-hike-from-the-trailhead.

On the summit of Hop Valley Peak's central summit. The south summit beckons in the near-distance.

"Hop Valley Peak" (7,500)

This is the aesthetic tri-summited red peak northeast of (and across Hop Valley from) Red Butte. Although the south summit is the most aesthetic (and the only one visible from the trailhead), the north summit is the highest. We'll be discussing the north summit here.

Views from the summit of the seldom-visited Hurricane Canyon system are interesting. Looking west to the spire of Red Butte isn't a waste of time either.

RT Mileage: 6.5
RT Elevation Gain: 2,400'
Time Required: 6-8 hours
Latitude: +37.3761
Longitude: -113.1097
FA: Unknown; we found no signs of prior visitation on the central or main (north) summit.
Etymology: The peak hovers over Hop Valley. Maybe I should endeavor to think more imaginatively.
Star Rating: **

The view to Hop Valley Peak-South (left) and Red Butte (right) from the summit of Hop Valley Peak.

Route: Southwest Ridge (class 3+)

A GPS is handy for this route, as the route-finding is particularly challenging.

Follow the Hop Valley Trail north to a gate. Go through the gate and continue for less than 0.5 mile to a point where you can gain the watercourse that drains from the hanging valley southeast of Hop Valley Peak. Note a small, north-south canyon immediately south-southwest of Hop Valley Peak's south summit (not the main watercourse that runs north-south to the south of Hop Valley Peak's north summit before bending southwest and dropping quickly). Leave the trail and get into the watercourse, following it to a point where you can gain the rib that leads to the flattish area just south of Hop Valley Peak's south summit's south ridge *(say what?)*.

Gain the rib at a likely-looking point a mere 50-75 feet west of the mouth of the small, north-south canyon (class 3 access can be found) and start up. Alternatively, the small canyon to the immediate east can be ascended (class 4-5 moves in a handful of spots) but this may be better utilized on the descent. Follow the rib up (some route-finding required to keep it a scramble), staying further east (rather than getting drawn west) when practical, until the terrain substantially levels out and you approach the steep cliffs of Hop Valley Peak's awesome, red south summit mass (and impressive south ridge).

Before reaching the cliffs, cut east over a low rib and drop easily (class 1-2) to the hanging valley. Head up the valley through tedious brush (it's not necessary to drop all the way to the bottom of the valley, though the brush tends to be less tedious there) until you can gain a very brushy slope leading to the saddle between the south and central summits. Gain the saddle and work 100 feet north along the cliffs on the southwestern edge of the central summit until you can head 150 feet east-northeast up a steep and loose talus chute. Before reaching the top of the chute, cut left (north) at an easy exit and traverse 100 feet to a sort of saddle.

From the saddle, head up an easy slope until you can gain the north ridge of the central summit. Follow the class 2 ridge south for 50-75 feet until you can drop down the east side (class 2) and gain the initially mellow southwest ridge of the main summit. (Before dropping to the ridge, you might as well walk the final 50 feet of ridge [class 2-3] to the 7,350-foot central summit.)

Once on the southwest ridge, scramble toward the north summit 0.2 mile away, wandering on and sometimes just below the crest. If you encounter anything more difficult than class 3, look harder. At one point near the Central-North saddle, you'll need to drop east from the crest into a gully (there's a steep and narrow slot/notch to the west), descending a very steep, 15-foot patch of manzanita right away. As soon as you get to the base of the manzanita, rather than continue down the gully, gain a dirty chimney with a tree at its base to the immediate north-northeast. Climb the 20-foot chimney (arguably the route's crux; class 3-4) to a flat perch with a healthy tree at its top. From there, continue northeast to the semi-inspiring summit.

For the descent, return to the base of the crux chimney. Once there, rather than climb back up the steep manzanita slope, head down the gully and follow the watercourse into the hanging valley, bypassing a dryfall on the right. At a point southeast of Hop Valley Peak's south summit, leave the watercourse and aim southwest for an indistinct saddle directly south of the south summit (this is another spot where a GPS and/or topo map comes in handy). On the other side of this saddle is the head of the canyon that will take you back down to the base of the rib you climbed near the start of the route.

Does this all sound confusing? As I said, the route-finding is tricky; the terrain is extremely complex.

Once you find the correct descent canyon, descend. If you encounter anything more challenging than the occasional class 4-5 move, you're probably in the wrong drainage. We encountered nothing that required a rappel. Once at the mouth of the canyon, follow the wash out until it reaches the Hop Valley Trail a short distance away. Hang a left and walk the trail out.

DB and Bryan Long celebrate on the summit of Hop Valley Peak-South. After an earlier failed attempt on this hard-earned peak with other friends, Bryan was game to join us for another attempt—he even volunteered his neck, back and shoulders for a shoulder stand-partner assist, a necessary ingredient for our eventual success.

"Hop Valley Peak – South" (7,480)

Hop Valley Peak's aesthetic, red south summit is the hardest of the three Hop Valley Peak summits to reach. My first attempt, under cover of spring snow, proved fruitless, as my partners and I were initially excited to find an amazing scrambling route that offered promise yet only sent us scurrying around the entire peak, creeping up gullies and climbing steep grooves in search of soon-to-be-discovered dead-ends. As we began our final retreat that cold afternoon, I spotted something that offered promise, real promise, possibility—but our morale was shot and so we slouched off and headed for Oscar's.

A couple of months later, some partners and I returned to take a peek at that possibility I'd spotted. It goes! Not necessarily with ease, but it goes nonetheless.

RT Mileage: 5
RT Elevation Gain: 2,000'
Time Required: 6-8 hours
Latitude: +37.3732
Longitude: -113.1124
FKA: Courtney Purcell, DB and Bryan Long (May 9, 2010)
Etymology: This is the more rugged, more colorful, and far more aesthetic south summit of Hop Valley Peak.
Star Rating: ****

Route: South Face (YDS 5.0 A0)

Follow the directions given for Hop Valley Peak to the area of the hanging valley directly south of our objective's summit. From here, find your way north-northwest to a key gully split by a pretty orange outcropping at its top. The gully is south of the summit mass of our objective peak. I put a small cairn in an alcove near the base of the orange outcropping, and another in a hidden slot a bit north of the gully. One hundred yards north of the top of the gully is a wide crack in a large block. If the lighting is wrong, the crack can be hard to spot. Scramble to the base of the crack, which is steep, very awkward, and has a nasty run-out (a down-sloping dirt ledge about four feet wide, with a 50-foot vertical drop below it).

Utilize a shoulder stand off your partner (or some other goofy method; otherwise, it's perhaps awkward YDS 5.7) to negotiate the first 8-feet of weirdness and get into an easy class 5 chimney that leads to a large bush. Drop down the backside of the block you're on to gain a ledge, which can be followed around an exposed corner to a steep gully. Scramble the steep gully then walk easily to the highpoint.

A 30m rope is recommended for the route.

Bryan Long and DB approaching the summit of Hop Valley Peak-South

Long Point (7,155)

Long Point is south of Langston Mountain, with its summit closely west-southwest of the high saddle separating the stair-stepped south fork of Beartrap Canyon and the brushy north fork of (the unofficially named) Hurricane Canyon.

The peak can be approached from either the north fork of Hurricane Canyon (easiest), the south fork of Beartrap Canyon (absurdly long but with a clear, cool spring offering drinking water a bit below the southeast fork confluence) or via a traverse from Langston Mountain (which I've not personally done).

RT Mileage: 13 (via Hurricane Canyon)
RT Elevation Gain: 2,000' (via Hurricane Canyon)
Time Required: 8-10 hours
Latitude: +37.4098
Longitude: -113.1150
FKA: Courtney Purcell (October 9, 2010)
Etymology: Unknown
Star Rating: **

Route: East Slope via Hurricane Canyon (class 4)
From the Hop Valley Trailhead, follow the trail north into Hop Valley until Hurricane Canyon comes in on the right. Hurricane Canyon is the second significant drainage on the right south of Langston Canyon. It meets Hop Valley roughly west of the summit of Hop Valley Peak.

Leave the trail and walk up the canyon for several hundred yards until it forks. Take the left fork north into the north fork of Hurricane Canyon. Ascend the canyon to the saddle at its head, just east-northeast of Long Point's summit. The frequently unpleasant canyon does not require ropes, though one should expect tough scrambling in places.

A bit of bushwhacking from the saddle takes one to the crest above, where you'll scramble southwest for about 0.5 mile to the rocky viewpoint of the summit.

Arch Peak from the summit of Burnt Hill

"Arch Peak" (7,134)

This beautiful, red slickrock peak forms the west wall of lower Langston Canyon, southwest of Langston Mountain. Along the route, you'll likely encounter a sweet arch, inside of which I put a cairn.

Arch Peak has 454' of prominence.

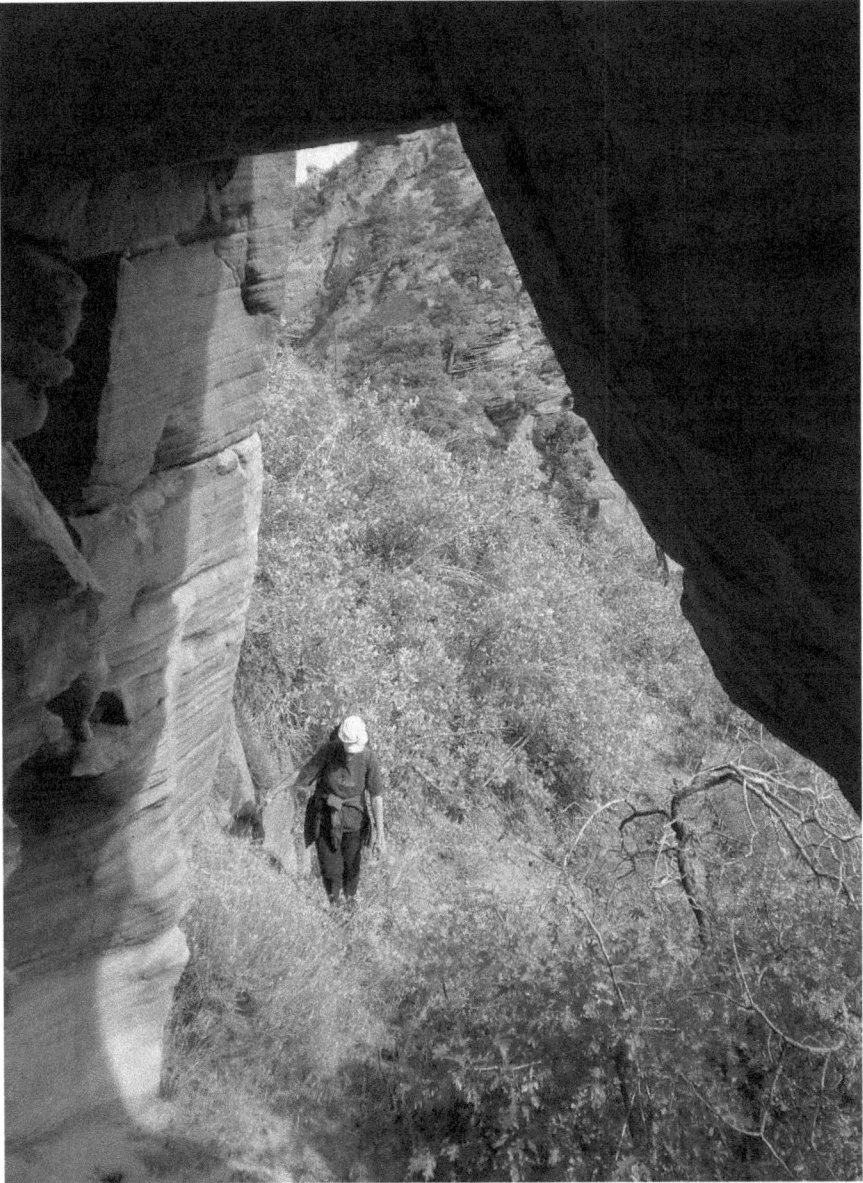

The namesake arch on Arch Peak

RT Mileage: 10
RT Elevation Gain: 1,800'
Time Required: 8-10 hours
Latitude: +37.4052
Longitude: -113.1293

FKA: Courtney Purcell and DB (October 29, 2010)
Etymology: Named for an awesome arch not far below the summit
Star Rating: ***

This massive alcove is on the northwest corner of Langston Mountain. It can be seen from Arch Peak and other unlikely spots nearby. One of these days it would be neat to hike to the base of the alcove to get a better perspective of the cliffs above.

Route: Northeast Ridge (class 3-4)
Follow the directions given for Langston Mountain into the north fork of upper Langston Canyon. At a point east of the saddle northeast of our objective's summit, leave the canyon and scramble (class 2) west to the saddle. Keep your eyes peeled for the peak's namesake arch along the way.

From the saddle, scramble the northeast ridge (class 3-4) to the highpoint.

Langston Mountain (7,453)

Langston Mountain is the most obscure, remote mountain in the Zion backcountry that can be hiked via trail. Of course, that trail was constructed in the early 1900's and shortly after abandoned, thereby making it virtually impossible to find and follow beneath all of the vegetation that now obscures it. Regardless, Langston Mountain is a fine mountain with an astonishingly beautiful approach through both Hop Valley and Langston Canyon. Middle Langston Canyon is one of the most special and spectacular places in Zion National Park.

Labor up lovely Langston leaving little litter!

With a good head for route-finding, a high tolerance for brush, and skill at boulder hopping, one can follow the route my partners and I first pieced together in April 2008. Some of it follows the old stock trail that once led to the ponderosa pine grove growing on the mountain's summit, while much of it explores the rugged canyon bottom adjacent to it.

RT Mileage: 13
RT Elevation Gain: 2,000'
Time required: 10-12 hours
Latitude: +37.4216
Longitude: -113.1233
FA: Unknown
Etymology: Named for Lorin Langston, a kitchen worker at the Zion National Park lodge in the 1930s.
Star Rating: ***

Route: Langston Canyon (class 3)
From the trailhead, follow the Hop Valley Trail north for about four miles to Langston Canyon. It is the third significant canyon on the right after dropping into Hop Valley. Once in Langston Canyon, follow the initially sandy wash until it becomes bouldery. From there, boulder hop (class 2-3) up-canyon for about 0.5 mile to the first fork you encounter. The fork may not be apparent, as the left (north) fork presents itself to you as a 40-foot dryfall. Scramble up the steep and brushy slope to the left of the dryfall until

you can traverse right to gain the slickrock just above the dryfall. There are some nice potholes here.

Beautiful pothole features in Langston Canyon

Cross the watercourse and look for an easy way to gain the ridge that separates the two forks of the canyon. It will be just in front of you and gained via class 2 terrain. Gain the crest of the ridge and head northeast above the two forks of Langston Canyon on either side of you. The views along the ridge crest are fantastic.

After about 0.5 mile the ridge peters out and you can hike down to the left (north) to gain the north fork of upper Langston Canyon. Once in upper Langston Canyon, follow the north fork toward its head. Along the way, you may notice an old retaining wall still surviving in the wash bottom. Just beyond is a stunning, bright orange and red alcove framed by a thick grove of ponderosa pine and fir trees. Gorgeous!

The canyon eventually narrows and more boulder hopping and scrambling (class 3) in the watercourse should be expected. Much of the old stock trail is visible on the bench to the right of the watercourse, though brush is often thick and the trail easily lost. Gain the head of Langston Canyon and follow the steep sand and brush slope north toward the summit area. There, you'll encounter a wonderful grove of mature ponderosa pines.

Just a bit to the northwest is the true highpoint of the mountain. The views from the highpoint, particularly of Gregory Butte and Timber Top Mountain, are phenomenal.

Cave Knoll Trailhead

From the UT-9/Kolob Terrace Road junction, follow the paved Kolob Terrace Road for 13.2 miles to a dirt road on the right. Park on the wide shoulder.

The peaks in this subsection are roughly arranged from shortest-hike-from-the-trailhead to longest-hike-from-the-trailhead.

The shadowed cragginess of Hop Valley Peak-South from near the summit of Firepit Knoll

Spendlove Knoll (6,895)

Standing out from the slickrock and hoodoo-rich environment of much of Zion, Spendlove Knoll and its higher neighbor, Firepit Knoll, are basaltic features with recognizable volcanic forms. Climbing Spendlove Knoll once one late winter morning, I caught the attention of a group of mule deer near the summit enjoying the views and the warming weather.

RT Mileage: 0.75
RT Elevation Gain: 400'
Time required: 1 hour

Latitude: +37.3371
Longitude: -113.1094
FA: Unknown
Etymology: Named for the Spendlove family, who were early settlers in the area.
Star Rating: *

Route: North Slope (class 1)

From the road shoulder, walk back west along the road less than 0.25 mile until you are at a point below the north slope of Spendlove Knoll. Once there, simply head up. Although some brush is to be expected, most of it can be avoided with a little wandering around.

Firepit Knoll (7,265)

Like its neighbor Spendlove Knoll, this volcanic feature stands out from the craggy reds and oranges of much of Zion National Park. Unlike Spendlove, this higher peak has a beautifully formed 360-degree crater just below its summit.

The views of Burnt Mountain, Pine Valley Peak and Red Butte from the summit are absolutely terrific, particularly in winter when the distant Pine Valley Mountains are covered in snow, contrasting sharply with the brilliant red of nearby Red Butte.

RT Mileage: 0.5
RT Elevation Gain: 700'
Time required: 1 hour
Latitude: +37.3498
Longitude: -113.1043
FA: Unknown
Etymology: The mountain is a cinder cone that once had active magma activity in its crater area.
Star Rating: *

Route: South Slope (class 1)

PRIVATE PROPERTY: Historically, one could simply head up from the road, avoiding most of the brush with a little weaving around. Since my only visit to the knoll, a large home has been built along the route, thus causing concern for private property. Consult a map to determine a legal approach. In any case, I strongly discourage folks from crossing private land without permission.

Alternatively, friends have avoided crossing private property by climbing the mountain on its southwest side (class 2) from near Hop Valley Trailhead.

Looking south to the slickrock paradise of Cave Knoll on a cold winter morning

Cave Knoll (6,518)

Cave Knoll is a nice little peak that offers interesting (though never terribly difficult) route-finding up, over and around hoodoos, little canyons, slabs and constantly stimulating terrain leading to a small summit with fantastic views of Pine Valley Peak and the Guardian Angels.

Doing the peak one winter, I followed cougar prints in the snow to within 75 feet of the summit.

Despite an embarrassing and shameful 135' of prominence, Cave Knoll is a cool and worthwhile stop on your tireless Zion adventures.

RT Mileage: 4
RT Elevation Gain: 500'
Time required: 3-5 hours
Latitude: +37.3218
Longitude: -113.1028
FA: Unknown
Etymology: Named for a cave-like slot that can be seen on the mountain's west face.
Star Rating: ***

Jobs Heads from the south. (Photo by Andy Archibald)

Route: Hoodoo Ridge (North Ridge) – class 3

From the parking area, walk south along the dirt road for 0.25 mile before leaving it and working your way cross-country to the southwest toward the base of Spendlove Knoll. Although there's plenty of brush to be dealt with, some animal trails can be followed efficiently to the base of the volcanic dome.

Contour around the base of the mountain and aim for the point where the gray/black basalt of Spendlove Knoll's south ridge meets the red sandstone of Cave Knoll's north ridge. The transition should be apparent. Work your way to the crest (or just below it) of the sandstone ridge, where the going becomes rather pleasant.

Once on the crest, head south toward the peak. Lots of stimulating and enjoyable route-finding will be required to keep the difficulty in the class 2-3 range, as many terrain obstacles will present themselves. As you approach the peak, you will find yourself forced off the crest from time to time. Generally speaking, trending along the east side of the crest is better than the west.

As you near the summit, wander your way up steepening terrain, approaching the final crags from the east/northeast. I climbed the summit pyramid via class 3 slabs on its northeast face.

Route: Traverse from Tinaja Knoll (class 3)
From the summit of Tinaja Knoll, it's an enjoyable exercise to drop northeast and traverse the sandstone crest around to the northeast side of Cave Knoll, where you pick up the "standard" route. Alternatively, a more direct class 4 line via the bowl east of the Cave Knoll's summit can be utilized.

Jobs Head Trailhead
From the UT-9/Kolob Terrace Road junction, follow the paved Kolob Terrace Road for 14.3 miles to where it crosses Pine Spring Wash. Park in a pull-out just west of the wash.

    The peaks in this subsection are roughly arranged from shortest-hike-from-the-trailhead to longest-hike-from-the-trailhead.

Double-A climbing Jobs Head

Jobs Head (7,233)
While the National Geographical *Trails Illustrated #214* 'topographic map' refers to a nearby high, impressive cliff as 'Jobs Head', their 'outdoor recreation map' calls Jobs Head the small, detached mountain just southeast of the cliff. Today, we're calling the little mountain Jobs Head—and a quality objective.

    Jobs Head has 153' of prominence.

Belaying Double-A during a snow climb of Jobs Head. This dicey attempt on the mountain in less-than-ideal conditions ended in failure, as we soon turned back at steep and exposed, brittle, down-sloping ledges. Not recommended. Interestingly enough, we returned a week later after the snow had burned off and summited.

RT Mileage: 2.5
RT Elevation Gain: 725'
Time required: 2-5 hours
Latitude: +37.3574
Longitude: -113.0881
FKA: Courtney Purcell, DB and Andy Archibald (November 16, 2008)
Etymology: Job is the name of a biblical character. Perhaps some aspect of the geologic feature resembles a head, I dunno.
Star Rating: ****

Route: North Ridge (class 3)

From the parking area, drop directly east into Pine Spring Wash (aka Pole Canyon) just as it passes under the road and follow it north about 1.1 mile until you reach the confluence with a small drainage coming in from the southwest from Jobs Head's north saddle. (Alternatively, one could hike over slickrock to the north and intersect Pine Spring Wash just east of the southern nose of Jobs Head.) From the wash, looking southwest, bear slightly right of the three cuts visible on the northeast face of Jobs Head to the drainage leading to the saddle (class 2). (The saddle can also be reached from the west via more convoluted and brushy terrain (class 2). The west side has three drainages near the saddle. The drainages can be used to access or exit the area near the saddle and adjacent ridge.)

From the saddle, hang a left and meander up Jobs Head's north ridge. Soon reaching a narrowing part of the ridge, scramble up a short crack (5 feet; class 3) just below a large pine on the narrow crest. Move past the large pine and step up to a ledge which can be traversed south to a V-notch.

From the notch, scramble left up 10 feet of exposed, down-sloping, brittle class 3 slabs to a platform next to a dying bush. Walk past the bush to the right then scramble left up another 10 feet of class 3 short ledges (exposed) to regain the crest in a small notch with bushes on both sides. Work 10 feet upward to the next level. At least two options are available. This level leads to the base of a crumbly false summit.

Bypass the false summit via an exposed, narrow ledge (class 2) on its right. Carefully follow the ledge around the corner until you can work back onto the crest next to a healthy tree just south of the false summit. Continue 20 feet south to the base of the next crag, which can be scrambled up via a dirty ramp on its right side. This is the summit!

According to Andy...

From the saddle north of Jobs Head, it is a worthwhile class 3-4 scramble to the minor summit to the north. This higher summit looks down on Jobs Head.

Route: Northeast Chimney (YDS 5.5)

Follow the directions given for the North Ridge route to the confluence with a small drainage coming in from the southwest from Jobs Head's north saddle. (There are three cuts apparent in the face when looking southwest from Pine Spring Wash. You'll be taking the left-most cut which is just right of the visible highpoint of Jobs Head.) Hang a left and head up the drainage. Soon, a smaller drainage will come in on the left. It leads to two narrow chimneys on the northeast face of Jobs Head.

Heading up the smaller drainage, aim for the southern of the two chimneys, both of which should be plainly visible on the face. Both chimneys are steep, have trees in them and end in notches on the north ridge of the peak. The southern chimney has a large pine halfway up it.

Reach the base of the southern chimney and head up. The crux moves (YDS 5.5) are near the bottom, and the chimney tightens about halfway up just before you reach a healthy pine on your right. Continuing past the pine, the chimney tightens again though the going is only class 3-4. Above the tightest part, the chimney opens up on its right side as it steepens. There's an awkward dying bush in your way here. This is the point where the North Ridge route comes in on the right via an exposed, narrow traverse from a large pine (described above).

From here, follow the directions already given for the remainder of the North Ridge route.

A 50m rope is recommended for this route.

Route: Northeast Cleft (YDS 5.5)

This route is more dirty, more unpleasant and has more loose rock than the other two routes I describe.

Follow the directions given for the Northeast Chimney route to the base of the chimney. Rather than climb that chimney, step left and climb a short, awkward chimney (6 feet; YDS 5.0) to a platform below another narrow chimney (8 feet) just right of a small, scrappy tree. Rather than climb directly up this narrow chimney, it will be necessary to climb over/around it (YDS 5.5).

Above the narrow chimney, continue up the cleft to a steep crack/chimney with a dead tree lying in it. Climbing up (10 feet; class 4), move past a loose, flattish spot and then continue up the cleft via steep class 3 terrain that leads to an appallingly loose rubble slope (short, thank goodness) below a notch in the crest above. Gain the crest via a 10-foot class 3 chimney then carefully step left to gain the flattish terrain near the base of a crumbly, red crag one might assume is the summit. This is the false summit described in the North Ridge route. From here, follow the directions already given to the summit.

A 50m rope is recommended for this route.

From the northeast side of Jobs Head one can make out the sharp, V-notch (left of center) that forms at the top of the northeast chimney route. (Photo by Andy Archibald)

"Jobs Head Plateau" (7,950)

Jobs Head Plateau is the high plateau looming over the diminutive Jobs Head, to the southeast. The Plateau is bordered by Pipe Spring Wash on the east and upper Hop Valley on the west.

Starting from the saddle north of Jobs Head, the route is pleasant (though brushy) and without significant difficulty. The views are excellent.

RT Mileage: 5
RT Elevation Gain: 1,400'
Time Required: 3-4 hours
Latitude: +37.3677
Longitude: -113.1014
FA: Unknown
Etymology: This is the plateau above Jobs Head. Adding a bit of confusion to the matter, certain maps show the plateau to be the officially named Jobs Head itself.
Star Rating: **

Route: South Gully (class 3)

Follow the directions given for Jobs Head's North Ridge route to the saddle north of that peak. From the saddle, scramble a short distance up the feature on its north side until you can cut left to find a neat hidden slot that drops into the prominent gully draining south from the southeast corner of Jobs Head Plateau.

Scramble up the gully (absurdly steep dirt and brush) to the head, where you can cut right to gain the rim of the plateau. Awesome views here! The summit of the plateau is a bushwhack to the northwest.

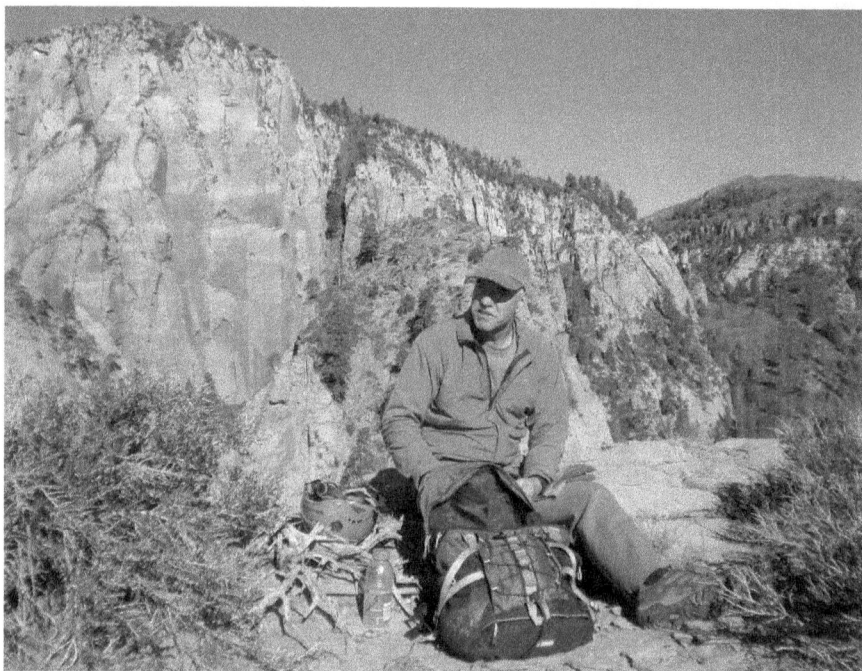

Double-A on the summit of Jobs Head. The route to Jobs Head Plateau ascends the prominent gully visible over Double's right shoulder.

Wildcat Trailhead

From the UT-9/Kolob Terrace Road junction, follow the paved Kolob Terrace Road for 15.4 miles to the signed Wildcat Trailhead on the right. The trailhead has a restroom (usually with hand sanitizer) and adequate parking for at least 10 vehicles.

The peaks in this subsection are roughly arranged from shortest-hike-from-the-trailhead to longest-hike-from-the-trailhead.

Aptly named, over the years the Park Service has occasionally posted signs here warning visitors of recent mountain lion sightings in the area.

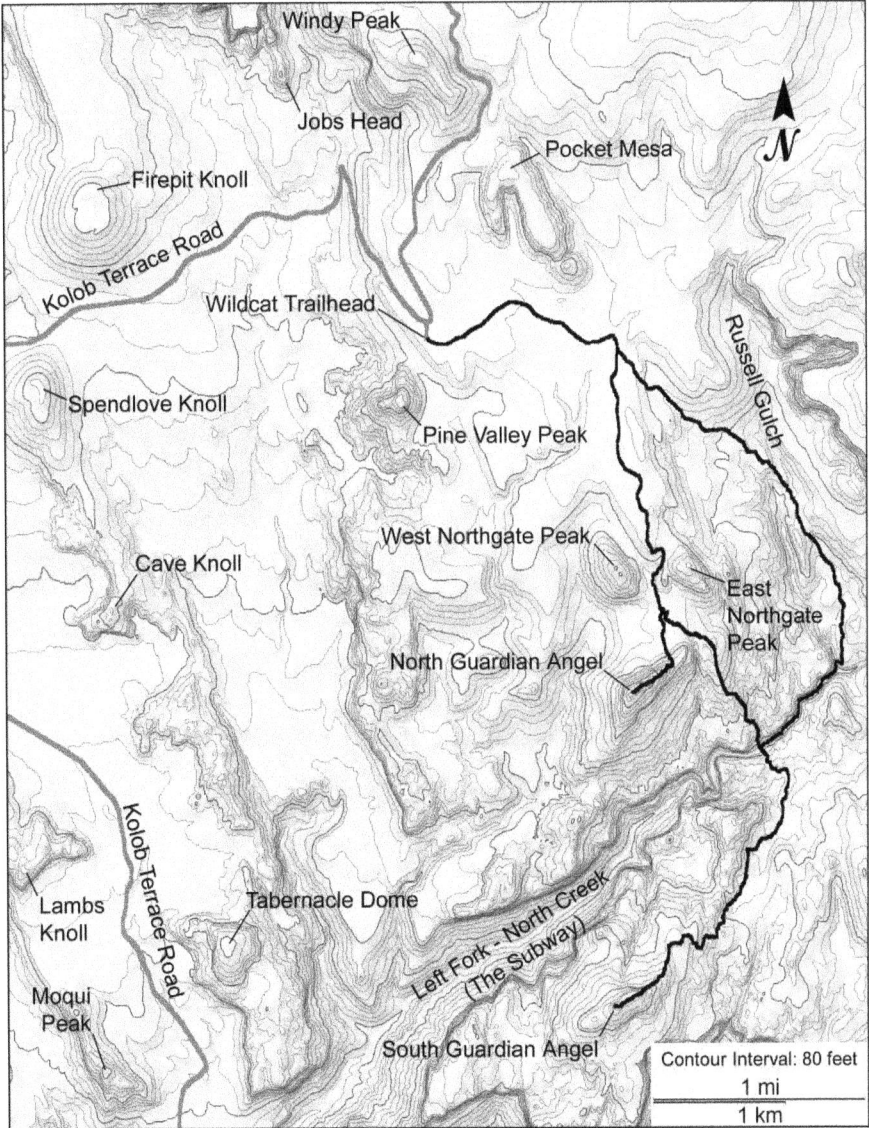

Map of the Wildcat Trailhead area

The big southeast face of Jobs Head Plateau on a wintry March morning

Pine Valley Peak (7,428)

Pine Valley Peak is the fine-looking, small mountain hovering next to the Wildcat Trailhead. Most folks stopping at the trailhead, intent on visiting the famous Subway (or just there to use the bathroom), pass by without so much as a glance at the peak. Upon close inspection, steep and slabby faces appear to offer little in the way of good, protectable climbing or scrambling routes. Though the route described below is at times heinous (and the only one I've done), friends of mine have climbed a relatively easy, low-class 5 route near the route I describe, and I've heard of at least one person piecing together a class 3 route to the summit.

RT Mileage: 1
RT Elevation Gain: 500'
Time Required: 3-4 hours
Latitude: +37.3355
Longitude: -113.0780
FA: Unknown, though Ram made an ascent of the northeast face many years ago. I believe we found some of his old rappel slings on our ascent.
Etymology: The prominent and particularly eye-catching peak lies on the western edge of Pine Valley.

Star Rating: **

Pine Valley Peak from the north-northwest

Route: Northeast Face (YDS 5.5)

From the Wildcat Trailhead, pick up an obscure trail through the brush that heads southwest toward the base of Pine Valley Peak. The approach takes five minutes. Scramble up class 3-4 terrain near the northeast base of the mountain and work your way up to an abrupt wall on the mountain's north face. Reaching it, drop easily about 50 feet to the east until you find low-angle slabs leading upward.

Gain the initial run-out slab (YDS 5.5) and head up for about 20 feet until you can line up with a prominent crack that runs up the northeast face of the mountain. Continue up the crack for roughly 180 feet (YDS 5.3) to a tree with a sling around it. Above the slung tree scramble up easy terrain until you encounter another section of steep terrain on the mountain's north face.

Starting at a short and loose, outside corner (YDS 5.5) on the right side of the face (minimal, sketchy protection off a small bush), continue up a sort of chimney (careful—really bad rock; YDS 5.5, protecting off of a small bush) then angle left (YDS 5.3) across slabs and toward some large trees at the top of the pitch. One of the trees should have a sling around it.

From here work left, then wander easily to the summit. Enjoy the views. To descend, retrace your steps. A single rope rappel works fine for the top technical section, and a double rope rappel does the trick for the lower one.

Two 60m ropes, a selection of nuts, and several long slings are recommended for the route.

Mellow terrain on Wildcat Mountain

"Wildcat Mountain" (7,635)

An easy hike to a minor summit with wilderness views of the higher elevations of Kolob Terrace.

RT Mileage: 6
RT Elevation Gain: 600'
Time Required: 3-4 hours
Latitude: +37.3511
Longitude: -113.0368
FA: Unknown
Etymology: On the day we hiked up the mountain (from the *Wildcat* Trailhead, no less), there was a NPS sign at the trailhead saying there'd been a recent mountain lion sighting in the area. To name the mountain in honor of the circumstances seemed appropriate.
Star Rating: *

Route: Northwest Slope (class 1)
From the trailhead, follow the trail 2.5 miles toward the West Rim Trail. In an open meadow, leave the trail on its right side and bushwhack to the summit. The summit affords decent (albeit distant) views into Phantom Valley, as well as closer views of upper Wildcat Canyon, The Hourglass and Greatheart Mesa.

Reaching the summit of East Northgate Peak

East Northgate Peak (7,153)
East Northgate Peak and West Northgate Peak frame a classic image of North Guardian Angel from the end of the official Northgate Peaks Trail. This is one of those hikes that is a delight to do periodically, just 'cause.

RT Mileage: 6
RT Elevation Gain: 400'
Time Required: 2-3 hours
Latitude: +37.3247
Longitude: -113.0533
FA: Unknown
Etymology: See West Northgate Peak
Star Rating: ***

Getting to the Mountain:

Follow the directions given for West Northgate Peak to the overlook between it and East Northgate Peak. From the overlook, approach as necessary for the route you have in mind. Getting to the bottom of the peak is technically insignificant, as a well-used trail leads right to its base from the overlook.

Routes:

The east face is extremely steep. The south and west faces appear to be more moderate. *According to Ram*...a loose, vegetated weakness near the east edge of the south face lends easy access to the top.

North Slope: There's a class 2 use trail that can be picked up near the eastern edge of the slope. Alternatively, pick any number of lines elsewhere on the slope/face. Most of these lines are in the class 2-4 range.

For an alternative approach to the north face routes, one can follow the directions given for Little Northgate to the Little Northgate-East Northgate Peak saddle via Russell Gulch. From there, follow a north-trending ledge to the right until it narrows considerably and dead-ends mere feet from easier terrain at the base of East Northgate Peak's north face. Drop a bit then pick up a ramp that puts you back on the north face, utilizing any number of route options to get to the summit from there. This alternative approach requires a Subway permit.

West Northgate Peak (7,267)

The Northgate Peaks are overshadowed by their more impressive and enigmatic next-door neighbor, North Guardian Angel. Still, these little puppies are fine peaks in their own right, and their summits are owners of striking views.

This is a charming and very scenic area—my wife and I considered having our wedding at the Northgate Peaks overlook, but abandoned the idea after tripping over all of the park's red tape. Instead, we had it at George Barker Park in Springdale—drama-free!

Even if one doesn't want to make the ascent of the peak, it's a wonderful, pleasant hike from the trailhead to the overlook. Be mindful of the rattlesnake that lives in the basalt at the end of the official trail, where you'll probably want to have a snack and some water.

RT Mileage: 6
RT Elevation Gain: 500'
Time Required: 3-4 hours
Latitude: +37.3241
Longitude: -113.0592
FA: Who knows?

Etymology: According to the USGS, the peaks are named "because of their position at the head of a difficult passageway."
Star Rating: ***

This view looks north to the south face of West Northgate Peak from the lower slopes of North Guardian Angel. The ramp visible on the face provides access to the summit via a couple of route possibilities.

Getting to the Mountain:

From the trailhead, follow the trail for about 0.9 mile to its junction with the Connector Trail. Stay left and continue for a couple hundred yards to another junction, signed for Northgate Peaks Trail. Follow the Northgate Peaks Trail (ignoring yet another junction, this one for The Subway, about 100 yards later) for about 1.5 miles to its end at an overlook of North Guardian Angel. North Guardian will be directly in front of you, while East Northgate Peak will be to your left and West Northgate Peak will be to your right. Look for a use trail heading down to the left (east) from the overlook and follow it until it essentially disappears a hundred yards later near the base of East Northgate Peak.

From here, approach as necessary for the route you have in mind. The approach to the bottom of the peak is elementary (though brushy in places) and technically insignificant. I've always found the small grove of pines just south of the overlook to be an enchanting spot.

Routes:

The easiest route on the mountain appears to be the north face. The peak's west face is very steep, as is the east face, and the south face offers easy-to-moderate level technical climbing routes.

South Face (YDS 5.4): Follow steep slabs and a prominent shallow gully until difficulties become large. At that point, working to the west increases the difficulty, while working to the east decreases the difficulty. Assuming you'll take the easiest of the three options (continuing straight up being the third), start traversing to the right (toward the southeast face), aiming for a shallow gully that will lead you to broken ledges and ultimately easier terrain taking you to the summit.

Although this is essentially a scrambling route, a 60m is recommended.

Southeast Face (YDS 5.3): Follow steep slabs, ledges and gullies. If one looks very hard, and reads slab steepness well, class 3-4 seems to be possible, though YDS 5.0-5.3 is more likely to be encountered. Harder lines do lurk, so be prepared.

Although this is essentially a scrambling route, a 60m is recommended.

East Face (class 3-4): Utilizing this as a descent route, one can scramble to within about 60 feet of the bottom of the steep stuff before cliffing out. From there, traverse south above the significant difficulties and eventually onto the southeast face to follow a reasonable way down.

This route is a bit contrived.

According to Ram…

The north face is an easy class 2-3 scrambling route that features a class 4 move or two a little more than halfway up the face.

Also, following the prominent gully (YDS 5.4) on the south face described above to the flattish, treed area at its head, continue west over frictional low class 5 terrain to ledges that wrap around to the southwest face. There, easier terrain allows access to the top.

"Little Northgate" (6,812)

This nubbin slightly southeast of the summit of East Northgate Peak caught my eye a couple years before I took the time to find a route up it. Although certainly not a big challenge, getting to the summit does require more effort than it might appear.

The views from the summit are outstanding.

Little Northgate (left) and East Northgate Peak from Russell Gulch

RT Mileage: 7
RT Elevation Gain: 500'
Time Required: 3-4 hours
Latitude: +37.3240
Longitude: -113.0499
FKA: Courtney Purcell (October 17, 2010)
Etymology: This is my uninspired named for the little, easternmost summit in the Northgate Peaks complex.
Star Rating: **

Route: West Face (class 2-3)

Follow the directions given for East Northgate Peak to the base of that peak's northwest face. Heading clockwise around the peak for 50 yards, a class 2-3 break can be found in a sudden cliff at your feet. Work to the base of the cliff and continues clockwise around its base to the East Northgate-Little Northgate saddle. From there, easy but loose slabs lead east to the summit.

For an excellent tour, you can drop back to the saddle and then follow the brushy canyon 0.25 mile south to a class 2 exit into a red slickrock bowl on the west. The canyon is non-technical to this point. The lovely slickrock bowl can be hiked to a point northeast of North Guardian Angel. From there, a short off-trail hike leads back to the Northgate Peaks overlook.

As an alternative approach, follow the directions given for West Northgate Peak to the junction of the Northgate Peaks Trail and the trail to the Subway. Leave the Northgate Peaks Trail and follow the Subway route (look carefully for cairns while crossing the slickrock) to a point near where the route crosses Russell Gulch. Leave the Subway route and make for the minor west fork of Russell Gulch, whose lesser south fork (of the west fork) ends at the Little Northgate-East Northgate Peak saddle. This is relatively complex terrain, so you may need to look around a bit to find a suitable route. This charming, obscure canyon can be scrambled (class 2-3) to the saddle. This alternative approach requires a Subway permit.

DB approaching the summit of Carls Peak

"Carls Peak" (6,600)

This minor peak sits atop the red cliffs above Lee Valley, south of Pine Valley Peak and northeast of Tabernacle Dome.

Carls Peak has 240' of prominence.

RT Mileage: 6
RT Elevation Gain: 1,000'
Time Required: 2-4 hours
Latitude: +37.3114

Longitude: -113.0776
FA: Unknown; we (myself, DB and Pedro Yamagata) found no signs of prior visitation to the summit on October 16, 2010.
Etymology: I once found a beautiful set of antlers below the summit of Palmetto Mountain, near Magrudor Mountain in Nevada. Ever the sentimental type, I named it (the antlers) Carl, took it hiking with me on Clinton Peak near Las Vegas, and eventually allowed it to settle on our coffee table at home. Anyway, not far from the base of Carls Peak, I found another nice set of antlers. Pedro Yamagata, who was with DB and I, named the antlers 'Carls Junior'. So I hauled them to the top of this little peak and interred them on the summit of the now-dubbed 'Carls Peak'!
Star Rating: **

Tabernacle Dome from Carls Peak

Route: Northeast Face (class 2)

Follow the Wildcat Trail for 0.8 mile east to where it crosses Little Creek (dry). Leave the trail and follow the lovely (especially in fall, when the leaves are changing), rocky (and brush-free) creek bed to a point east of Carls Peak. Here, a windy, brushy wash heads initially west from the main drainage to the northeastern base of Carls Peak. Easy scrambling from there leads to the summit hoodoo and its interesting view of Tabernacle Dome.

Harlan Stockman resting on the summit of Jumbled Knoll. South Guardian Angel is in the background.

"Jumbled Knoll" (6,280)

Jumbled Knoll is southeast of Carls Peak and southwest of Red Cone, straddling the divide between Little Creek and the Left Fork of North Creek. From the summit, the views of the higher peaks surrounding it are outstanding.

The peak has a pathetic 240' of prominence which seems particularly pronounced next to the famous and classic, hulking slickrock dome just to the northeast.

RT Mileage: 6
RT Elevation Gain: 1,200'
Time Required: 3-5 hours
Latitude: +37.3046
Longitude: -113.0689
FKA: Courtney Purcell, DB and Harlan Stockman (October 16, 2010). Hugh de Q or Pedro Yamagata might have been with us too.
Etymology: This knoll is a weird collection of jumbled crags and hoodoos. It would be a fun place to just wander around and get weird.
Star Rating: **

Route: Northeast Ridge (class 3)
Follow the directions given for Red Cone to the confluence of Little Creek and the drainage coming down from the West Northgate Peak-North Guardian Angel saddle. Complex terrain lies ahead. Head up to gain the northeast ridge of the peak. Class 2-3 terrain can be found leading to the upper mountain, which consists of a collection of funky crags and hoodoos, three of which are of comparable height. We placed a cairn atop the northernmost crag (class 3).

An interesting view of North Guardian Angel from the slopes of Jumbled Knoll

"Red Cone" (6,440)
Of the three Little Creek peaks southwest of North Guardian Angel, this is the most striking and aesthetic.

Red Cone has 240' of prominence.

RT Mileage: 6
RT Elevation Gain: 1,300'
Time Required: 3-5 hours
Latitude: +37.3079
Longitude: -113.0628
FKA: Courtney Purcell, DB and Harlan Stockman (October 16, 2010)
Etymology: The summit is a red hoodoo.

Star Rating: **

Looking down on Red Cone from the southwest ridge of North Guardian Angel

Route: Southwest Face (class 3)

Follow the directions given for Carls Peak into Little Creek but continue down Little Creek to its confluence with the drainage coming down from the West Northgate Peak-North Guardian Angel saddle. Alternatively, one can follow the directions given for the southwest ridge route of North Guardian Angel to gain the saddle then head down the drainage to the confluence. Both approaches are non-technical.

From the confluence, wander complex and sometimes brushy terrain to the southwest side of Red Cone. Find a break in the cliffs (at least one class 2 weakness exists) then wander to the highest hoodoo. From its east-northeast base, a quick, class 3 scramble leads to the top.

North Guardian Angel (7,408)

Like its legendary and more physically-challenging sister, South Guardian Angel, North Guardian Angel is a classic peak of Zion National Park. The impressive Guardian Angels stand guard over the Left Fork of North Creek, home of the world famous Subway, an awe-inspiring semi-technical canyon.

Both peaks belong on every mountain explorer's to-do list.

A seldom-seen view of North Guardian Angel

RT Mileage: 6
RT Elevation Gain: 800'
Time Required: 4-6 hours
Latitude: +37.3162
Longitude: -113.0583
FKA: Arkel Erb (1960's)
Etymology: North Guardian Angel and her near-twin sister South Guardian Angel, which stand across from each other on opposite sides of the Left Fork of North Creek, were named as guardians of this portion of the park. Both peaks are undisputed classics.
Star Rating: ****

Route: Northeast Ridge (class 4)

Follow the directions given for East Northgate Peak to the base of that peak's northwest face. Hike to the flattish, brushy area between the Northgate Peaks to pick up a use trail that head south toward the base of North Guardian Angel's northeast ridge. Aim for the base of a shallow saddle on the shoulder near the eastern end of the ridge. Once the base of the mountain is reached, scramble class 3 slabs and ledges to the saddle above. From the saddle, hang a right and begin ascending the northeast ridge.

Bryan Long scrambling the southwest ridge of North Guardian Angel

You'll immediately come to the first significant obstacle: a steep and semi-exposed 50-foot crack in the center of the ridge. Look to the right (north) side of the ridge for an exposed class 3-4 slab and ledge system you can use to regain the crest of the slabby ridge above the initial crack. Alternatively, the crack can be climbed directly (YDS 5.5).

Scramble from here to the summit, following signs of use and generally the easiest line. Although steep and exposed in places, most of the route is class 2-3. There are several short class 4 sections, with minor variations possible. Generally speaking, easier terrain can be found on the left (south) side of the ridge, though one should try to stay near the crest as often as feasible. If you're climbing something harder than class 4, you're off-route. The terrain mellows out as you near the top.

Many parties will want a 60m rope so that several sections of the route can be rappelled on the return. Other parties may feel that the route is easily done without a rope. Decide wisely—this is not a place for mistakes.

Route: Southwest Ridge (YDS 5.2)

Follow the directions given for the approach to the northeast ridge to the flattish, brushy area between West Northgate Peak and East Northgate Peak. Once there, angle west/southwest toward the indistinct saddle of West Northgate Peak and North Guardian Angel. Route-finding will be required to keep the journey from becoming an agonizing bushwhack (though an essentially brush-free path does exist).

When you break through the brush, you find yourself on the edge of a splendid wonderland of slickrock and delicious ledges. There, look for a ledge at about the same elevation that works across slickrock all the way around to the west face of North Guardian Angel. Following it, the going is wonderfully aesthetic.

Once below the west face, continue across the slickrock at the same elevation until you find yourself at the base of the southwest ridge. Scramble up class 2 slabs to gain the crest of the ridge above. A hundred feet up, you'll come to a flattish area with a very minor crag to your right. The crag is a fine vantage point to scope out much of the steep ridge above you. The flattish area is known as Scorpion Notch.

Heading up the mostly class 2-3 ridge, you'll encounter two distinct YDS 5.0-5.2 slabby sections, both of which offer about 80-100 feet of climbing. Above the second class 5 section, hike up to the base of the very steep upper ridge and traverse right for 100 feet until you can gain a groove (one class 4 move) that allows access to mellower terrain above. There, work left for 50 feet and climb a short YDS 5.0 face that puts you back on the crest of the ridge. From there, walk the class 2-3 summit ridge to the top.

A 60m rope is recommended for this route.

According to Ram...

Both of the class 5 slabby portions of the southwest ridge can be bypassed via class 3 terrain right of the crest. The upper bypass utilizes a blind ledge system around a hugely exposed corner. Above that, one climbs through the class 4 groove already mentioned and then bypasses the last YDS 5.0 face via class 2 terrain on the right. Easy ground leads to the summit. Utilizing these variations, the entire southwest ridge can be done class 3 (except for the single class 4 move in the groove), making it the easiest route on the mountain.

Aaron Ramras on the southwest ridge of North Guardian Angel

"Das Peak" (6,164)

Diminutive Das Peak, with its meager 284' of prominence, offers interesting views of the Left Fork of North Creek and the higher peaks surrounding it.

RT Mileage: 8
RT Elevation Gain: 1,800'
Time Required: 5-7 hours
Latitude: +37.3150
Longitude: -113.0401
FKA: Courtney Purcell (November 12, 2010)
Etymology: The peak sits just south of where the Das Boot canyoneering route ends at Russell Gulch.

Star Rating: *

Route: South Face (class 3)
Follow any of the approaches given for South Guardian Angel to the wash that runs along the south side of Das Peak. At least two different class 3 routes on the south face go to the summit.

The view north from the summit of Subway Peak

"Subway Peak" (6,347)

Subway Peak is a minor but glorious peak northeast of South Guardian Angel and southeast of North Guardian Angel, clinging to the cliffs above the heart of the Subway.

The peak has 307' of prominence.

RT Mileage: 8
RT Elevation Gain: 2,000'
Time Required: 5-7 hours
Latitude: +37.3078
Longitude: -113.0496
FKA: Courtney Purcell (November 12, 2010)
Etymology: The peak hovers just over the Subway.
Star Rating: **

Route: Northeast Ridge (class 3)

Follow any of the approaches to South Guardian Angel to where the wash heading southwest toward the amphitheater passes along the east side of Subway Peak. Scramble west to gain the peak's northeast ridge at a feasible spot. Head up. The excellent ridge has an incredibly cool notch mid-way up. Scramble past the notch and cruise to the summit, where the views are certain to inspire.

Rams Peak (left) from near the confluence of Wildcat Canyon and the Left Fork of North Creek. A convenient seep marked on the topo map is nearby. South Guardian Angel is at distant-right.

"Rams Peak" (7,111)

Rams Peak, clearly visible to those approaching the Subway via Russell Gulch, is connected to Greatheart Mesa by its gnarly, loose and dangerous southeast ridge. Both peaks sit on the east side of the Left Fork of North Creek and are clearly visible from near the start of the Subway route at the Northgate Peaks Trail.

A "delightful backcountry summit," an ascent of Rams Peak can also be combined with a technical descent of Das Boot and the Subway for an awesome day in and around the Left Fork of North Creek. If doing either or both of the Das Boot/Subway descent options, remember that both require canyoneering permits.

RT Mileage: 8
RT Elevation Gain: 2,500'
Time Required: 6-8 hours
Latitude: +37.3203
Longitude: -113.0233
FKA: Steve Ramras (October 1998)
Etymology: In 2005, Steve Ramras (aka 'Ram') described Peak 7,111 to me as a "delightful backcountry summit" he'd explored once upon a time. He said that the summit could easily be attained via either its north or south-southwest ridges. With winter quickly approaching, he urged me to check it out before the snows fell. Well, I didn't make it that fall, but I did make it eventually.

A buddy and I decided to check out the peak before dropping into the Left Fork of North Creek for a romp through Das Boot and the Subway one spring. With an early morning start, crossing in then back out of the Left Fork, we explored our way up Peak 7,111's south-southwest ridge. We found easy scrambling, great scenery, and soon enough, a tranquil, brushy summit. Thanks Ram!

I later told Ram I wanted to dub the peak "Rams Peak" in his honor. He declined the gesture, but I did it anyway!
Star Rating: **

The elegant pyramid of Rams Peak

Route: South-southwest Ridge (class 3)
This route requires a permit.

Follow the directions given for West Northgate Peak to the junction of the Northgate Peaks Trail and the trail to the Subway. Leave the Northgate Peaks Trail and follow the Subway route (look carefully for cairns while crossing the slickrock). At the point where the trail crosses Russell Gulch (you will be at the top of a short dryfall, which is on your immediately right, as the trail continues straight ahead and out of the Gulch), leave the trail, exiting left, and aim for a sort of low pass up to the left. Soon gaining the slickrock pass, continue along a bench, working roughly east, until you can pick up a prominent drainage (complex terrain here) that heads southeast toward the Left Fork. Dropping down the drainage, a prominent ridge should be on your right, and you should be aiming for a very prominent drainage running southeast toward Greatheart Mesa. As you continue down the drainage, sometimes on slickrock, other times fighting brush, and sometimes down-climbing steep slabs (with route-finding, no harder than class 3), you'll soon find yourself at the canyon rim above the Left Fork.

Depending on the exact point where you meet the canyon rim, a number of terrain features may confront you and some additional route-finding may be required to find a suitable point to drop-in. Whether by a steep, dirty slope, a short, down-climbable face or a short rappel off a tree, find your way into the bottom of the canyon. If you dropped in up-canyon from the optimal spot (which is virtually impossible to describe in words), expect to encounter a cold wade (or swim) back down-canyon to where you ultimately need to be. This is the start of the popular Das Boot canyoneering route.

Once in the bottom of the Left Fork, you'll need to find a way back out the other (east) side and into a low-angle slickrock drainage. This is the same drainage you could see that headed southeast up toward Greatheart Mesa as you approached. The ticket to climbing out the east side of the canyon is just barely (50 feet) up-canyon from where the bottom of the low-angle slickrock drainage dumps into the Left Fork. It's also in a particular part of the Left Fork where one can usually cross from bank-to-bank without getting wet (unusual in this part of the canyon). This spot offers the only reasonable climb-out to the east side: a narrow, dirty chimney/ramp.

Climb up the dirty chimney/ramp (class 2) and out of the canyon then angle back right on narrow, exposed ledges leading into the low-angle slickrock drainage. From here, bushwhack up the drainage a couple hundred yards until you can exit easily onto a semi-open area on your left. Once there, route-find your way over gentle terrain to the base of a large chute coming down from the mountain. The base of the chute is due west of the summit.

The head of the chute is a notch along the south-southwest ridge of the mountain.

With some route-finding involved, gain the chute and head up to the notch. If you're dealing with terrain harder than class 3, you're likely off-route. Once the notch is gained, head up the south-southwest ridge. Generally, sticking near the crest, often passing on either side of it, should get one to the summit via class 2-3 scrambling. The summit itself is lightly treed and brushy.

To descend, retrace your steps...or, see below.

Other Descent Options:

If one has more time to kill (and appropriate equipment with them), an optional descent of Das Boot or the Subway makes for an awesome day out. Das Boot and the Subway are simply names for different portions of the same canyon—the Left Fork of North Creek. Das Boot is immediately up-stream of the Subway, and both slots are fantastically beautiful and worth visiting (for those with appropriate canyoneering experience). Das Boot and the Subway are cold, with Das Boot (which features a substantial amount of cold water swimming and wading) being the colder of the two. Even in high summer, wetsuits are recommended for Das Boot. The Subway will require a car shuttle (leaving one car at the Left Fork Trailhead and one car at the Wildcat Trailhead).

1) To do Das Boot (4BII), head down-canyon from the point where the route to Rams Peak crosses the Left Fork of North Creek. Several challenging down-climbs and at least one mandatory rappel (30-meter rope is sufficient) will be found. After about two hours of splashing through Das Boot, and just below the final rappel down a fluted section of canyon into a cold swimming hole, you reach the confluence of the Left Fork and Russell Gulch. If not opting to descend the Subway as well, hang a right into Russell Gulch and reverse the directions back to the Wildcat Trailhead, as provided for South Guardian Angel;

2) To also do the Subway (4BIII, including Das Booth), make your way through Das Boot and then continue past the Russell Gulch confluence and on down-canyon, following the Subway descent directions to the Left Fork Trailhead (as provided for South Guardian Angel). Expect 3-4 short rappels (30-meter rope is sufficient).

Greatheart Mesa (7,410)
CLOSED TO RECREATIONAL USE—RNA

Greatheart Mesa is a sprawling, glorious peak in the Left Fork region of the Kolob Terrace of Zion. When approaching The Subway, one can't help but notice this big, steep-walled mountain.

The peak has 1125' of prominence.

RT Mileage: 11
RT Elevation Gain: 4,100'
Time Required: 9-11 hours
Latitude: +37.3088
Longitude: -113.0251
FA: Unknown
Etymology: Steve Allen writes in *Utah's Canyon Country Place Names, Volume 1*, that the peak was named for "Christiana's guide in the story of Pilgrims Progress."
Star Rating: ***

Greatheart Mesa (upper-left) from Zippy

Route: North Ridge (class 4)

This route requires a permit.

Follow the directions given for Rams Peak to the notch at the top of the gully on that peak's south-southwest ridge. From the notch, head left up the ridge for 50 feet to a steep chute dropping into the bowl on the other (east) side of the ridge. Head down (class 4 in a couple short spots), cross the bowl and then scramble up to the (north-south) ridge connecting Rams Peak and Greatheart Mesa. Traverse south along the ridge, either downclimbing a steep and loose step midway or bypassing it on the right (west). As the final cliffs below Greatheart Mesa are approached, work up and right to a short (12-foot) and awkward, brushy slab (class 3) that forms a break in the final cliffs. The RNA begins at the mesa-top. As such, the true summit is closed to recreational use.

A 30m rope is recommended for the route.

Rams Peak (left) and the northern shoulder of Greatheart Mesa from the slickrock above Das Boot. A few minutes after this picture was taken, we rescued a woman who'd become stranded.

South Guardian Angel (7,164)

Welcome to beautifulZion National Park's legendary South Guardian Angel—the frequently sought after (but rarely achieved) little sister of the heralded North Guardian Angel. The impressive North Guardian Angel and South Guardian Angel stand guard over western Zion's Left Fork of North Creek—home of the world famous Subway, an awe-inspiring semi-technical slot canyon.

The ultra-reclusive South Guardian Angel is a worthy adversary and the final objective of many a DPS (Sierra Club "Desert Peaks Section") list-ticker. Many have tried and failed to reach this fabled summit on the first try, myself included. Nestled deep in the backcountry, this Guardian Angel (unlike its challenging—also class 4 by its standard route—but easily accessible neighbor, North Guardian Angel) takes some work to get to. But it's worth it—the sexy slickrock of the elegant northeast ridge is not to be missed.

RT Mileage: 12
RT Elevation Gain: 3,000'
Time Required: 5-12 hours
Latitude: +37.2954
Longitude: -113.0598
FKA: Arkel Erb (1960s)
Etymology: North Guardian Angel and South Guardian Angel, near-twins posted on opposing sides of the Left Fork of North Creek, were named as guardians of this portion of the park.
Star Rating: ****

Approach option #1 (Direct via Northgate Peaks):
This approach does *not* require a permit.

This approach is renowned for its subtle complexity. Despite a massive increase in the number of cairns and the use of the route in the years since I first covered it, route-finding on the descent is still tricky.

Follow the directions given for the northeast ridge route on North Guardian Angel to a point near the base of that peak's northeast ridge. Hike east through flattish terrain until you can cut to the right over a low sandstone hill just east of a gap at the base of North Guardian Angel's northeast ridge. Cruise down the backside, slowly trending left across several chutes and ribs, ultimately trying to locate a steep, dirty chute that dumps one in the Left Fork of North Creek, immediately opposite the "jug handle" arch described in approach option #2. Follow the remainder of that route to the amphitheater.

Approach option #2 (Russell Gulch & The Subway):
This approach requires a Subway permit.

Follow the directions given for West Northgate Peak to the junction of the Northgate Peaks Trail and the Subway trail. Follow the intermittent Subway trail down toward Russell Gulch. At times the route becomes a little hard to follow, though an abundance of cairns facilitates matters. In a couple of miles you'll find yourself walking along the trail as it overlooks a steep-walled canyon below—this is the Left Fork of North Creek, and the entrance to the world famous Subway.

Follow the trail steeply down into the very bottom of Russell Gulch. You'll encounter a pool of water, which you'll wade across then walk 100 yards to the confluence with the Left Fork of North Creek. Hang a right and head downstream, working through various obstacles, including a short rappel (12-15 foot) down a large polished boulder (I'm told there's a rabbit hole on the far left that allows one to scramble easily past this obstacle) and a mandatory swim through a couple of ice-cold potholes, for about 0.5 mile until you come to a portion of the canyon that looks a touch like a subway tunnel, with a flat, rock shelf about waist-high on the left side.

Perhaps 30 feet beyond the prominent "shelf" feature on the south side of the canyon, at or slightly above eye level, is a smallish sandstone arch that resembles the handle of a jug. The feature is partially obscured by trees and brush, but large enough that those looking for it should have little problem finding it. This point marks the exit from the Left Fork. From the "jug handle," your objective is to head up the steep chute above. The going in the chute is not too bad, with just a few obstacles to overcome. The first obstacle is about 15 feet above and just to the left of the "jug handle," where a short and minimally exposed class 3 move or two puts you on a ledge next to a tree. From there, climb a short (8-foot) class 4 wall to the next ledge above. Fifteen feet beyond the class 4 section is a hardy tree. In the event you feel uncomfortable down-climbing the class 4 section on the return, this tree makes for a nice anchor.

Continuing up the chute a short distance, it divides. Head left and immediately come to an exit blocked by a chockstone. The chockstone is easily climbed around with a couple of class 3 moves. Once above the chockstone, you'll encounter a use trail heading up to the left. Follow it. The use trail switchbacks up a couple hundred feet to a notch at the top of the canyon cliffs. You're out of the canyon.

From the groove, head southeast for 100 yards to a wash. Follow the wash east for a couple hundred yards until it turns abruptly south as another wash comes in from the east. Continue up the wash south then southwest to where it ends in a sort of sandstone amphitheater near the base of the northeast ridge of South Guardian Angel.

Approach option #3 (Overland via Das Boot Entry):
This approach requires a permit.

Follow the directions given for Rams Peak to the shallow slickrock drainage immediately east of the start of the Das Boot canyoneering route. Scramble 40 feet up the drainage until you can exit to the right up a steep, pine needle slope. From here, there's no easy way to describe where to go. Generally, hike south over and around a view obstacles to gain the flattish plateau southeast of Das Peak. Next, get into the wash that flows west along the south side of Das Peak and head down-stream (bypassing obstacles on the left). Follow the stream course west to its confluence with another wash coming in from the west. The stream course turns abruptly south at the confluence. Here, the route coincides with the final portion of approach option #2. Follow the route to the amphitheater.

Route: Northeast Ridge (class 3-4)
Once at the amphitheater, get onto the slickrock and start scrambling up. Frequent cairns mark an optimal route. Generally, head up and trend southwest. It won't be long before South Guardian Angel comes bursting into view and the access to the northeast ridge will be apparent. Gain the northeast ridge and follow it steeply upward over class 2-3 slabs and ledges to the summit ridge, which is followed westerly to the highpoint. Shortly before the summit is a steep and exposed class 3 slabby section for which some parties set a handline.

Alternative descent option #1 (The Subway—Left Fork of North Creek: 3BIII):
A Subway permit is required.

In cooler months, expect cold (and potentially treacherous), icy conditions. In spring, high water volume in the narrow canyon could make the going extremely dangerous and/or impossible. Some may wish to wear a wetsuit for the canyon, even in summer. During the summer monsoon season, flashflooding can be a concern. A car spot will need to be arranged beforehand, leaving a car at the Left Fork Trailhead.

Descend to the "jug handle" arch mentioned in approach options #1 and #2. Head down-canyon through the Left Fork of North Creek. Various obstacles are encountered along the way, including a few rappels up to 30 feet, swimming through icy-cold pools, and some short down-climbs over wet rock. The scenery is outstanding, and you will not be let down.

Once the "Subway" itself (referring to a subway tunnel-like feature in the canyon) is reached, you are near the end of the most spectacular part of the canyon. Continue downstream for a few more miles, crossing and re-crossing the creek as necessary (often on bits of use trail), until you come to a park sign with an arrow on it. The sign is right next to the edge of the creek and is difficult to miss. From the arrow, follow a good trail as it winds its way steeply up 400 vertical feet and out of the canyon to the rim above. The trail then takes you to the Left Fork Trailhead in about a mile.

Alternative descent option #2 (West Cliffs):
This descent option requires a Subway permit.

A car spot will need to be arranged beforehand, leaving a car at the Left Fork Trailhead. This descent option is non-technical, except for a single rappel near the bottom of the route.

From the summit, descend generally southwest for several hundred vertical feet to gain the vegetated plateau at the base of the dome of the mountain. With a bit of route-finding, hike west to the far western tip of the plateau, atop the cliffs overlooking the Rosebud-South Guardian Angel saddle. Here, some funky down-climbing and then a 65-foot rappel put one on easy ground near the saddle. From here, follow the directions given for Rosebud to the Left Fork Trailhead.

Congrats—you've just completed a full traverse of South Guardian Angel.

The sleek beauty of South Guardian Angel. I've been tirelessly exploring every nook and cranny of the backcountry of Zion National Park for the last 13 years, trying to find something that equals or exceeds the beauty of this peak—thus far, I've not found its equal. It may not be my favorite peak, but it's the prettiest I've seen.

"Turkey Peak" (6,127)

Diminutive Turkey Peak is southeast of South Guardian Angel in a glorious and ultra-convoluted portion of the park. The peak has 327' of prominence.

RT Mileage: 12-14
RT Elevation Gain: 2,500'
Time Required: 8-10 hours
Latitude: +37.2899
Longitude: -113.0460
FKA: Courtney Purcell, DB, Andy Archibald, Sarah & Dominic Meiser (November 24, 2011)
Etymology: After climbing this peak on Thanksgiving Day, our party decided to call it Turkey Peak.
Star Rating: **

Outrageous views from the vicinity of The Hourglass

Route: East Slope (class 2-3)

Follow one of the approaches given for South Guardian Angel to the complex terrain on the south side of the Left Fork of North Creek. From here, there's no easy way to describe where to go. A number of viable approaches may be utilized.

Perhaps the most straightforward approach is to make for the gap slightly northeast of Guardian Angel Pass. The gap is at approximately +37.3043 -113.0413. Head south from the gap down the drainage to its confluence with a more substantial drainage coming in from Greatheart Mesa. Leave both drainages and work south-ish through some dirty, steep stuff to attain the pleasant, sandy area just east of Turkey Peak. A short walk from here leads to the highpoint, where we built a cairn.

"The Hourglass" (7,204)
CLOSED TO RECREATIONAL USE—RNA

The Hourglass is a splendid peak deep in the Zion backcountry behind Rams Peak and Greatheart Mesa, towering above the upper Right Fork of North Creek. The views from high on the mountain go deep into Phantom Valley to Church Mesa, as well as to Inclined Temple, Ivins Mountain and elsewhere.

RT Mileage: 15
RT Elevation Gain: 2,000'
Time Required: 12-14 hours
Latitude: +37.3111
Longitude: -113.0112
Etymology: I named the peak for a huge hourglass-shaped feature (requires imagination) on the big, steep west face of the peak's north ridge.
Star Rating: ***

Route: Northwest Ridge (class 3-4)
From the Wildcat Trailhead, follow the Wildcat Trail several miles to where it crosses the shallow, forested head of Wildcat Canyon. Wildcat Canyon is not signed; however, it's hard to miss the huge canyon as you approach it. Fighting thick vegetation, walk into Wildcat Canyon and work your way down. Although brushy, the going is easy for a mile or two, after which the bottom of the canyon narrows and the going gets more tedious. Although it can be done in a number of places, when the canyon begins to narrow up considerably work to the flattish bench above you to the right and follow easy terrain and/or game trails further down the canyon. Continuing along the bench above the slot on your left, you'll eventually encounter a slot canyon before you. This is the upper portion of the Left Fork of North Creek.

Work into the slot via a number of possible walk-down routes. Walking down the Left Fork for a short distance (well under 0.25 mile), exit left as soon as you find easy terrain that allows you to do so then work south-southeast to a nearby seep next to two potholes in an open area of slickrock. The seep is marked on the topo map and is 100 yards east of the point where the Left Fork briefly heads south near the toe of The Hourglass's northwest ridge. (The seep might be the first drinkable water you've seen thus far. Treat it before consumption.)

From the area of the seep, head south to gain the northwest ridge of The Hourglass. Heading up the ridge, the going is initially easy and the route-finding elementary. As you approach a significant false peak on the ridge, you can climb up and over it or bypass it by working exposed class 2 ledges on its left (east) side. Regaining the crest of the ridge at the saddle immediately beyond the sub-peak, you'll be confronted by a striking, large, colorful spire on the crest. Work around it on the left by gaining a 3-inch wide ledge just beyond the saddle and traversing 10-15 feet to flat ground. The exposure here is small.

Scrambling the northwest ridge of The Hourglass

Continue south through a small notch and walk 50-75 feet beyond this very colorful portion of the ridge until you can regain the ridge crest via class 2 scrambling. There, you are confronted with another sub-peak. Instead of trying to work up and over the sub-peak, cross to the west side of the crest and drop just enough to start traversing southeast along a series of narrow, rubbly ledges to gain a steep but easy chute that you can see heading directly up the northwest face of the mountain. A spicy couple of moves may be required to get to the chute. Once there, you have left the northwest ridge (which will be to your left) and are now on the northwest face.

With some zig-zagging here and there to avoid a few rock band obstacles, generally work the chute upward toward the flattish summit plateau above. Several steep, exposed class 3-4 scrambling sections may be encountered unless you work hard to keep it easier. The RNA begins at the mesa-top. As such, the true summit is closed to recreational use.

To descend, retrace your steps. Alternatively, you can continue down the chute to a point a couple hundred vertical feet below the point where you originally gained it on your traverse from the ridge and exit right as soon as easy scrambling to moderate slabs allows. From there, route-find your way northwest (avoiding a slot that forms on your left) to a point where class 2 slabs allow you to meander your way back onto the northwest ridge not far from its toe.

Alternative Approach Option (The Hammerhead: 3AIV, for the combo):

A shorter but more technical approach would be to take the West Rim Trail toward Potato Hollow. Leave the trail here and work through tedious brush (GPS helpful) to the head of The Hammerhead, which is approx. 0.2 mile southeast of Point 7,325. Rappel into the canyon from a large tree at its head (look for slings) then negotiate several downclimbs and rappels up to about 165 feet. You will eventually reach the mouth of the canyon. From there, do a semi-tricky traverse right to escape the drainage and gain the easy terrain to the northwest. Once on the easier terrain, traverse northwest to a point where you can readily gain the northwest ridge of The Hourglass.

For this variation, you'll need to bring appropriate technical equipment (including that needed for establishing natural rappel anchors). You are also required to obtain a canyoneering permit. You'll want to spot a car at the appropriate exit point.

Alternative descent option #1 (Full Right Fork of North Creek: 4BVI, for the combo):

With proper planning, an ascent of The Hourglass can be combined with a descent of the Right Fork of North Creek. This option will require 3 days of your time, a canyoneering permit, full wetsuits, harness/helmet, rappel device, several carabiners, a 50-meter rope, drybags, sufficient food and the capacity to carry lots of water, a water filter, 50 feet of webbing and a spotted car at the Right Fork Trailhead. This experience is classic and requires advanced canyoneering skills.

Here's the low-down:

From the toe of the ridge, hike east and follow the gentle drainage southeast to the col about a mile away. A couple of nice bivy spots can be found here. (Ideally, you would have started from the trailhead early enough on day 1 to reach the col by day's end after doing the peak.)

Rising early on day 2, note the semi-complex topography on the southeast side of the col. Drop down class 2-3 terrain to gain the drainage immediately below. Negotiating a short rappel or two, the drainage will soon slot up and get wet and cold. Move through the slot for 2-4 hours (working through several anchor challenges), until the canyon briefly opens up to nice, sunny slabs on your left and then re-slots and begins a bend to the right. Continue down-canyon and work through easier terrain and a handful of fun obstacles, including a long (100-yard), cold swim through a narrow channel. Near the end of day 2, you'll come to a stunning area known as the Grand Alcove. The Grand Alcove is a giant, colorful alcove with fresh water pouring out from seeps all along the canyon wall. This is the first good drinking water you've encountered since the seep the day before. Make camp at the Grand Alcove, or consider moving along a bit further to shorten the hike out on day 3. Work a ledge above the canyon bottom on the left side of the drainage then do two short rappels to regain the bottom of the canyon. Once there, continue along. Suitable camp spots thin out shortly hereafter.

On day three, negotiate some waterfalls (can generally be bypassed, though one called Barrier Falls requires a 60-foot rappel down a steep, slippery slab) and then complex, bouldery terrain until you reach the mellow streambed that meanders four miles out to the confluence of the Right and Left Forks of North Creek at the base of the black, lava slope below Kolob Terrace Road. From the confluence, head 0.5 mile further down the creek and look for the unsigned Right Fork Trail (easy to miss) on the right. I've been up this spot at least a dozen times and still tend to screw it up.

Alternative descent option #2 (Full Left Fork of North Creek: 4BIV, for the combo):
This variation is appropriate for canyoneers with advanced skills during summer through early fall. A full wetsuit is needed, even in the heat of mid-summer. Plan on 1-2 days to complete the entire route (through the Subway), though quick and efficient parties can certainly do it in a reasonable (albeit longish) day. Don't forget a canyoneering permit and to spot a car at the appropriate exit point. In addition to standard technical canyoneering gear (see above), bring a water filter and plenty of food.

Once down from the peak, enter the Left Fork near the seep (don't forget to fill up!) then start down-canyon toward Das Boot (and lower, the Subway), negotiating a number of tricky, wet downclimbs and rappels from natural anchors. Like Das Boot, the portion of the Left Fork below the seep is tricky, technical, very cold—and very fun. Exit the canyon on the right using either the Das Boot or Subway approach directions given for South Guardian Angel.

A 50m rope is adequate for the route.

"Dead Tree Peak" (6,805)

Dead Tree Peak is in one of my favorite parts of the Zion backcountry. Few venture back into this wild and wonderful, rugged and rough country, sublime and poetic with slickrock, hoodoos, potholes and cliffs.

Dead Tree Peak has 525' of prominence. It is a good peak in a fine chunk of backcountry.

RT Mileage: 16
RT Elevation Gain: 4,600'
Time Required: 10-12 hours
Latitude: +37.2962
Longitude: -113.0196
FKA: Courtney Purcell, James Hiebert, Bryan Long and Sarah & Dominic Meiser (November 23, 2012)
Etymology: Although ours was the first known ascent of the peak, we found a curious small piling of rocks atop the highpoint. I moved the "cairn" to an adjacent dead tree, for which the peak was named.
Star Rating: ***

Rabbits Ears (center) and Dead Tree Peak (right) from near the head of Stevenson Canyon. Iron Lion and its stunning northeast buttress are visible rising above Stevenson Canyon. Out of view to the left is Great White Dome. Stevenson Peak is behind the photographer.

Route: Northwest Face (class 3-4)

Follow the directions given for Turkey Peak to the substantial drainage coming down from Greatheart Mesa. (It is worth mentioning that a number of variations to the approach down to this wash have been utilized; unfortunately, they're so tricky to describe that I won't bother. In nearly all cases, they begin southeast of the gap that is northeast of Guardian Angel Pass.)

Hike up the charming, though at-times-brushy, wash toward the gap between Greatheart Mesa and Dead Tree Peak to a point northwest of the summit of Dead Tree Peak, where ramping slabs lead directly toward the summit.

Scramble up the slabs (steep; class 3) for about 200' until you pick up a convenient but exposed and narrow ledge that heads southwest directly for the saddle between Dead Tree Peak and Elkhorn Peak. From the saddle, scramble up Dead Tree Peak's northwest face. Although the ascent seemed like reasonable class 3, during the descent several in our group of strong scramblers utilized a handline around a bush for a 20' section near the top.

Dominic Meiser relaxes on the summit of Rabbit Ears. North Guardian Angel is at top-center. What appears to be mellowish, gentle terrain between the two peaks is actually a wonderland of rugged country—hoodoos and slots and potholes and other bits of goodness.

"Elkhorn Peak" (6,680)

Elkhorn Peak is a delightful moderate scramble deep in the backcountry south of Greatheart Mesa. This is No-Man's Land. There's no easy way in or out.

The peak has 320' of prominence.

RT Mileage: 16
RT Elevation Gain: 4,600'
Time Required: 10-12 hours
Latitude: +37.2945
Longitude: -113.0257
FKA: Courtney Purcell, James Hiebert, Bryan Long and Sarah & Dominic Meiser (November 23, 2012)
Etymology: On the approach to the peak, we found a massive elk antler, which we took turns lugging across miles of rugged country, through a narrow slot, past thick brush, down walls, up ramps, and ultimately to the summit of this peak, where we left it.
Star Rating: ****

Route: Northeast Ridge (class 3)

Follow the directions given for Dead Tree Peak to the saddle between it and Elkhorn Peak. Leave the saddle and scramble Elkhorn Peak's northeast ridge to the top.

"Rabbit Ears" (6,840)

Rabbit Ears (560' of prominence) is a really sweet peak in an outstanding position above the Right Fork of North Creek, west of Ivins Mountain and south of Elkhorn Peak. The views are terrific.

The southwest summit is the highpoint. The northeast summit is called Iron Lion.

RT Mileage: 16-17
RT Elevation Gain: 4,800'
Time Required: 12 hours
Latitude: +37.2865
Longitude: -113.0256
FKA: Sarah & Dominic Meiser and Courtney Purcell (November 29, 2013)
Etymology: Once on the summit of North Guardian Angel at dusk with my pal Aron Ralston, I was pointing out a peak several rugged miles distant to the southeast that I'd yet to do. He asked me, "Do you mean the one that looks like rabbit ears?" Indeed. So when my partners and I climbed it a year or so later, we decided to keep the name.
Star Rating: ****

Route: North Face (class 4)

Follow the directions given for Dead Tree Peak to the saddle between it and Elkhorn Peak. Proceed southwest from the saddle across a wooded plateau to a trio of steep slickrock buttresses leading up the north face of Rabbit Ears. Starting up the rightmost buttress, enjoyable class 3 scrambling (trending left as necessary to avoid steeper, more exposed terrain) funnels you onto steep dirt below the final rock band just before the summit. From here, a 50-foot, dirty class 4 scramble up the loose upper north face leads to the top. We roped up for the ascent of this upper portion (a tree or two can be slung for protection) and subsequently rappelled it on the descent. Due to anchor limitations, play it safe and bring a 60m rope and about 30 feet of webbing.

According to Darin Berdinka...

Iron Lion

The aesthetic northeast buttress of Iron Lion can be climbed directly at III 5.9 and has been named The Kingdom. Access is via Stevenson Canyon (rappels to 170'). Climb the obvious brushy weakness on the north side of the buttress then another five pitches to 5.9 on the crest. Exposed 4th class scrambling on good rock leads to easier terrain and the summit. Descend via Rabbit Ears (class 4 from Iron Lion to Rabbit Ears) then rappel and downclimb a series of obvious trees on the canyon wall due north of the start of the route. When exiting Stevenson Canyon to the Right Fork, deep pools can be avoided by staying high and to descenders' left before rappelling near the mouth of the canyon.

Medium rack to 3" including LA and Angle pitons. Double 60m ropes required for the descent.

Stevenson Peak

This peak is 1.5 miles northeast of Rabbit Ears.

Climb the northeast ridge via 3rd class scrambling and a single short pitch of 5.7 (#1 Camalot for protection) in an obvious corner. Descend the route with a single rappel from trees.

Great White Dome

This beautiful peak is 0.5 mile south of Stevenson Peak.

From the summit of Stevenson Peak descend the south ridge via exposed downclimbing and two single rope rappels. From here the ridgeline is followed on chossy 3rd and 4th class rock with the occasional low-5th class boulder move. The final 100' to the summit plateau are steep and exposed and may require a rope. Crossing the summit plateau to the marginally higher high point is prohibited by the Park Service [RNA]. To descend reverse the route to the base of Stevenson Peak. A double rope rappel to the west is followed by exposed 3ʳᵈ class downclimbing to a dirt ridge lying against the lower slabs.

Pocket Mesa Trailhead

From the UT-9/Kolob Terrace Road junction, follow the paved Kolob Terrace Road for 16.3 miles to a dirt pull-out on the left side of the road. Park at the pull-out.

The peaks in this subsection are roughly arranged from shortest-hike-from-the-trailhead to longest-hike-from-the-trailhead.

Pocket Mesa (7,500+)

Though Pocket Mesa's south and southeast cliffs are impressive while walking the Wildcat Trail toward the Subway, when approaching the small peak from Kolob Terrace Road, the objective is less than inspiring. Regardless, this easy, named peak offers nice views of this portion of the park.

RT Mileage: 0.5
RT Elevation Gain: 250'
Time Required: 1 hour
Latitude: +37.3508
Longitude: -113.0689
FA: Unknown
Etymology: In *Utah's Canyon Country Place Names, Volume 2*, Steve Allen notes that the USGS provided the name for "the deep recesses in the south face of this white-cliff mountain."
Star Rating: *

Route: Northwest Face (class 2)
From the pull-out, walk up the road less than 0.25 mile to a point where you can cut east through the forest and easily reach the northwest face of Pocket Mesa. Climb to the flattish summit area via any of several class 2 lines on the face. As I recall, the highpoint itself is not obvious.

"Windy Peak" (7,888)

Windy Peak is a heavily vegetated high summit that offers commanding views of the entire Kolob Terrace. As evidenced by all the hoof prints and game trails criss-crossing much of the peak, it's also popular with the local elk crowd.

Although it can't be seen via the standard route, the west face of Windy Peak features a huge (500-foot tall) face housing a giant alcove. The "Windy Alcove" can best be viewed from the summit of nearby Jobs Head.

Windy Peak has 328' of prominence.

A massive alcove in the west face of Windy Peak, as seen from Jobs Head

RT Mileage: 1
RT Elevation Gain: 800'
Time Required: 1 hour
Latitude: +37.3585
Longitude: -113.0766
FA: Unknown
Etymology: Labeled simply as "BM 7888" on the map, I found extremely cold and windy conditions during an early spring ascent of the peak.
Star Rating: **

Route: Southeast Ridge (class 1)

From the pull-out, head northeast up easy slopes to gain the southeast ridge of the peak. With a little looking around, you should be able to pick up good game trails that will take you all the way to the summit.

Alternatively, the southeast ridge can be followed directly from the road, 0.25 mile northeast of the pull-out. This variation is not as pleasant.

According to Andy...

A more rigorous hike can be had by starting at the Jobs Head Trailhead (or the sharp U-turn in the road just past the Jobs Head Trailhead) and hiking up obvious weaknesses in Windy Peak's southwest face. Both of these options require more substantial uphill hiking.

Amazing scenery from just off the West Rim Trail

West Rim Trailhead

From the UT-9/Kolob Terrace Road junction, follow the paved Kolob Terrace Road for 19.9 miles to a dirt road on your right signed for Lava Point and the West Rim Trail. Turning onto this road, the first section to a fork (the right fork goes to Lava Point) is generally graded and in good shape. Taking the left fork toward the West Rim Trailhead for another 1.4 miles, the road deteriorates and can become impassable if it has rained recently. Passenger cars usually make it to the West Rim Trailhead (about 2.4 miles from Kolob Terrace Road) during dry conditions.

Kolob Terrace Road is closed below Wildcat Trailhead during the winter months. It is not uncommon during spring and fall for the road to the West Rim Trailhead to be gated (and therefore closed to vehicular traffic) shortly beyond the fork. If that's the case, one can park outside the gate and walk the 1.4 miles down the road to the trailhead, or head to Lava Point, where Barney's Trail (behind the campground) can be used as an excellent shortcut down to the road.

The peaks in this subsection are roughly arranged from shortest-hike-from-the-trailhead to longest-hike-from-the-trailhead.

Goose Creek Knoll (7,660)

Goose Creek Knoll is likely the easiest (and most lame) "peak" in this guide. The named summit sits just north of the popular West Rim Trailhead. When the road's open to the trailhead, you can drive right to the base and then slouch your way almost effortlessly to the top.

The peak has 120' of prominence.

RT Mileage: 0.25 mile
RT Elevation Gain: 150'
Time Required: 15 minutes
Latitude: +37.3837
Longitude: -113.0224
FA: Some anonymous psycho from years past, I'm sure.
Etymology: The knoll lies at the head of Goose Creek.
Star Rating: *

Route: Southwest Slope (class 2)

From the West Rim Trailhead, walk 100 yards back up the road toward Lava Point. Leave the road and simply head up the southwest slope of the "peak," fighting brush the whole way to the top. Good stuff!

Goose Creek Wilderness Highpoint (7,020)

Although I believe this un-prominent (0' of prominence) highpoint is just outside of Zion National Park, signage nearby keeps things ambiguous. Regardless, it takes just a pleasant stroll along a lonely dirt road to get there.

RT Mileage: 5
RT Elevation Gain: 500'
Time Required: 2-3 hours
Latitude: +37.3751
Longitude: -112.9959
FA: Unknown
Etymology: This is the highpoint of Goose Creek Wilderness.
Star Rating: *

Route: Via the Road (class 1)

From the West Rim Trailhead, hike east past the gate and down the road (not the West Rim Trail), keeping to the main road that initially heads northwest but generally heads southeast. With a GPS, locate and walk to the "summit," which seems to be about 15 feet right of the road.

Awesome views from Never Done Mountain

"Goose Creek Peak" (6,840)

This peak is in a nice, quiet part of the park. Most of the route is walking along a lonely dirt road; the rest is pleasant, class 1 hiking through forest.

RT Mileage: 7
RT Elevation Gain: 1,500'
Time Required: 3-5 hours
Latitude: +37.3607
Longitude: -112.9833
FA: Unknown
Etymology: The minor peak (240' of prominence) hovers over central Goose Creek.
Star Rating: *

Route: Northeast Slope (class 1)

From the West Rim Trailhead, hike east past the gate and down the road (not the West Rim Trail), keeping to the main road that initially heads northwest but generally heads southeast. You will leave the park and eventually re-enter it. After re-entering the park, at a point north-northeast of Goose Creek Peak, leave the road and head south across easy terrain that soon descends toward the saddle connecting the plateau you're on with Goose Creek Peak (to the south-southwest). It's easy going (class 1) all the way to the saddle.

From the saddle, simply hike southwest to the summit.

"Krishna Point" (6,280)
CLOSED TO RECREATIONAL USE—RNA
This minor peak (240' of prominence) holds a special place in my heart.

Krishna Point is due west of Goose Creek Peak.

Latitude: +37.3600
Longitude: -112.9889
Etymology: The essence of Krishna seems to dwell near the mountain.

"Never Done Mountain" (7,325)
A nice trail (and short off-trail) hike to a stunning viewpoint. I've always loved this part of Kolob Terrace, as the gently sublimity of a stroll along the West Rim Trail couples so nicely with the intensity of the views that occasionally open to the west.

RT Mileage: 12.8
RT Elevation Gain: 1,650
Time Required: 5-7 hours
Latitude: +37.3131
Longitude: -112.9966
FA: Unknown
Etymology: While on the summit one day, my partner Andy Archibald commented on how the views inspired him to explore more and more of Zion. Instead of the same reaction, the views reminded me of how much more I still had *left to do* in the park. Andy then coined the name "Never Done" for the mountain. Ha!
Star Rating: **

Route: West Rim Trail (class 1)
Follow the West Rim Trail south for a bit under six miles, passing through Potato Hollow and re-ascending to a highpoint along the trail on a vegetated ridge immediately east of the summit. You'll pass through a beautiful bit of forest just below this point. Leave the trail and walk easily to the highpoint. We built a cairn on the summit. From the top, there are awesome views of Church Mesa, The Hamster, Zippy, Ivins Mountain, Inclined Temple and the great white domes south of Greatheart Mesa.

Aaah, views from Horse Pasture Plateau…

Horse Pasture Plateau (7,350)

Horse Pasture Plateau is the highpoint of the West Rim Trail. The highpoint itself has only marginal views; fortunately, by walking a mere 50 feet off the trail, the views expand into an improbably classic panorama that includes Phantom Valley, the Right Fork drainage, and dozens of rarely (and some never) climbed peaks.

For those who care about prominence, Horse Pasture Plateau has 375 feet of the stuff.

RT Mileage: 16 (from Zion Canyon) / 15 (from West Rim Trailhead)
RT Elevation Gain: 3,800 (from Zion Canyon) / 2,400 (from West Rim Trailhead)
Time Required: 6-10 hours
Latitude: +37.2963
Longitude: -112.9897
FA: Unknown
Etymology: Early settlers used to let their horses and cattle graze up on this rolling plateau.
Star Rating: ***

Route: West Rim Trail (class 1)
From the West Rim Trailhead, follow the trail over undulating, mellow terrain to the summit. While the scenery along this route does not possess the sustained visual dramatics of the lower West Rim Trail approach from the Grotto Trailhead, this section of the trail is more serene and much less traveled.

Route: From Zion Canyon (class 1)
From the Grotto Trailhead, take the main trail past Angels Landing on up to the plateau leading to the summit of this peak. This is a straightforward, long-ish trail hike with excellent scenery.

The small, forested summit of Imlay Point during the final approach

"Imlay Point" (6,365)

Although minor in stature, Imlay Point is a nice peak with excellent views. The peak is in an isolated area yet it's a very reasonable hike from the West Rim Trailhead. Thanks to a seemingly healthy deer and elk population, game trails allow one to move fairly freely along the off-trail portion of the approach, largely avoiding what should be a horrible brush slog.

RT Mileage: 15
RT Elevation Gain: 3,000'
Time Required: 6-8 hours
Latitude: +37.3242
Longitude: -112.9684
FKA: Courtney Purcell (October 12, 2013)
Etymology: This minor summit sits near the northern rim of middle Imlay Canyon, northwest of the two Imlay Sneak routes.
Star Rating: **

Route: North Ridge (class 2)

From the West Rim Trailhead, follow the trail south to a point northwest of Imlay Point, where the trail bends right and begins to descend toward Potato Hollow. Leave the trail and follow the wooded ridge initially east-southeast then northeast as it heads toward Corral Hollow. At a point north-northwest of the summit of Imlay Point, the ridge bends sharply southeast toward its terminus, due north of the summit of our objective. A convenient class 2 weakness in the south face of the ridge allows one to scramble rubbly garbage to the base of Imlay Point. From here, a simple hike leads to the summit.

Imlay Point is the small, pointy, wooded summit near the center of the photo

"Buddha Point" (6,360)

CLOSED TO RECREATIONAL USE—RNA

Buddha Point sits across the deep chasm of the main fork of Goose Creek from Krishna Point in a seldom-visited and interesting portion of Zion. The peak has 320' of prominence.

Latitude: +37.3589
Longitude: -112.9913
Etymology: Few mountains in the backcountry of Zion exude Buddha-nature more than this one.

Andy Archibald catches his breath just below the summit of Corral Hollow Peak

"Corral Hollow Peak" (6,805)

Corral Hollow Peak is a large, well-guarded mountain between Corral Hollow and Imlay Canyon. It is bordered on the east by the Zion Narrows and on the west by the north forks of Imlay Canyon. The mountain's massive west and southwest faces are jaw-dropping when viewed from either of the lower Imlay Sneak Routes.

The mountain is dirty, dangerous, and not easy to climb. I failed on my first attempt to climb the peak with a very talented team, with various partners peeling off and turning around here and there along the route as the ugliness became real. I returned with one member of that team a couple of years later, and we were able to overcome the crux with some well-planned creativity.

Corral Hollow Peak has 605' of prominence, which is misleading when you consider what a hulking mountain it is.

RT Mileage: 16
RT Elevation Gain: 4,800'
Time Required: 11-14 hours
Latitude: +37.3214
Longitude: -112.9607
FKA: Andy Archibald & Courtney Purcell (May 13, 2015)
Etymology: This big peak hovers over the mellow middle section of Corral Hollow.
Star Rating: **

Route: North Ridge (YDS 5.2 A0)

Follow the directions given for Imlay Point to a point just above the saddle at the base of that peak. Next, follow game trails east as they descend toward the south fork of Corral Hollow, which drains from the north face of Corral Hollow Peak. Easily cross the south fork of Corral Hollow then scramble up steep dirt and pine needles to gain the crest of the peak's north ridge, which is the thin ridge immediately east of the south fork of Corral Hollow. The going is initially mellow.

Ascend the steepening ridge to the final headwall. Anticipate a couple of dirty class 4-5 steps that must be negotiated before reaching an 80-foot YDS 5.2 slab/groove (trees and bushes can be slung for protection) just below the headwall. Above the slab/groove, scramble 30 feet left to a pine at the headwall. Although three options present themselves at the headwall, the safest is probably a steep and dirty 20-foot slab (perhaps YDS 5.9) 15 feet above you on the right. There's a dirty seam on the right side of the slab and two decent trees at the top of the slab. You'll need to get creative to overcome this section.

Above the crux, scramble up 30 feet of dirty class 3 terrain to reach the flattish plateau below the summit cap. Traverse west along the base of the cliffs of the summit cap then cut south until you can pick up a class 3 break in the cliffs just northwest of the highpoint. Battling brush takes you to the summit, where we built a cairn out of fallen logs.

At least three rappels should be expected on the descent of the ridge. Helmets are strongly encouraged.

Two 30m ropes are recommended for the route.

The author on the summit of Avalokiteshvara Temple

Zion Canyon

Zion Canyon—this is what all the hype's about. Carved by the Virgin River, which flows out to the town of Springdale and beyond into Lake Mead from above the Temple of Sinawava, the high-walled multi-colored canyon is lined with majestic, impossible-to-climb-looking peaks. As it turns out, many of these peaks can be scrambled with little or no technical effort required. Great stuff.

The park's main entrance, administrative buildings, and visitor center, as well as the backcountry desk, human history museum, and two campgrounds, are found here.

Getting There:
From I-15 in St. George, Utah, head north to exit 16 (UT-9) then exit and follow UT-9 east toward the park. At 12.4 miles, UT-9 will turn right in La Verkin, Utah. Continuing on UT-9 for 30.3 miles from I-15, you'll soon reach the charming community of Springdale, Utah. Springdale lies just outside of the main park entrance.

Alternatively, from St. George, you can follow I-15 north to exit 27 (UT-17). Exit and take UT-17 six miles (passing through Toquerville) and then turn left onto UT-9 in La Verkin. Continue from there.

DB in Zion Canyon

22. Mount Kinesava
23. The West Temple
24. Three Marys (East)
25. Three Marys (Middle)
26. North Sentinel
27. Mount Moroni
28. Lady Mountain
29. Angels Landing
30. The Organ
31. Mount Majestic
32. Cathedral Mountain
33. Refrigerator Peak
34. Twin Peak
35. Sneak Peak
36. The Bodhisattva
37. Johnson Mountain
38. Middle Johnson
39. North Johnson
40. The Watchman
41. G2
42. Bridge Mountain
43. Mount Spry
44. Twin Brothers
45. Mountain of the Sun

46. Cable Mountain
47. Observation B.M.
48. Flagpole Mountain
49. Deertrap Mountain
50. Progeny Peak
51. Ant Hill
54. Stevensworth Peak
55. Destination Peak
56. Gifford Peak
57. Hepworth Peak
58. Roof Peak
59. Red Jenny
60. Jenny Peak
61. Little Jenny Peak
62. Lost Peak
70. No Mans Mountain
79. The East Temple
81. The Sentinel

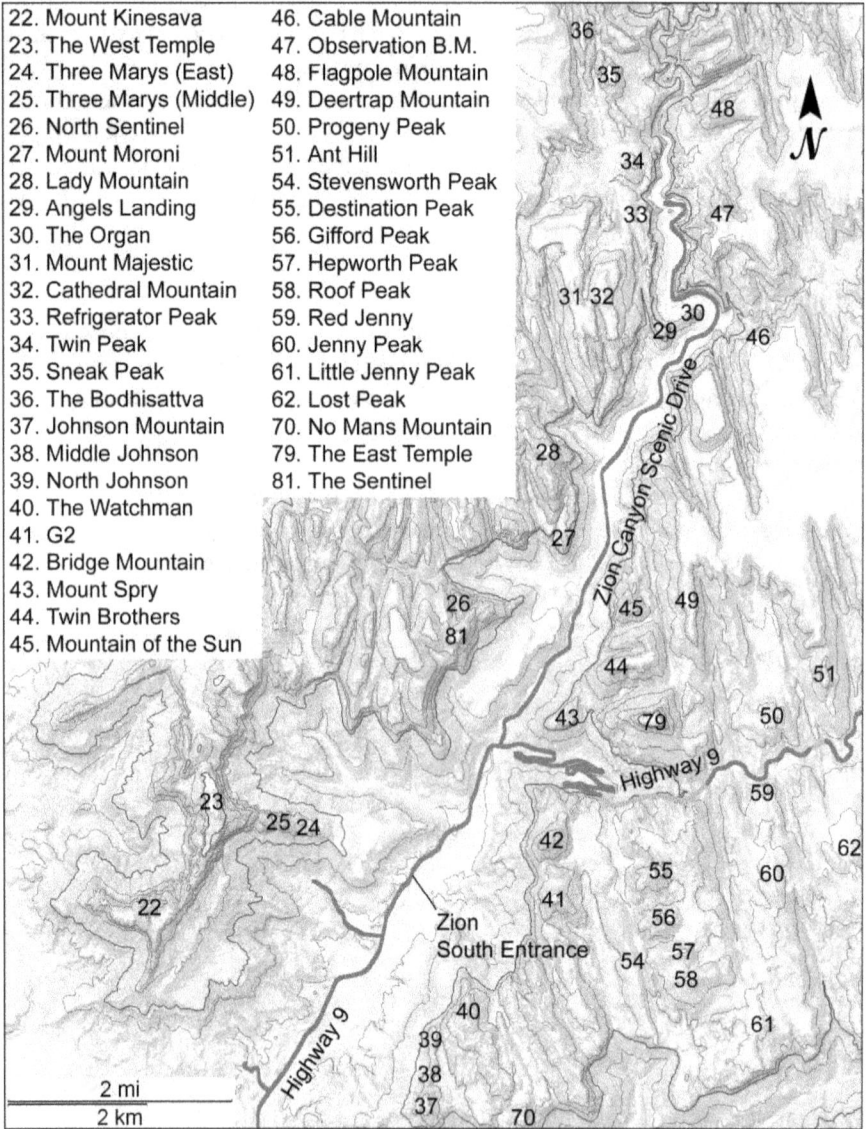

Map of Zion Canyon. The numbers utilized here are specific only to this map.

Chinle Trailhead

As you leave Rockville to enter Springdale on UT-9, turn left into the signed Anasazi Plateau community. About 100 yards along the driveway, look for an easy-to-miss dirt road on your right. Follow the dirt road 100 yards to a signed parking area. This is the Chinle Trailhead.

The peaks in this subsection are roughly arranged from shortest-hike-from-the-trailhead to longest-hike-from-the-trailhead.

The gorgeous south face of Mount Kinesava from near Rockville Bench Peak

"Rockville Bench Peak" (4,386)

Bordered by fine BLM mountain biking terrain to the immediate south and overshadowed by Mount Kinesava's looming presence to the north, Rockville Bench Peak doesn't seem to get a lot of traffic. Still, the hike to the highpoint of Rockville Bench is a fine one and the views are quite nice. While you're at it, you might consider bagging the fun class 4 boulder just east of the summit. You might find my cairn on top.

RT Mileage: 5
RT Elevation Gain: 800'
Time Required: 2-3 hours
Latitude: +37.1725
Longitude: -113.0419

FA: Unknown
Etymology: This small peak is the highpoint of Rockville Bench.
Star Rating: **

Route: East Ridge (class 1-2)

From the trailhead, follow the Chinle Trail to the park boundary. Just inside the boundary gate, follow the fence line left until it meets the east ridge. Follow the ridge to the highpoint.

Johnson Mountain Trailhead

PRIVATE PROPERTY: This is not a trailhead, per se, as private property in this area complicates access. As development in this area occurs, access may change. Please be sure to respect any private property. An accurate local map will assist you in making sure you access this part of the park without infringing upon anyone's property rights.

Parking either in Springdale or near the Watchman Campground (just inside of the park), look up at the Johnson Mountain ridge (the north-south trending ridge that runs parallel to The Watchman massif to its east). The Johnson Mountain ridge and The Watchman are separated by a canyon (a wash, really). You need to aim for the west side of the Johnson Mountain ridge.

If parking in Springdale, the approach will involve crossing the Virgin River. Fortunately, in case of high water there are a couple of bridges you might be able to use, such as the one directly across UT-9 from Bit & Spur. Again, please stay off of private land as you hike in to the park boundary.

This "trailhead" starts at the western base of the Johnson Mountain ridge.

The peaks in this subsection are roughly arranged from shortest-hike-from-the-trailhead to longest-hike-from-the-trailhead.

"Mount Allgood" (5,788)

Mount Allgood (which I called North Johnson in the first edition of this book) is the nice-looking spire-like northern summit of Johnson Mountain. It is especially aesthetic when viewed from points near the center of Springdale.

The peak is a fine, short hike and scramble. The views from the summit perch inspire.

RT Mileage: 3
RT Elevation Gain: 2,000'
Time Required: 3-5 hours
Latitude: +37.1812
Longitude: -112.9854
FKA: Joe French & Bryan Bird (2002)

Etymology: Unknown
Star Rating: ***

DB and Double-A on the summit of Mount Allgood

Route: South Ridge (class 4)

Follow the directions given for the east face route on Johnson Mountain above the sandy notch and up to the low rock band on the crest of the Johnson Mountain ridge. From the crest, head north along the ridge (class 2-3), soon bypassing a large crag on its left, and hike to the base of the final summit crag. A class 3 move past some brush up a groove near the southeast corner of the summit crag allows access to the final class 2-3 moves north to the highpoint.

Alternatively, one can continue north along the eastern base of the summit crag to a drop-off. A class 4 slab move left leads to a YDS 5.3 chimney/chute that puts one within a few feet of the highpoint.

"Middle Johnson" (6,056)

The middle of Johnson's three prominent summits, Middle Johnson provides fantastic views of Johnson Mountain and The Watchman from its summit. The views up Zion Canyon and across to Mount Kinesava and The West Temple aren't bad either.

RT Mileage: 4
RT Elevation Gain: 2,300'
Time Required: 4-6 hours
Latitude: +37.1769
Longitude: -112.9855
FA: Unknown
Etymology: This is the middle of Johnson Mountain's three prominent summits.
Star Rating: ***

Route: Southeast Face (YDS 5.0)

Follow the directions given for Johnson Mountain into the wash between Johnson Mountain and The Watchman. Proceed south down the wash for about 0.25 mile (downclimbing a 15-foot class 3 dryfall along the way) until a minor canyon comes in on the right. The canyon runs down from the saddle between Middle Johnson and Johnson Mountain.

Gain class 2 terrain on the left (south) side of the minor canyon and head up while paralleling the canyon. When the natural track leads you right back into the watercourse, cross over and then continue up the drainage, now paralleling the minor canyon on your left. Leave the canyon when a dryfall blocking further progress is encountered and angle to the right toward a shallow gully that heads up the upper southeast face of Middle Johnson. The gully is largely class 2-3 but has a single unexposed YDS 5.0 move across a slab on its right side about mid-way up. From the upper gully, work right until you can gain class 2-3 ledges that lead to the highpoint.

Route: North Ridge (YDS 5.0)

This route is shorter but less aesthetic than the southeast face route.

Follow the directions given for the east face route on Johnson Mountain above the sandy notch and up to the low rock band on the crest of the Johnson Mountain ridge. Head south on the crest for 20 feet until steeper terrain forces you left. Continue south just below (and left of) the crest on class 2 terrain, soon passing below the summit of a minor sub-peak just northeast of Middle Johnson. Below the summit of the sub-peak, head down class 2 ledges until you can work right into a minor drainage coming down from Middle Johnson and the northeastern sub-peak. Cross the minor drainage, gain the shallow gully on Middle Johnson's upper southeast face, and head up. The gully is largely class 2-3 but has a single unexposed YDS 5.0 move across a slab on its right side about mid-way up. In the upper gully, work right until you can gain class 2-3 ledges that lead to the highpoint.

The Watchman (6,555)

The Watchman is one of the most famous landmarks in Zion National Park. Its image has been featured on countless postcards, in calendars, and on the covers of books. Striking when viewed from just inside the park entrance near the visitor center, the mountain is seemingly impenetrable. Fortunately, for those with strong scrambling and route-finding skills, there does exist a single non-technical route to the summit of this glorious and much sought after peak.

The Watchman (left) from across Zion Canyon

RT Mileage: 5
RT Elevation Gain: 3,000'
Time Required: 6-8 hours
Latitude: +37.1848
Longitude: -112.9796
FKA: Stacy Allison-Austin & Mark Austin (1984)
Etymology: Originally known as Flanigan's Peak, for the Flanigan family of settlers of the area. Like The Sentinel, the Watchman name was later given as the two prominent mountains stand as lookouts over Zion Canyon.
Star Rating: ****

Route: West Face (class 4)

Follow the directions given for the east face route on Johnson Mountain above the sandy notch and up to the low rock band on the crest of the Johnson Mountain ridge. Before proceeding, look across the wash at the west face of The Watchman. Almost directly across from you, make out a prominent wide chute coming down from the upper mountain. The chute ends at a dry waterfall about 60 feet above the bottom of the wash. You want to get into this chute.

Leave the crest of the Johnson Mountain ridge and scramble down (class 3) to the wash. From the bottom of the wash, scramble up onto the steep terrain (crux) just left (north) of the dryfall below the prominent chute. This ledgy terrain, while short and sweet, consists of a few committing class 4 moves on poor rock. Once through them, about 50 feet above the floor of the wash, trend right, slightly upward, and find your way into the prominent chute.

(To avoid the crux near the bottom of the wash, it is possible to head south down the wash for about 0.25 mile until you can pick a way onto the cliffs above. A little route-finding will take you back north, landing you in the prominent chute immediately above the dry waterfall. This variation is class 3.)

Head up the prominent chute over enjoyable class 2-3 terrain. The occasional class 4 move may be encountered. Trend left as you ascend. Doing so, the terrain breaks up and becomes more complex at a level about 500 feet above the wash. A number of narrower chutes come into being at this time. Although several of the narrower chutes may lend passage (we found two that did), you may need to work around a little to find one that gives itself up more easily. We found one that went class 4, while the other necessitated low class 5 climbing through a chimney.

Once through one of the narrower chutes, continue up a short distance (again trending left) until you happen upon a flattish, vegetated area. It is the only one of its kind on the route. From the flattish area, avoid steeper terrain above by traversing around the upper mountain in a clockwise fashion. Just before the flattish area comes to an end at the steep, cliffy terrain on the edge of the northwest face of the peak, you'll encounter a break consisting of slabs and ledges in the upper cliffs. Heading up the break, you'll soon encounter substantially easier terrain. Follow dirt and talus slopes slightly upward and north until you reach the summit. A touch of class 3 scrambling can be expected as you approach the summit. The summit views are among the best to be found in the park, which is a considerable statement when you ponder the perspective offered from some of the high viewpoints in other parts of Zion.

Johnson Mountain (6,153)

When viewed from the town of Springdale, Zion National Park's Johnson Mountain blends in with its legendary neighbor, The Watchman, appearing somewhat insignificant by comparison. However, when viewed from points around The Watchman itself and from certain angles near the park's visitor's center, Johnson Mountain is seen for what it truly is—a very impressive, well-guarded peak that is worthy of attention.

With a cluster of three sub-peaks at the south end of the Johnson Mountain massif and a prominent summit at the northern end of the Johnson Mountain ridge, the true summit is a pyramid-like crag near the southern end of the massif.

Middle Johnson (left) and Johnson Mountain from Springdale

High cliffs on all sides, the only real weakness appears to be on the mountain's east face. There, one can find a number of breaks in the steep face, though the rotten quality of the rock and the difficulty of the climbing still make the endeavor "interesting."

RT Mileage: 6
RT Elevation Gain: 2,500'
Time Required: 5-7 hours
Latitude: +37.1742

Longitude: -112.9862

FA: Unknown

Etymology: The peak was named for Nephi Johnson, the first white explorer to visit Zion. Johnson was shown Zion Canyon by the Paiutes in November 1858.

Star Rating: ****

Route: East Face (YDS 5.8+R)

As you approach the base of the Johnson Mountain ridge, you may pick up a prominent use trail heading eastward toward a point in the ridge roughly halfway between Mount Allgood and Middle Johnson. Finding the use trail helps tremendously. Looking up at the ridge as you approach, you should be able to pick out a conspicuous weakness in the cliffs above. The weakness is a ledge/ramp system on the Johnson Mountain ridge, just a bit to the south of Mount Allgood. The use trail leads to the base of the weakness.

Follow this weakness (class 3, with two short class 4 sections) up to a sandy notch just below the crest of the Johnson Mountain ridge. Once at the notch, proceed south about 40 feet and scramble up onto a low band of rock on the left. There is a prominent, bushy tree at the easiest point to gain the top of the band. From the top of this rock band (which is actually the crest of the Johnson Mountain ridge), you'll be able to look east into the deep-ish wash that separates the Johnson Mountain massif from The Watchman.

Scramble down (class 3) to the wash. Once in the wash, follow it south over a few obstacles (the biggest one being a class 3 dry fall) for a bit over 0.25 mile until you're at a point that is more or less directly below the true summit of Johnson Mountain. Climb out of the wash to the west (class 3-5, depending on exact line chosen) and work up for 150-200 feet and trend slightly south until you encounter a prominent drainage coming down from the upper mountain. This drainage has a number of branches feeding into it from above. Once this drainage is located, seek out a particular branch (mostly slickrock and steep slabs as it ascends) that heads somewhat northwesterly to the upper mountain. To its right is a slabby/ledgy ridge. Look for cairns—we placed several.

Gain the ridge and follow it up for a few hundred feet of class 2-3 scrambling to a steeper slabby section just above a large, fallen dead tree. This is the route's crux. The crux (YDS 5.8+R) consists of 35-40 feet of climbing, first following a left-slanting seam and then pulling a slight bulge just above a small dead bush coming out of the seam 2/3 way up the slab. The rock is bad, and leading the crux is artwork. As usual, the followers have it much better, as there are adequate materials above to set up a decent belay.

Once through the crux, continue scrambling up class 2-3 slabs until you come to a cliff band with a class 2-3 weakness directly in front of you and several interesting shelter caves visible to the immediate left (south). The shelter caves (and the arch you'll find nearby) are worth exploring. Continue up through the weakness in the cliff band, noting the cliffy section above. This is the summit crag. Work up slightly, to the south side of the crag, where class 2 terrain leads to the summit.

A 50m rope is recommended for the route.

Looking back to No Mans Mountain (upper-right) during the approach to Stevens Peak

Route: East Face - South Chute (class 4)
This route variation is a bit harder to find and follow than the east face route.

Follow the directions given for the east route to the prominent drainage coming down from the upper mountain. This drainage has a number of branches feeding into it from above. Work to the south side of the main body of the drainage then continue a bit further south until you come to a steep, wide chute just beyond it. Cross over the chute, and just below a noticeably steeper portion of the chute work onto the rock face south of the chute. From there, negotiate class 4 terrain (look carefully) and start heading up. About halfway up along the chute to your right (north), climb over into the chute and continue up. The going should be mostly class 2-3.

Once the top of the chute is reached, work north along ledges and obstacles without gaining much elevation until you are at a point that is more or less directly below the main summit of the mountain (which is perhaps 150-175 feet above). Heading up from about that point, you should notice a cliff band with a class 2-3 weakness directly above and several interesting shelter caves visible to the left (south). Continue up through the weakness in the cliff band, noting the cliffy section above. This is the summit crag. Work up slightly to the south side of the crag, where class 2 terrain leads to the summit.

A 30m rope is useful for the route.

Johnson Mountain from No Mans Mountain

"No Mans Mountain" (6,200)

No Mans Mountain is among my (many) favorite peaks in Zion National Park. With a stunning approach through long-unexplored country, the route itself is improbable and sweet—and not as hard as the rating suggests. After the delightful slickrock slabs and ledges of the scramble up the mountain, the mellow sand dune area below the top gives the peak an "island in the sky" sort of vibe.

It's said that wild topography makes 95-percent of Zion National Park inaccessible—don't get lost in hoodoo land! The lovely red slickrock of Johnson Mountain, the long and still mostly-unexplored Watchman massif, and across the hanging valley to Stevens Peak, is a place that's long held my interest, thanks to a mention Ram made to me many years ago, speculating on that fiery furnace one could see across the way from The West Temple.

No Mans Mountain has 400' of prominence.

RT Mileage: 6
RT Elevation Gain: 3,000'
Time Required: 6-9 hours
Latitude: +37.1711
Longitude: -112.9703
FKA: Courtney Purcell (October 25, 2008)
Etymology: Although not far from Springdale, No Mans Mountain rests in an obscure, seldom-visited part of the park that feels nearly as remote as any place I've been in Zion. Indeed, the peak resides in a wonderful and varied "No Man's Land."
Star Rating: ****

Route: Northwest Face-Northeast Ridge (YDS 5.7)

Follow the directions given for Johnson Mountain into the wash between Johnson Mountain and The Watchman. Proceed south down the wash for perhaps 0.5 mile to a narrow 200-foot pour-off at its mouth. Along the way, the going is easy and generally brush-free, though one will need to down-climb a 15-foot class 3 dryfall along the way. Forty feet before the pour-off, exit the canyon on its east (left) side via a class 4 weakness then meander to easier terrain above.

From here, the topography is complex and difficult to describe. Without gaining (or losing) much in the way of elevation, work your way generally southeast across interesting terrain until you can get into a prominent wash that runs southwest from the col between No Mans Mountain and the unnamed red massif to its northwest. Many variations are possible, and it would be easy to get lost around here—be careful! The going should never be harder than the occasional short bit of class 3.

As the beautiful, red northwest face of No Mans Mountain comes into view, note a large gully gracefully coming down it. Follow the wash northeast toward the col, ultimately aiming for the base of the gully on the northwest face. Access into the gully is blocked by a 30-foot dryfall at its base, so work right for 100 feet to a slot with a chimney at its head. An initial class 4 move to get into the slot, followed by a couple YDS 5.0 moves in the chimney (exiting left), lands you on slabs. Work left for 100 feet until you can easily (class 2) get into the gully, some 100 feet above the top of the dryfall you saw from below. Head up delightful stair-step terrain on red slabs and ledges. Initially class 2, the gully steepens a bit more than halfway up. There, you'll need to negotiate a series of three steep steps, the highest of which requires a couple of YDS 5.4 moves to negotiate. Above the steps, twenty feet of class 3-4 slab scrambling leads to gentler slabs that bend left to a beautiful red, slabby saddle overlooking the seldom-seen valley east of The Watchman.

From the saddle, carefully step right (east) thirty feet to the base of a series of steps leading up to a landing just right of a clump of bushes on the northeast ridge. Scramble up the steps for 30 feet (class 3-4). Reach a 3-foot wide ledge just above a class 4 move past a bush then climb a 9-foot YDS 5.7 open book to a crumbly ledge next to a clump of bushes. Once on the ledge, scramble up and left for 30 feet (class 3-4), ignoring a weakness immediately above you, and then head left around a blind corner as soon as the terrain levels out. Step clockwise around the corner on a wide, bushy ledge and marvel at the remainder of the northeast ridge. It doesn't look promising, though the summit is only 150 feet away.

Follow the ledge around to a small saddle between two hoodoos on the ridge. Approach the southern of the two, and carefully walk down 10 feet to the right (west) until you can get onto an exposed 40-foot face (class 3-4) broken by a ledge halfway up. Carefully scramble up the face and onto the top of a hoodoo with a small bush perched atop it. From the top of this hoodoo, drop to the south over class 2 terrain and scramble to the next hoodoo (class 2). Downclimb 15 feet of class 3 slabs to a sandy bowl. Immediately across the bowl is the highest hoodoo, which is gained via class 2 scrambling.

A 50m rope is useful for the route.

Looking north to G1 (left of center) and G2 (right) from Stevens Peak

"Stevens Peak" (6,555)

Stevens Peak and its sister summit, G1, form an impressive barrier on the east side of Watchman Valley. The peak is wonderful, and an excursion into this part of Zion is classic. I know people who have done amazing tours up and over the Stevens Peak massif, starting at the Johnson Mountain Trailhead and finished at the Gifford Canyon Trailhead.

RT Mileage: 7
RT Elevation Gain: 4,500'
Time Required: 8-12 hours
Latitude: +37.1818
Longitude: -112.9657
FKA: Courtney Purcell, Bryan Long and Reed McCoy (October 24, 2010), though two of my other friends were through here a year or two prior. It is not known whether they visited the summit.
Etymology: Named for nearby Stevens Wash, which is two drainages east.
Star Rating: ****

Route: Southeast Ridge from the West (class 4-5)

Follow the directions given for No Mans Mountain to the area of the col separating that peak from the unnamed massif to its north-northwest. Left of the col, scramble through a notch that allows easy access to the plateau on the north side of No Mans Mountain. Hike east-northeast across the short plateau until you arrive at the cliffs overlooking Watchman Valley. Walk north a short distance along the top of the cliffs until you encounter a wonderfully improbable dark, deep slot (class 4) that breaks through the cliffs and dumps you out in Watchman Valley.

Travel east-northeast across the valley, working through and around obstacles encountered (I've usually found myself having to downclimb a short (8-10 foot) but very awkward class 4-5 chimney), to the base of Stevens Peak. Scramble up the easiest-looking line (usually class 2-3), trending left, until you gain the southeast ridge. Follow the ridge to the base of the summit block, which is a quick, class 4-5 scramble.

A return via the ascent route would be strenuous. With appropriate canyoneering skills and equipment, it's easiest (and quickest) to return via G1 and Whale Bone Canyon.

Alternative descent (Whale Bone Canyon: 3AII):

This canyon has some interesting stuff in it.

Follow the directions given for Whale Peak from the summit of Stevens Peak to the head of Whale Bone Canyon. Descending the canyon involves about 9 rappels up to 115 feet. You may need to establish the occasional anchor.

Below the technical difficulties, scramble down the canyon until you can easily cut right to pick up the Watchman Trail, which can be followed to the visitor center.

Two 50m ropes are recommended for the descent. A canyoneering permit is required.

Bryan Long and Reed McCoy working through Watchman Valley

"G1" (6,555)

Unlike its south sister, Stevens Peak, this peak is viewable from Zion Canyon. From the Zion Human History Museum, the peak's steep and impressive northern ramparts can be identified to the left (east) of The Watchman and to the right (south) of G2.

This is a quality objective. It is also known as Mount Greer.

It is interesting to note that G1 and Stevens Peak appear to share the same elevation.

RT Mileage: 8
RT Elevation Gain: 5,000'
Time Required: 9-13 hours
Latitude: +37.1880
Longitude: -112.9679
FKA: Brody and Jared Greer (spring 2005), though it is not known whether they went to the actual summit of the mountain or stopped at a lesser summit atop their climbing route from Zion Canyon
Etymology: I can only speculate, but: the "G" is for Greer and the "1" is for theirs being the first known ascent of the peak.
Star Rating: ****

The view north into Zion Canyon from G1

Route: South Slope (class 2-3)
Follow the directions given for Stevens Peak to the vicinity of the summit of that peak. Continue hiking northwest a short distance until you can drop easily north toward the saddle between the two peaks. From the area of the saddle, scramble up the south slope to the summit of G1.

A return via the ascent route would be strenuous. With appropriate canyoneering skills and equipment, it's easiest (and quickest) to return via Whale Bone Canyon.

Alternative descent (Whale Bone Canyon: 3AII):
This canyon has some interesting stuff in it.

Follow the directions given for Whale Peak from the summit of G1 to the head of Whale Bone Canyon. Descending the canyon involves about 9 rappels up to 115 feet. You may need to establish the occasional anchor.

Below the technical difficulties, scramble down the canyon until you can easily cut right to pick up the Watchman Trail, which can be followed to the visitor center.

Two 50m ropes are recommended for the descent. A canyoneering permit is required.

"Whale Peak" (6,280)

I'll introduce Whale Peak via a short story:

I'd long stared at the cluster of isolated peaks that would eventually come to be known to me as Stevens Peak, G1, and Whale Peak. I'd presumed them all to be most likely unclimbed, particularly the smallest, most isolated, and most uninteresting of the trio—Whale Peak.

In November 2010, Bryan Long, Reed McCoy and I set out for an attempt at all three of them. I'd scouted out most of an approach I reckoned held solid promise. As fortune would allow, my route allowed us great success, including the stumbling upon and subsequent descent of a particularly interesting deep and improbable slot. Soon, we surmounted the class 4-5 summit block of Stevens Peak, scrambled the rugged ridge north to G1 then found our way to the saddle east of that second peak. With weather threatening and the day growing somewhat long, we bailed on our last objective via an untested but ultimately rewarding route that offered us pioneer inscriptions and old wooden ladders. Whale Peak would have to wait for another day.

And so in April 2011, I recruited a threesome of fit souls to attempt a longer day that included the last of these obscurities. Nailing the route I'd pieced together only a few months earlier, we quickly cruised up and over Stevens Peak and G1, crossed to Whale Peak and tagged its obscure summit. I built a cairn atop the highest point, then we proceeded to drink, eat and enjoy the wonderful spring sun and the strange feeling of being among the first to touch the pinnacle of a place relatively difficult to reach. We returned via my inscription/ladder route.

RT Mileage: 10
RT Elevation Gain: 5,500'
Time Required: 10-14 hours
Latitude: +37.1844
Longitude: -112.9598
FKA: Courtney Purcell, Bob Sihler and Sarah & Dominic Meiser (April 20, 2011), though two of my other friends were through here a couple of years prior. It is not known whether they visited the summit.
Etymology: The peak is named for nearby Whale Bone Canyon, which was named by my friend Bryan Long. Bryan has some cool stories about whale bones and other things he's come across on his many travels around the globe.
Star Rating: ***

Route: Northwest Ridge (class 3-4)

Follow the directions given for G1 to the summit of that peak. Descend north-northwest from the summit, looking carefully for a ramp system that cuts sharply right and leads southeast toward the head of Whale Bone Canyon, which is the prominent north-draining canyon on the northeast side of G1. Some exposed class 3-4 scrambling should be anticipated in the lower portion of this ramp system.

Another canyon drains south-southeast from the divide between the two canyons. Cross this divide and scramble onto Whale Peak's northwest ridge, which is followed easily to the summit.

A return via the ascent route would be strenuous, perhaps prohibitively so for many parties—so beware. With appropriate canyoneering skills and equipment, it's easiest (and quickest) to return via Whale Bone Canyon.

Alternative descent (Whale Bone Canyon: 3AII):

This canyon has some interesting stuff in it.

Descending the canyon involves about 9 rappels up to 115 feet. You may need to establish the occasional anchor in this seldom-visited, dirty environment.

Below the technical difficulties, scramble down the canyon until you can easily cut right to pick up the Watchman Trail, which can be followed to the visitor center.

Two 50m ropes are recommended for the descent. A canyoneering permit is required.

Mount Kinesava Trailhead

Historically, this "trailhead" was off of Serendipity Lane in Springdale. Since that trailhead is no longer legally appropriate, I'll share the following option, which I've never used:

Just north of Oscar's (yum!) in Springdale, turn on Paradise Road and follow it north to the cemetery, where you'll park. Walk up the road past some buildings and continue up the drainage and through the cliffs then angle left to reach the beginnings of the respective routes.

Although the legality of this approach is unknown to me (as it passes through land apparently owned by the town of Springdale), I'm told by friends that this has become the new "standard" approach to the peaks in this subsection. I recommend you ensure this approach is legal prior to using it.

The peaks in this subsection are roughly arranged from shortest-hike-from-the-trailhead to longest-hike-from-the-trailhead.

Mount Kinesava (7,276)

Mount Kinesava is one of the highest peaks in one of the finest national parks the United States has to offer. With a commanding presence above the main entrance to Zion National Park, Mount Kinesava offers extraordinary views of much of the park—from Zion Canyon itself, to both the rugged and topographically-complex eastern and western regions of the park, as well as to the red rock dreamlands to the south and outside of the park, including Eagle Crags, Canaan Mountain, and the mystical (mythical?) beyond.

As if that's not enough, the mountain's view of its neighbor, The West Temple (and of The West Temple's knife-edge south ridge), is absolutely astounding. The two stunning peaks are separated by a deep notch and The West Temple's gorgeous, serrated south ridge.

Mount Kinesava features an enjoyable (and rather direct) route up its east face. Likely the easiest route possible on this sheer-walled peak, it goes 4th class with less than five miles and about 3,200 feet of gain car-to-car. Like nearly every other big peak in the park, Mount Kinesava also hosts a number of established technical routes on its impressive faces, as well as a stunning YDS 5.7 route on its south ridge, which has been dubbed Cowboy Ridge.

RT Mileage: 5
RT Elevation Gain: 3,200'
Time Required: 7-9 hours
Latitude: +37.1976
Longitude: -113.0305
FA: Considering that there is a large panel of petroglyphs just below the summit, it seems that Native Americans made ascents during prerecorded times.

Etymology: Paiute legend had it that Kinesava was a mysterious spirit with changeable moods. Kinesava would often roll rocks down from the heights of the mountain or light fires on the tops of the surrounding peaks.

Star Rating: ****

Route: East Face (class 4)

Prior to starting, it helps to stop in Springdale to identify the route, which is clearly visible from town. From the center of Springdale, Mount Kinesava is the southernmost high peak on the left (looking up-canyon) side of the highway. Make note of a prominent brushy weakness in the east face that works from lower-left to upper-right. The weakness ends at the plateau just below Mount Kinesava's summit pyramid. This is your goal. From the cemetery, your perspective of the weakness changes—it is now visible as the left-most vegetated ramp on the face, and only the very bottom portion of the route is visible.

Once at the lower-left corner of the weakness on Mount Kinesava's east face, work your way up and right. Appearing at certain times as a ramp system (and at other times as a bouldery gully), the objective is clear—stay high (but not quite hugging the cliffs of the east face) and follow this ramp/gully/weakness to its top. The top of the weakness is clearly visible on the approach to the base of the east face, as well as much of the way up. Travel along the ramp/gully/weakness is mostly class 2-3, with several short sections of class 4. Route-finding is not difficult, as it is best to simply keep following the weakness up and to the north until it ends, though one may have to look around at times to keep the terrain in the class 4 realm (particularly if you are hugging the cliffs of the east face along the way). Harder variations are easily found.

You will travel up the ramp/gully/weakness for 1,800-2,000 vertical feet to its end at the eastern edge of a vegetated plateau. The spectacular plateau is surrounded on all sides by hoodoos, pyramids, and other cool-looking features. It is wise to mark this area, as finding this access point on the return is crucial.

Cut west across the plateau to the white-colored pyramid appearing to be the highest. It is to the immediate left of a much lower white pyramid, and to the right of a more cliffy, craggy area. From the base of the high, white pyramid (the summit pyramid, incidentally), head up its east face. The left side of the face consists primarily of steep slabs and faces, and the right side consists of gentler terrain (mostly loose class 2-3 stuff), while a broken fin (frequently loose class 4-5.easy) splits the two sides in half. After 400-500 feet of gain, you'll reach the top of the pyramid (and the summit of the mountain). The views are astonishing.

The awe-inspiring south face of Mount Kinesava

The West Temple (7,810)

One of the most famous landmarks in the celebrated park, this monstrous, seemingly unconquerable big-walled, classic mountain boasts the highest vertical sandstone face in North America. The massive east face commands the attention of anyone passing through the main entrance to the park near the town of Springdale, Utah.

Sitting just northeast of the beautiful Mount Kinesava, the often-photographed West Temple was named by John Wesley Powell, who also named its sister peak, The East Temple, which sits across Zion Canyon above the Zion-Mt. Carmel Tunnel. Some Zion locals still refer to The West Temple by its original name, though—The Steamboat. A cool name, I think.

The West Temple was first climbed in 1933 by the brothers, Norman and Newell Crawford, and over the years a number of routes have been established on the mountain, most of them highly technical. There are no non-technical routes to the summit, though the easiest route (via the exposed south ridge) is a long scramble over ridiculously loose rock with only a short YDS 5.6 pitch near the end. There is a considerable amount of treacherous travel on this route, so be careful—people have died here.

RT Mileage: 7
RT Elevation Gain: 4,200'
Time Required: 9-11 hours
Latitude: +37.2107
Longitude: -113.0206
FKA: Norman Crawford and Newell Crawford (members of an 8-person team) in 1933
Etymology: Once known by most settlers in nearby Virgin (and still known to some) as The Steamboat (for the mountain's similarity to a steamboat when viewed from the west), the peak's current name was assigned by John Wesley Powell in the 1860s. Prior to its modern names, the Paiutes called the mountain "Temp-o-i-tin-car-ur," which roughly translates to "mountain without a trail."
Star Rating: ****

Route: South Ridge (YDS 5.6)

From Springdale, Mount Kinesava is the southernmost high peak on the west side of the highway. The West Temple is the larger (and even more impressive) peak to the north of Mount Kinesava. The two peaks are connected by a long, serrated ridge with a prominent notch near the Mount Kinesava end. Make note of a clearly visible brushy weakness near the north end of Mount Kinesava's east face. The weakness works from lower-left to upper-right and heads directly for the distinct deep notch in the ridge between the two peaks. This notch, and the weakness leading to it, is your goal. (Note that this weakness is not the same weakness that takes you up Mount Kinesava; Kinesava's weakness is further south on Kinesava's face.)

Once at the base of the weakness, you should be able to look to the north and clearly make out the notch above. Work your way to it. Although getting to the notch is a bit difficult to describe in any detail, your goal is typically in sight, the path of least resistance is generally easy to discern, and the terrain should never exceed class 3.

Once at the notch, take a breather and look down into the cirque on the other side—impressive. On the north (right) side of the notch, climb up into either of two short chutes (the one on the left, just behind a large, flat slab of rock, is the easier of the two to climb up and out of) until you exit out onto the south ridge of The West Temple.

Once on the ridge crest, the rest of the journey is clear. Head north to the mountain's glaring headwall high above in the distance. Travel along the ridge, sometimes on the crest, sometimes on either side of it, roaming around towers, along ledges, up and down ramps, climbing up and down a tree, and over the summit of a sub-peak along the way in a convoluted manner until you come to the headwall below the summit plateau. Watch out for some poorly placed cairns along the way.

(A few extra words about working north from the summit of the sub-peak, which has been called "Wussie Peak" by Ram and company in honor of the many folks who have been too intimidated to continue on from that point: A few feet short of the summit of Wussie Peak, drop back south about 20 vertical feet to pick up conspicuous, east-facing, frightening-looking ledges (class 2 and loose). There, traverse left on the ledges to a tree down-climb.)

The going for the bulk of the ridge is largely class 2-3, with several (3 or 4) short and sketchy sections of class 4 (or low class 5). The ridge is largely comprised of loose, exposed rock. At one point, you'll encounter a short YDS 5.8-ish wall with minimal exposure that may nevertheless prove challenging to work through. This wall can be avoided by traversing ledges on the left around a corner to a heinously loose, 50-foot chute/chimney (class 4) leading to easier ground. As you near the base of the headwall just below the summit plateau of the mountain, approach it from the east side of the ridge crest. Surmounting a short class 4+ wall, the most apparent weakness in the headwall, something resembling a dihedral, will present itself.

The headwall here goes at YDS 5.6. The rock is poor, the exposure is eye-opening but not extreme, but this short pitch is protected by several bolts, with a solid-appearing two-bolt anchor at the top (3-4 feet below the mesa). Climbing up the first dihedral-like portion of the feature for about 25 feet (just past a bush), get into the next dihedral-like feature to its right. Follow it 50-60 feet to the top. From the top of the headwall, scramble onto the mesa.

From here, the summit cap is 0.5 mile to the north across the manzanita-covered plateau. There's a large scree/talus chute on the south side of the cap. The chute leads to the summit.

A 50m rope and 6 quick draws are recommended for the route.

Three Marys Trailhead

While in Springdale, look for Lion Boulevard on the west side of UT-9. Lion Blvd. is 0.6 mile before the park entrance. Once on Lion Blvd., follow it west about a mile to a closed gate at the entrance to the O.C. Amphitheater. Park in a turn-out just outside the gate.

The peaks in this subsection are roughly arranged from shortest-hike-from-the-trailhead to longest-hike-from-the-trailhead.

Before you leave the car, I recommend you grab your helmet—the gully leading to the east summit above is a loose and dangerous place, the scene of much rock tumbling.

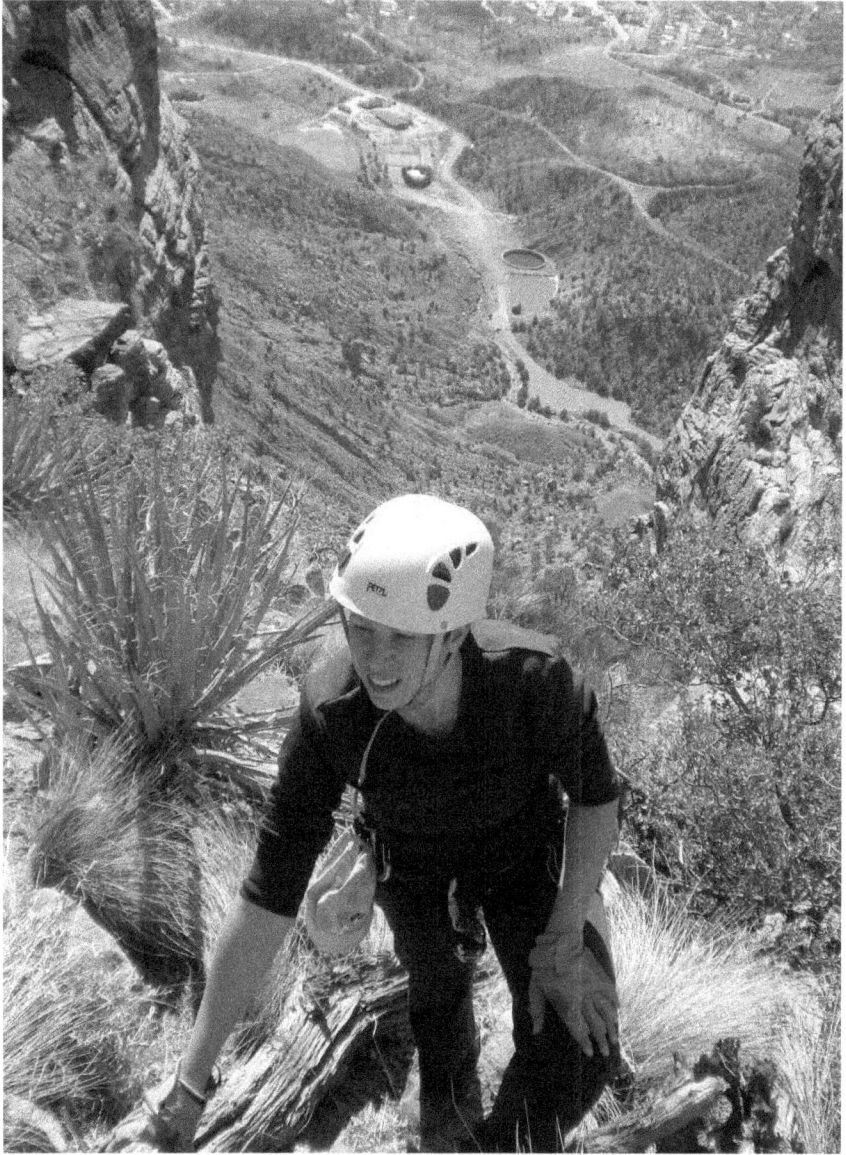

DB climbing East Mary

Three Marys—East Mary (6,000)

Though slight in elevation, the Three Marys are considered a part of the noble Towers of the Virgin on the west side of Zion Canyon. Stacked up and flowing east in descending order of elevation, the highest of the Three Marys (circa 6,400 feet) is a significant technical endeavor beyond my abilities or interest. Though still *technically* technical in their difficulties, East Mary and Middle Mary are much more mellow—mostly light (class 2-3) scrambles with the occasional steep step thrown in for fun.

The views from East Mary are phenomenal.

Scrambling to the base of Three Marys-East

RT Mileage: 2
RT Elevation Gain: 2,000'
Time Required: 4-6 hours
Latitude: +37.2076
Longitude: -113.0059
FA: Unknown; I found a cairn and register on the summit.
Etymology: The peaks were named for the three biblical Marys who came to the sepulcher of Jesus in the Gospels.
Star Rating: **

Route: South Chute (YDS 5.4)

From the parking area, the park boundary is a mere few hundred feet north, near the base of the large cliff band before you. As steep and unpleasant as it is, head due north to the base of the cliffs. Upon reaching the base of the cliff band, carefully contour west until you reach the first (and only) significant break—a dirt and vegetated ridge line flowing south from East Mary above you. Gain the ridge line and follow it up to the cliffs at the base of East Mary. While doing so, note the prominent chute immediately east of the sheer, vertical cliffs on the peak's south face. You need to aim for the bottom of this chute.

Once at the base of the cliffs, easily gain a ramp that heads up and right toward the chute in question. A 15-foot scramble (class 3-4) along a slab/arête feature adjacent to the cliff on your left will lead to an exposed 10-foot slab traverse to the right, landing you at the base of the first crux—a 12-foot YDS 5.2 face immediately below a small but healthy tree.

Negotiate the face and continue up a 6-foot class 4 wall then up the chute. Soon, you'll encounter the second crux of the route—a dirty, virtually unprotectable chimney (YDS 5.4) with plenty of loose stuff. Fortunately, the chimney is only about 10-12 feet high. (This second crux can be avoided by climbing a steep chimney just left and around the corner from it. This chimney, also about 10-12 feet high, is slightly easier—perhaps YDS 5.0.)

Working through the second crux, the chute forks. Angle left, staying in the main chute as it parallels the steep cliffs on your left. Difficulties ease as you approach the saddle at the top of the chute. There, a terrific view of the rest of the Towers of the Virgin opens before you. Ignore the semi-prominent sub-peak to your right, and turn left and immediately enter the convenient narrow chute that breaks through the cliffs and allows continued passage toward the upper mountain. Once through the 80-foot chute angle left and route-find your way to the top. Any number of variations are possible.

The summit views are terrific, including an impressive view of The West Temple immediately above you, Meridian Tower, The Watchman, Bridge Mountain, and The East Temple.

A 30m rope is recommended for the route. An assortment of nuts may help protect the route.

Three Marys—Middle Mary (6,298)

The middle (in west-to-east order *and* elevation) of the Three Marys—Middle Mary—shares terrific summits views, as well as particularly striking views of both West Temple's monstrous east face and the scary cliffs separating you from an ascent of the very close West Mary.

With a nice amount of fun class 2-3 scrambling, and a short class 5 crux on the traverse from East Mary, an ascent of Middle Mary from East Mary is short and rewarding. The final, exposed climb onto the summit boulder is an excellent finish.

The view toward The East Temple and Twin Brothers from Three Marys

RT Mileage: 3
RT Elevation Gain: 2,500'
Time Required: 5-7 hours
Latitude: +37.2082
Longitude: -113.0092
FKA: Dave Anderson (May 1977)
Etymology: The Three Marys were named for the three biblical Marys who came to the sepulcher of Jesus in the Gospels.
Star Rating: ***

Route: East Face (YDS 5.2)
Follow the directions given to the summit of East Mary, keeping in mind that the lower Mary is more technically challenging.

From East Mary's summit, follow the ridge down to the saddle between East Mary and Middle Mary. With a little route-finding, the going is only class 2-3. Along the way, try to spot weaknesses in Middle Mary's steep east face. With most of the difficulties found 2/3 way up the face, it'll be a challenge to piece together a feasible way…but it can be done.

The view west to The West Temple and West Mary from the summit of Middle Mary

From the saddle, angle slightly left and then start heading up the easiest terrain you can find. The winding route is not terribly difficult, and the route-finding stimulating. Soon reaching significantly steepening terrain, look around for a way through. Although easier passage could possibly be found, I found two reasonable weaknesses:

1) A steep, essentially unprotectable 15-foot chimney (YDS 5.2) that was dripping water from snowmelt above it. Capped by a bushy slab, you'll need to exit left at the top of the chimney and then continue up easier ground. The chimney is near the northern edge of the peak's east face, about 2/3 way up the face;

2) Just south and around the corner from the chimney is a downclimb to an exposed notch and short (8-foot) slab climb (with a decent finger crack on its right side) leading to a dirty and loose chimney. The slab is about YDS 5.2. The easy (class 3) chimney can be followed to easier ground.

Beyond the crux, continue up easier ground to the final summit boulder, a nicely positioned perch with huge exposure. Class 2-3 scrambling on the west-northwest side of the boulder lends easiest access to the top.

A 30m rope is recommended for the route. An assortment of nuts may help protect the route, though I found it to be a reasonable solo with plenty of care.

Sand Bench Trailhead

Following UT-9 for 1.5 miles once inside the park, you will come to a junction. At the junction, UT-9 continues straight ahead toward the Zion-Mt. Carmel Tunnel and a 6-mile long side road (Zion Canyon Scenic Drive) heads off to the left. Turn left and follow the road further into Zion Canyon and the goodies that eagerly anticipate your arrival.

Note: Although this road is open to cars during the relatively slow wintry times, the rest of the year it is open only to shuttles, those staying at Zion Lodge, and those with special permits. The shuttle is free, and runs regularly during the long days of the busy season. It typically runs from dark-to-very dark (generally about 6 a.m. to about 10 p.m., though hours vary with the seasons). Shuttle hours are posted at shuttle stops.

Whether via personal vehicle or shuttle, head to the signed Court of the Patriarchs stop along the main road in the canyon. It is the first stop north of Canyon Junction. The stop also serves as the Sand Bench Trailhead. The Sand Bench Trail is popular with the horse-riding tourist crowd, of which I was once a member.

Interesting views east from the summit of North Sentinel

"North Sentinel" (7,058)

After my second failed attempt of its parent peak, North Sentinel served as a consolation prize. With surprising prominence (363 feet of the stuff) and beauty, were it not for the chossy, unsafe and sometimes terrifying nature of its ascent, this hidden peak could (arguably) be a classic. We found no signs of prior visitation on the summit.

As one might imagine, the views from the top are pretty cool, though all the neighboring exposed choss gets to be unnerving. Still, don't forget a camera—you'll probably never want to return.

RT Mileage: 4
RT Elevation Gain: 2,800'
Time Required: 8-10 hours
Latitude: +37.2354
Longitude: -112.9803
FKA: Courtney Purcell and Rick Kent (September 20, 2008)
Etymology: North Sentinel is the detached north summit of The Sentinel massif
Star Rating: **

The view south to The Sentinel from the summit of North Sentinel

Route: East Face (YDS 5.7)

From the Court of the Patriarchs shuttle stop, walk the service road for 100 yards and then gain a trail (the Sand Bench Trail) that continues west and crosses a bridge over the Virgin River. Just past the bridge, take the left fork of the trail and walk another 150 yards until the trail forks again. Taking the next left fork, head up the good trail and follow it for about 0.5 mile to a point where it passes below the east face of The Sentinel.

Leave the trail and head up the steep, trail-less slope until you can gain a deep wash that takes one up to the base of the east face. At times it may be easier to travel the slopes on either side of the drainage. The drainage will end at a 30-foot steep, slabby face below a loose, rotten chimney-face system. Climb the slabby face (YDS 5.0), exit left and then continue up, trending left until you can get into a more pronounced chute system that heads north. Encountering a loose chimney (YDS 5.4), climb through, again trending left, and continue up the main, widening chute to its head. Once at the head, angle up and left to a shallow saddle that overlooks a hidden, ponderosa pine-filled drainage to the immediately west.

From the shallow saddle, drop into the drainage and traverse steep dirty slopes clockwise to a large pine at about 11 o'clock. Behind the pine, gain a small, slabby ledge and then step left into another chute that runs south. Fifty feet up the chute, you'll encounter a tricky chimney with a tentative chockstone at the top. Climb through the chimney (8'; YDS 5.7) and then continue up to another chimney with a small tree growing on its right side halfway up. Climb through this next chimney (15'; YDS 5.2), aiding off the small tree, and continue scrambling up steep, loose, scary terrain for another 100 vertical feet to the flattish terrain at the head of the chute.

From here, do an upward traverse to the left (staying below major difficulties) and make for the loose, craggy saddle between The Sentinel and North Sentinel. Once there, head north/northwest along the ridge, soon coming to a steep face barring further easy progress along the ridge. The short face (10') might be hard, were it not for a dead tree growing near the top of it. One can aid up the face with the assistance of the tree (while it lasts) at about YDS 5.2. Once above this short face, angle right and then continue along sandy, loose ledges below the crest of the ridge. Soon, the red summit layer comes into view. There's a large dead tree right at a break in the layer. Approach the dead tree and climb a short chimney left of the tree then step left, climb up through another dead tree and then scramble easily to the highpoint. The view into "Sentinel Chasm," a seemingly bottomless canyon draining toward Birch Creek from the Sentinel, is awesome.

On the descent, the YDS 5.2 face on the final ridge can be rappelled from a healthy tree at the top of the face. Additionally, the loose and unpleasant YDS 5.7 and YDS 5.2 chimneys can be avoided by route-finding your way further north/northeast down a minor, craggy ridge from the flattish terrain at the head of the chute. Perhaps 50 feet from the flattish area (and 15 feet below and west of the crest), a large ponderosa with a sling around it can be used to rappel about 60 feet down to the hidden drainage you traversed through earlier. Alternatively, one can continue down the craggy ridge for another 50 feet or so, downclimb 10 feet of loose class 3 terrain then rappel 50 feet from a tree to the same hidden drainage. Lastly, the YDS 5.0 slabby face and loose YDS 5.4 chimney encountered early on the route can be avoided by continuing straight down the wide chute until forced to downclimb a 12-foot class 4-5 crack (or a harder chimney on its right). Thirty feet beyond the crack is a low juniper with slings around it. Rappel 30 feet from the juniper to easy terrain. Thirty feet below the juniper is a small ponderosa that anchors a 90-foot rappel to the drainage at the base of the east face.

A 60m rope, several long slings, and a set of nuts are recommended for the route.

The view northwest up Birch Creek from the summit of North Sentinel

Emerald Pools Trailhead

Following UT-9 for 1.5 miles once inside the park, you will come to a junction (Canyon Junction). At the junction, UT-9 continues straight ahead toward the Zion-Mt. Carmel Tunnel and a 6-mile long side road (Zion

Canyon Scenic Drive) heads off to the left. Turn left and follow the road further into Zion Canyon.

Note: Although this road is open to cars during the relatively slow wintry times, the rest of the year it is open only to shuttles, those staying at Zion Lodge, and those with special permits. The shuttle is free, and runs regularly during the long days of the busy season. It typically runs dark-to-very dark (pre-6 a.m. to about 10 p.m., though hours vary with the seasons).

Whether by personal vehicle or shuttle, head to Zion Lodge, which is 3.25 miles up-canyon from Canyon Junction. You'll find food, lodging, drinking water, restrooms and wild turkeys here. The Emerald Pools Trailhead is directly across the street from Zion Lodge.

The peaks in this subsection are roughly arranged from shortest-hike-from-the-trailhead to longest-hike-from-the-trailhead.

DB on the summit of Lady Mountain-East Spur

Lady Mountain – East Spur (5,934)

The prominent east spur of Lady Mountain is a fine, detached mini-peak with spectacular, wild views. Although the route is a bit brushy in places, it's a worthwhile endeavor. The summit itself is an exposed, aesthetic block perched above Zion Canyon.

It's easy to ignore this little summit with Lady Mountain so close, but those who head for this summit should not be disappointed.

The author at the first crux on the Lady Mountain route (Photo by Mike Schasch)

RT Mileage: 2
RT Elevation Gain: 1,700'
Time Required: 3-5 hours
Latitude: +37.25408
Longitude: -112.96340

FKA: Curt Haire & Wes Hall (July 1975) via Chimney Sweep (on East Face)
Etymology: Although the first ascent party called this feature the *North* Spur, this spur of Lady Mountain is actually on the mountain's *east* side.
Star Rating: **

Route: West Col (YDS 5.0)

Follow the directions given for Lady Mountain through the first crux (the exposed, overhung chimney; YDS 5.0). One hundred feet past the crux, the trail bends right and a 100-foot long red rock staircase presents itself. Visible at the top of the staircase is a gully leading to the col west of the East Spur (and east of Lady Mountain itself). Walk halfway up the staircase to a large, fallen tree on your right, step over the tree and walk 30 feet right, stepping over a chimney to gain the gully. Head up the gully (a number of short class 4 sections must be negotiated to reach the col). Immediately before the col, go right and work the easiest line (class 2-3) to the summit, where you'll find three points of approximately equal elevation. The southernmost is the most aesthetic.

A 30m rope is recommended for the route.

Mount Moroni (5,667)

Mount Moroni is the small, red-cliffed mountain situated immediately southwest of and above Zion Lodge and below Jacob, one of the park's celebrated Three Patriarchs. The other two patriarchs are Abraham and Isaac, both of which sit to the west of Jacob. The Three Patriarchs were named by Reverend Fisher, who also named Great White Throne and Angels Landing.

Mount Moroni is part of a craggy ridge running south from the vicinity of the old Lady Mountain trail on the Jacob-Lady Mountain massif. The named peak, a prominent crag near the southern tip of the ridge, is actually slightly lower than an unnamed point a few crags north of it.

Mount Moroni (a fine, little peak in its own right) is an excellent bonus for the motivated scrambler traveling up or down nearby Lady Mountain. Its summit has seen relatively few.

RT Mileage: 3
RT Elevation Gain: 1,800'
Time Required: 4-6 hours
Latitude: +37.2433
Longitude: -112.9638
FA: Unknown, though a number of challenging technical routes were put up by Brian Smoot and others on the mountain's east and southeast faces starting in the mid-1980's.

Etymology: Like many features in the park, early Mormon ranchers named the peak after themes from the *Book of Mormon*—this one for Moroni, a major figure in the book.

Star Rating: **

Route: North Ridge (YDS 5.0)

The first part of this route follows the old Lady Mountain trail. The rest of the route is an enjoyable, crag-bagging fest.

Follow the directions given for Lady Mountain through the first crux (the exposed, overhung chimney; YDS 5.0). Continuing along the old trail past the crux, the route soon traverses south below the east face of Lady Mountain, eventually making a right turn when it reaches a steep, dirty chute heading south and upward toward a chimney-like slot. There is a large dead tree lying horizontally across the bottom of the chute. If you find yourself coming to a 12-foot right-facing open book, you've gone too far—this is the 2nd crux on the Lady Mountain route.

Backtrack less than five minutes (about 100 feet) from the open book to the steep, dirty chute then leave the old trail and head up the loose chute with the fallen tree at its base. Be careful not to knock rocks down on those in your party coming up behind you. Fighting brush to reach the head of the chute, continue south for a short bit (100 feet or so) over brushy terrain until you find yourself at the shallow saddle between Mount Moroni and Jacob, the much higher peak above. Traverse left and south to the base of the red, craggy ridge heading south to Mount Moroni. Gain the ridge and follow it south, up and over several crags, toward the named peak at its southern end. With many variations possible, the easiest way to traverse the crags along the ridge requires a couple short sections of class 4 (or low 5) scrambling.

Eventually passing over a prominent crag (the highpoint of the ridge, actually), you'll come to a lesser crag. This lesser crag is separated from the crag to its south by a deep cleft. Once the cleft is reached, route-find your way down and west toward the wash below for about 200 feet until you can regain the ridge above. Doing so, the crag above you, immediately south of the deep cleft, requires a short bit of exposed (and committing) class 5 climbing to surmount.

Either bag this crag (the hardest of the bunch) or continue south a hundred feet or so below the ridge crest toward the summit of Mount Moroni, the next crag to the south. It is the highest crag at the southern end of the ridge.

Route-finding a bit, you'll likely need to work your way around a few short cliff bands and across a thickly brushy "saddle" to the terrain below the northwest face of Mount Moroni's summit crag. Once below the northwest face of the summit crag, work your way up, traversing across the north and northeast faces, until you find class 3 terrain allowing you to gain the highpoint. Success!

A 30m rope is recommended for the route.

The author works through the second crux on the Lady Mountain route. (I've climbed this crux numerous times, and I swear each time I end up finagling it in a new and inventive ungraceful way.) Photo by Mike Schasch

Route: West Wash (YDS 5.0)

This route is an easier (but less enjoyable) way to bag Mount Moroni than the North Ridge route. It shares the same crux as the North Ridge route.

Follow the directions given for the North Ridge route to the shallow saddle between Mount Moroni and Jacob. Ahead and to your left is the red, craggy north ridge of Mount Moroni. To your right are the cliffs of Jacob. Straight ahead is a brushy wash. Drop into the wash and follow it south for less than 0.5 mile until you are below the northwest face of Mount Moroni's summit crag. You'll know you're roughly there when the brushy wash opens up briefly into a 200-foot stretch of unvegetated slickrock. Moroni will be to the southeast.

Route-finding a bit, you'll likely need to work your way around a few short cliff bands and up to the terrain below the northwest face of Moroni's summit crag. Once below the northwest face of the summit crag, work your way up, traversing across the north and northeast faces, until you find class 3 terrain allowing you to gain the highpoint.

A 30m rope is recommended for the route.

Lady Mountain (6,945)

Lady Mountain is the high, cliffy mountain sitting directly across the road from the Zion Lodge. Viewing its east face from the lodge, it's easy enough to imagine that the route up is technical…but to think that the route is almost entirely class 2-3—impossible!

In 1924 the National Park Service oversaw the construction of an amazing trail up the mountain's imposing east face. Due to a couple of steep sections that were certainly not "trail-able," the NPS had ladders and cables installed to be used as aids. After a number of rescues and deaths, in 1978 the ladders and cables were removed and the trail was allowed to deteriorate. Today, the route is still relatively easy to follow. Painted arrows, a remnant of earlier visitation, are also visible in places. The former locations of the ladders are where this route becomes 5th class.

RT Mileage: 3.5
RT Elevation Gain: 2,700'
Time Required: 5-7 hours
Latitude: +37.2542
Longitude: -112.9664
FKA: Quite likely crew members involved in constructing the amazing 1924 trail up the mountain.
Etymology: Early pioneers named the mountain after a feature on the east face that resembled a woman's figure. In the late 1910s, early climbers of the mountain formed a group called the Mount Zion Mountaineers and

petitioned to have the name changed to Mount Zion. The petition didn't go through, and the Lady Mountain name remained.

Star Rating: ****

Route: East Face (YDS 5.4)

From Zion Lodge, cross the road and a footbridge then head left on the trail. After 100 yards, angle right as the trail splits. The trail here is no longer maintained, officially closed, and should be considered a "route." Follow the route for about 0.25 mile to an interpretive sign overlooking the Virgin River. Fifty feet beyond the sign, leave the obvious route and head left up a good use trail that leads to a headwall above. Once the headwall is reached, follow trail, painted arrows, cairns, and use common sense to work your way up the mountain. Expect several exposed scrambling sections along the way.

There are two short climbing sections: the first is an exposed chimney (YDS 5.0) with a bit of an overhang. It is short and sweet. There is an eye-bolt at the top of the chimney, as well as a bolt and hanger at the bottom. The second climbing section is a right-facing dihedral (YDS 5.4). A very helpful chipped hold which is nearly always buried under vegetation on the ledge keeps the route YDS 5.4. This 12-foot section has minimal exposure.

Continuing along, you'll eventually reach a saddle. The saddle connects Lady Mountain (right) with Jacob (left). Although it is *right there*, Jacob requires difficult 5th class climbing on questionable rock to surmount. My hat's off to you if you can do it.

From the saddle hang a right and spend a few minutes working your way along a class 2 use trail to the top of Lady Mountain. The views are excellent, particularly down into nearby Behunin Canyon.

A 30m rope is recommended for the route.

"Lady of the Cliff" (6,850)

Lady of the Cliff is a small but excellent summit with extraordinary views into Heaps Canyon and Jacob Canyon, whose head is at the base of the peak's east face.

RT Mileage: 4
RT Elevation Gain: 3,300'
Time Required: 5-8 hours
Latitude: +37.2560
Longitude: -112.9707
FKA: Jared Campbell & Buzz Burrell (April 10, 2009)
Etymology: This dainty but worthwhile overlook sits at the saddle connecting *Lady* Mountain with the unofficially named *Cliff* Dwelling Mountain (Peak 6,945).

Star Rating: ****

Mike Schasch descending Lady Mountain's northwest ridge en route to Lady of the Cliff

Route: Northeast Face (YDS 5.2)

Follow the directions given for Lady Mountain (YDS 5.4) to essentially the summit of that peak. From the gentle, manzanita-covered slope 75 yards from the summit, leave the beaten path and descend to the top of Lady Mountain's northwest ridge, where the views really begin to open up. Locate a class 3 weakness involving an exposed step-around above a short tree downclimb to breach the initial cliff and reach steep class 2-3 slabs leading toward the base of Lady of the Cliff. Beyond the slabs of Lady Mountain's northwest ridge, at a large crag blocking continued progress along the ridge, angle left of the crest to traverse class 2 (but spooky) dinner plates leading to the notch at the head of Jacob Canyon.

Walk to the base of our peak's northeast face then climb a 40-foot YDS 5.2 pitch to a belay at a large pine. A bush 30 feet up the pitch could be slung for protection. From the pine, walk 30 feet to the right on a dirty ledge then scramble to the next level above. Next, angle 80 feet to the right to find a class 3 groove that leads to class 1-2 slopes toward the summit. A pine tree graces the highpoint.

A 30m rope is recommended for the route.

Isaac (center) from the approach to Lady of the Cliff

Grotto Trailhead

Following UT-9 for 1.5 miles once inside the park, you will come to a junction (Canyon Junction). At the junction, UT-9 continues straight ahead toward the Zion-Mt. Carmel Tunnel and a 6-mile long side road (Zion Canyon Scenic Drive) heads off to the left. Turn left and follow the road further into Zion Canyon.

Note: Although this road is open to cars during the relatively slow wintry times, the rest of the year it is open only to shuttles and those with special permits. The shuttle is free, and runs regularly during the long days of the busy season. It typically runs from dark-to-very dark (generally about 6 a.m. to about 10 p.m., though hours vary with the seasons). Shuttle hours are posted at shuttle stops.

Whether by personal vehicle or shuttle, head to the Grotto Trailhead, which is 3.75 miles up-canyon from Canyon Junction. There is parking here, as well as bathrooms, drinking water, picnic tables, glorious scenery—and a cool breeze on a summer morning.

The peaks in this subsection are roughly arranged from shortest-hike-from-the-trailhead to longest-hike-from-the-trailhead.

Could this be the busiest trailhead in the park? Probably so.

The view north up Zion Canyon from Angels Landing

Angels Landing (5,785)

Angels Landing is unquestionably the most popular mountaintop hiking objective in Zion National Park. On late summer weekends, hundreds of people a day make their way to the top. Angels Landing is a Zion classic, and its narrow summit ridge is unforgettable.

RT Mileage: 5
RT Elevation Gain: 1,500'
Time Required: 2-4 hours
Latitude: +37.2693
Longitude: -112.9479
FKA: Most likely crew members involved in the 1924-25 construction of Walter's Wiggles and the Angels Landing Trail.

Etymology: In 1916, Rev. Frederick Fisher and his friends were exploring the area when Fisher looked up at the towering monolith and said "only an angel could land on it." The name stuck.
Star Rating: ****

Route: Standard Trail (class 3)

From the Grotto, cross the bridge on the other side of the road, hang a right, and follow the trail toward Angels Landing and the West Rim. The trail eventually steepens and passes through a portion of Refrigerator Canyon, then ascends Walter's Wiggles—a series of 21 tight, steep switchbacks in the trail. Walter's Wiggles was named for Zion's first superintendent (Walter Ruesch), who in 1924 helped design the switchbacks.

The trail flattens immediately above the Wiggles, and you arrive at Scout Lookout, the point where the Angels Landing Trail and the West Rim Trail intersect. Look to the right—Angels Landing looms nearby. Follow the obvious route toward the summit. Steep, narrow and hugely exposed in places, the Park Service had chains installed to be used as handlines in several spots along the route. Steps have also been carved in places to facilitate matters. The terrain levels out just as you approach the summit. The views of Zion Canyon from the top are phenomenal.

"Refrigerator Peak" (6,011)

Although minor, Refrigerator Peak is a popular objective for those hiking the West Rim Trail above Scout Lookout (and Angels Landing). With a narrow(ish) summit ridge, the views from the summit are sublime.

Few summits in Zion disappoint. This is not one of them.

RT Mileage: 5
RT Elevation Gain: 1,800'
Time Required: 3-5 hours
Latitude: +37.2832
Longitude: -112.9526
FA: Unknown
Etymology: The peak lies at the head of Refrigerator Canyon.
Star Rating: **

Route: South Ridge (class 2)

Follow the directions given for Sneak Peak to the level(ish) yellow slickrock area with the "shoeprint" signs. From here, Refrigerator Peak is just to the north. At a point that looks right, leave the trail and walk the remaining 100 vertical feet to the summit.

Mountain of Mystery (left) and Flagpole Mountain from the summit of Refrigerator Peak

Route: West Face (class 3)

Follow the directions given for Sneak Peak to the level(ish) yellow slickrock area with the "shoeprint" signs. Continuing north along the trail for another 100 yards or so, as you pass by the head of Refrigerator Canyon (on your left), leave the trail and scramble east up the mountain toward the summit. Several variations are possible.

"Little Majestic" (6,185)

This is a minor summit near Refrigerator Peak. The two are separated by both Refrigerator Canyon and a neighboring tributary of Telephone Canyon, though a cool strip of land can be walked across—like a bridge—to improbably connect the two peaks. I have fond memories of unexpectedly finding and crossing this land bridge during a dark-time descent of nearby Hook Canyon.

The summit offers splendid views of The Bodhisattva, Mountain of Mystery, Flagpole Mountain, and Wynopits Mountain. It's sort of neat to think that it's this easy to find serenity and solitude so close to the masses along the trail and ridges below you.

DB enjoying the view east across Zion Canyon from the summit of Little Majestic

RT Mileage: 5
RT Elevation Gain: 1,800'
Time Required: 3-5 hours
Latitude: +37.28290
Longitude: -112.95712
FA: Unknown
Etymology: A little bump of a summit next to Mount Majestic
Star Rating: *

Route: Southeast Face (YDS 5.0)

Follow the directions given for the west face route on Refrigerator Peak to the head of Refrigerator Canyon. Here, leave the trail and cross the isthmus that puts one near the base of Little Majestic's southeast face. A vegetated groove, mostly easy with a couple of funky class 5 sections, can be followed to the nice, flat summit with a weird, bent tree.

Route: Southwest Slope (class 2)

From the base of the southeast face hike easily to the base of the southwest slope then up to the summit.

The steep and slabby northeast buttress of Cathedral Mountain from Majestic Spur. The buttress, which was climbed by Brian Cabe and Tom Jones, has been called Foolz Buttress.

"Majestic Spur" (6,329)

Majestic Spur is a little nubbin protruding from the northeastern wall of Mount Majestic. The summit offers a marginal view into Hook Canyon and better views out across Zion Canyon to the sweet peaks on the other side of the abyss.

Majestic Spur and its close neighbor to the east, Little Majestic, are approached from the isthmus of earth picked up from the popular trail right at the head of Refrigerator Canyon.

RT Mileage: 5
RT Elevation Gain: 1,800'
Time Required: 3-5 hours
Latitude: +37.28251
Longitude: -112.95902
FA: Unknown
Etymology: Majestic Spur is simply a spur of land on the northeastern side of Mount Majestic.
Star Rating: *

Route: Southwest Ridge via South Slope (class 2-3)
Follow the directions given for Little Majestic to the southwestern base of that peak. Continue west to gain Majestic Spur's south slope, which leads to the southwest ridge and then the small summit.

Twin Peak

"Twin Peak" (6,145)

Twin Peak is a minor peak on the ridge south of Sneak Peak. I hadn't thought much of the peak until I was struck by its interesting profile while standing on the east mesa near Flagpole Mountain. Still, it wasn't until even later that I looked at the mountain from the northwest and first noticed just how impressive its twin peaks are from that direction.

The south summit is the highpoint.

RT Mileage: 7
RT Elevation Gain: 2,500'
Time Required: 4-6 hours
Latitude: +37.2900
Longitude: -112.9531
FKA: Courtney Purcell (November 9, 2009)
Etymology: The mountain has two ("twin") summits, which are particularly striking when viewed from the northwest.

Star Rating: **

Route: Southwest Face (class 3)

Follow the directions given for Sneak Peak to the confluence of lower Telephone Canyon and the unnamed, minor canyon you walked over on the footbridge. Once at the confluence, scramble up slabs on the north side and then begin angling northeast toward the southwest face of Twin Peak. Once at the southwestern base of the peak, head up while looking for the easiest line of ascent. Some route-finding will be required, as one could easily find himself on class 4 (or harder) terrain. The going is steep and loose.

As you ascend, easier terrain should soon start leading you around toward the south face. Once on the south face, continue up, working east as difficulties increase. Near the top, one can scramble class 2 slabs and broken ledges on the southeast face that lead to the final class 2 scramble onto the small, exposed summit.

Route: Northwest Face (class 2+)

Follow the directions given for Sneak Peak toward the north saddle of Twin Peak. As you approach this saddle, head southeast up the northwest face of Twin Peak, ultimately aiming for a minor saddle between Twin Peak's main summit (right) and its lesser north summit (left). This minor saddle will be south of the more prominent Sneak Peak-Twin Peak saddle. With a little route-finding, the going should not be harder than class 2.

From the minor saddle, hang a right and scramble up 20-30 feet of class 2-3 terrain to the highpoint.

"Gunsight Point" (7,091)

This is a wonderful and incredibly scenic hike to one of the finest viewpoints in the park. The views from the slickrock and funky hoodoos just below the summit extend from across Zion Canyon to Deertrap Mountain to across Phantom Valley to Ivins Mountain.

RT Mileage: 15
RT Elevation Gain: 3,500'
Time Required: 5-8 hours
Latitude: +37.2717
Longitude: -112.9743
FA: Unknown
Etymology: The peak is named for Gunsight Canyon, which is immediately west.
Star Rating: ****

DB admiring the views into Phantom Valley from just below the summit of Gunsight Point

Route: Northwest Face (class 3)

From the Grotto Trailhead, follow the directions given for Horse Pasture Plateau to a point where the West Rim Trail passes above the long, narrow spit of land heading south out to the peak. Leave the West Rim Trail and follow a class 2 game trail through a break in the rim cliffs to the flattish plateau below. The good game trail continues south, avoiding virtually all of the brush, and passes a few lovely slickrock areas with hoodoos and other interesting features. The scenery is terrific. Gunsight Canyon is to the immediate west and Behunin Canyon is to the immediately east.

Reaching the northwest corner of the summit cap, scramble through a neat class 3 break to reach easier terrain above. Although the summit is only a 5-minute walk from here, it is brushy and the views are not good. The slickrock area at the top of the class 3 break is a wonderful spot for photography.

The Organ (4,920+)

The Organ is an aesthetic, narrow fin jutting out from Angels Landing at the Big Bend in Zion Canyon. Guarded by steep faces, The Organ requires excellent route-finding and solid climbing skills to reach its summit. Doing so, the climber is rewarded with awesome views of Weeping Rock (complete with a stunning 100-foot gushing waterfall in spring), Great White Throne,

Cable Mountain, Angels Landing, and of course, the Virgin River bending around its base.

DB returns to the West Rim from Gunsight Point. As for the entire route to Gunsight Point and back, the views are astonishing. Behind DB can be seen the walls of Mount Majestic and Castle Dome guarding the depths of Behunin Canyon. In the distance across Zion Canyon is Deertrap Mountain, Mountain of the Sun, and The East Temple.

RT Mileage: 1
RT Elevation Gain: 700'
Time Required: 5-7 hours
Latitude: +37.2709
Longitude: -112.9435
FKA: Jim Beyer & Courtney Simpkins (1978)
Etymology: Reverend Fisher named the feature for its resemblance to a pipe organ.
Star Rating: ****

Looking down on The Organ (center) from the summit of Cable Mountain

Getting to the Mountain:
One can approach the peak from the Grotto Trailhead, or continue another mile or so up Zion Canyon to the Weeping Rock trailhead.

Route: Southeast Chimney (YDS 5.6)
This, perhaps the easiest summit route on the feature, was first established in late 1978, though the ascentists did find evidence of prior exploration partway up.

Approaching the feature's southeast face from either the Grotto Trailhead or the Weeping Rock Trailhead (both of which will likely require a foot crossing of the Virgin River) note a prominent chimney near the center of the face. You need to aim for this.

Climb a short (6-8 feet) chimney or face below and about 70 feet left of the big chimney seen on the face. Once up, enter an interesting slot and then angle back right through brush, scrambling to a brushy flat spot at the base of the chimney in question. Either work up the 40-foot chimney (perhaps YDS 5.6) or climb the face (class 4) to its left and continue up to a possible belay. From here, step left into a more narrow 20-foot chimney (YDS 5.6). Exiting right from this chimney, you'll immediately encounter another chimney. This 50-foot chimney is tight but can be negotiated rather easily (class 4). Exiting right to a belay atop of chockstone, you'll encounter the tightest chimney (YDS 5.4) of the route—a 20-foot squeeze with an exit left at the top.

Exiting the squeeze chimney via an exposed step-across, climb the slab right next to you and get into a sandy slot that makes a decent belay. From the sand belay, step right through some brush and look up at the first semi-clean pitch of the route, a 120-foot chimney (YDS 5.6). Mostly quite easy, at one point you'll need to step right around a bulge and get into another chimney. A second bulge greets you just before the spacious belay above. From this spacious slab belay, scramble up a short slot and then step right and negotiate a lieback/undercling problem that stands as the final technical obstacle of the route. This 8-10 foot problem is easily negotiated with a little finesse.

From the top of the technical difficulties, angle up and rightward (class 2-3) for a couple hundred feet, looking for the easiest line of ascent, to the nicely exposed, tiny summit block. A hugely exposed class 3 couple of moves put you on the highpoint.

To descend, downclimb to the flattish spot above the lieback/undercling problem. From there, continue to route-find your way south, negotiating nothing harder than class 3 terrain. Encountering a couple of steep chimneys, downclimb (class 4) to a tree with a rappel sling on it. Rappel from the tree about 80 feet down to flattish terrain below. Continue route-finding south for a couple hundred feet until you find a small but healthy tree on the edge of the feature's south face. A sling or two should be around it. A clean rappel of about 180 feet from the tree lands you on terra firma at the base of the mountain. From there, a short walk back to the road follows. (Other descent options do exist, though one may have to look around a bit to find something that suits the skills, experience and available equipment of the party.)

Two 60m ropes are recommended for the route. An assortment of medium and large cams and nuts are useful for protection.

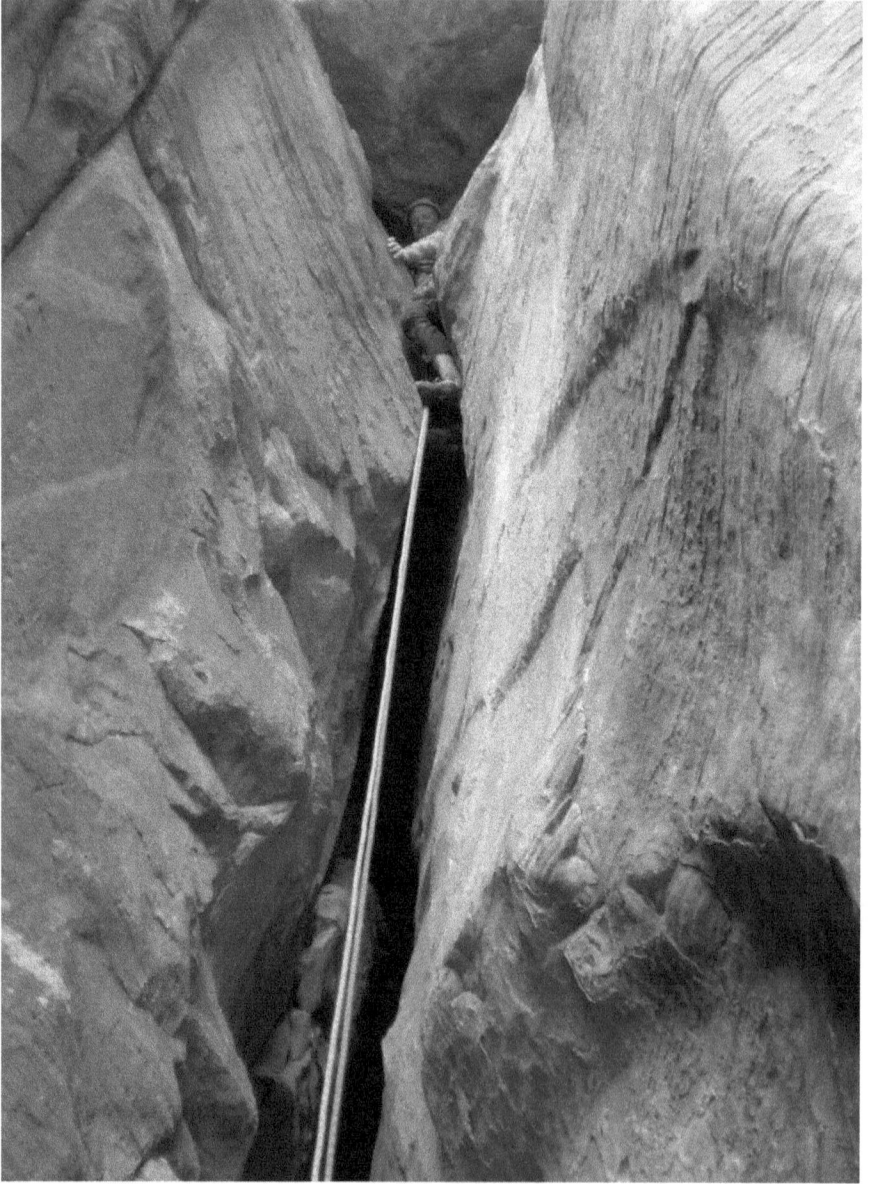

Dow Williams leading the "squeeze" pitch on the Southeast Chimney of The Organ

"Sneak Peak" (6,528)

This overlooked peak, tucked away in the backcountry near the West Rim Trail a couple of miles north-northwest of the fabled Angels Landing, has seen relatively few human feet. With plenty of steep terrain and loose rock scrambling, care must be taken to ensure one gets on and off this crumbly peak without incident.

Climbing Sneak Peak once in winter without any beta, I found narrow, icy ridge traverses, an unexpected rappel (on the ascent), and particularly brittle rock. Fortunately, I've since found a better variation that gets rid of the rappel and the narrow ridge stuff.

The views from the flat, manzanita-covered summit of Sneak Peak are interesting, particularly east to Mountain of Mystery and its gaping hanging canyon (Mountain of Mystery Canyon).

RT Mileage: 9
RT Elevation Gain: 3,000'
Time Required: 7-9 hours
Latitude: +37.3012
Longitude: -112.9564
FKA: Courtney Purcell & DB (January 19, 2009)
Etymology: Close at hand are the "Imlay *Sneak* Routes," two shortcut to one of Zion's classic canyoneering adventures.
Star Rating: **

Route: South Ridge (class 2+)

Follow the directions given for Angels Landing to the junction of the Angels Landing Trail and the West Rim Trail at Scout Lookout. Follow the West Rim Trail left. The trail will wander up through breathtaking scenery before briefly leveling off at a yellow slickrock area (with signs showing shoeprints on them) and then descending a bit. As you descend, the trail will make a couple of switchbacks and then cross a footbridge over a shallow slot.

Continue past the bridge for another 50 yards then leave the trail and head north on a use trail that parallels the slot on your right. The use trail reaches a point about 20 feet above the confluence of the slot on your right and lower Telephone Canyon. Look for a steep, dirt ramp on your right that allows access down to the confluence of the two drainages.

At the confluence scramble north up the other side and then hike north toward Sneak Peak, which should be visible in the distance. As you approach the saddle immediately north of Twin Peak (the minor peak 0.75 mile south of Sneak Peak) on your right, angle toward the saddle. It is gained via class 2 terrain.

Once on the saddle, follow the crest of the ridge north toward Sneak Peak. Reaching Point 6,228, which is 0.25 mile south of Sneak Peak, you'll come to cliffs barring further easy progress. Backtracking 50 feet, notice that you can easily drop about 75 feet to the northeast and pick up the ridge again. Rather than do that, drop to the steep, somewhat brushy terrain to the right of the ridge and work your way down about 300-400 vertical feet to the relatively flat terrain below and immediately east of the cliffs. Some route-finding may be required to avoid a few steeper sections on the way down, though the going is reasonable.

Once down, contour along the cliffs on your left to the base of a steep brush and slab area leading northwest up to a pine needle-filled chute with a large pine in it. This chute leads to a notch in the ridge crest immediately adjacent to the final steep face leading toward the summit. Work up to and through the pine needle chute to the notch then hang a right and follow the easiest line of ascent up the face to the northeast. Anything harder than class 2-3 is off-route.

Eventually gaining a final ridge leading to the summit, angle back left (northwest) on the narrow, brushy ridge until you reach the final band of cliffs leading up to the flat summit. A class 4 corner can be found on the left, while brushy class 2 terrain can be found on the right. Wander to the top and relax amongst the manzanita living there.

The toe of The Bodhisattva's south buttress

"The Bodhisattva" (6,630)

The Bodhisattva is an unassuming high peak straddling the Imlay Sneak Routes near the West Rim. The peak is east of the West Rim and northwest of Sneak Peak.

Without any obvious routes to the summit, the south buttress (not to be confused with the detached south *ridge*) is a fun and improbable route that requires some technical skill.

Once near the actual summit on the northwestern corner of the summit mesa, one will find that the true highpoint is a small-car-sized boulder balanced on two thin pegs of sandstone. Very cool.

RT Mileage: 10
RT Elevation Gain: 3,300'
Time Required: 8-12 hours
Latitude: +37.3074
Longitude: -112.9615
FKA: Courtney Purcell & DB (November 23, 2008)
Etymology: My name for it. For me, the mountain vibrates a sense of calm, centering and compassion.
Star Rating: ***

Route: South Buttress (YDS 5.5)

Follow the directions given for Sneak Peak to the confluence of lower Telephone Canyon and the minor slot below the footbridge. Once at the confluence, scramble north-northwest to gain a mellow and meandering sandy/brushy rib that leads to The Bodhisattva's south ridge. A use trail makes the going easy. As you near the base of the steep and imposing south ridge, leave the trail and drop into the wash to your left. You might need to look around for a walk-down route.

Hike north up the wash. About 0.25 mile south of a pass, the canyon forks and the main drainage stays left. The lesser right fork heads to the notch between the cliffy Bodhisattva and its detached south ridge. The south buttress looms between the two forks.

Gain a cleft in the lower buttress via a steep, loose dirt slope, and head up. Soon, a 40-foot crack (with poor protection) appears in the cleft—this is the route's crux. Climb through the crack and continue up the cleft past some unpleasant, steep pine needles and brush. The cleft ends at a clump of bushes below a slab. Climb the slab (15 feet; YDS 5.0) to gain steep but easier (albeit more loose and broken) terrain on (or very near) the crest of the buttress. Continue scrambling (class 3) up the buttress until a steep chute appears on the left. Step left into the chute when a class 2 weakness appears.

DB near the top of The Bodhisattva's south buttress

Once in the chute, head up steep pine needles to its head. There, continue up a red and broken (and very loose—careful!) chimney (25 feet; class 3-4) until you gain the summit mesa. The actual summit is a 0.25 mile walk to the north/northwest over gentle terrain. I'd think twice before stepping onto the highpoint, as it won't take much weight to send it careening down toward Imlay Canyon.

A 50m rope is recommended for the route. A small cam or two *may* help protect the crux.

Mount Majestic (6,956)

One of the large, seemingly impenetrable big-walled mountains of Zion National Park, Mount Majestic is seldom climbed. Not quite owing to the apparently unconquerable nature of its massive faces, nor to the technical abilities needed to overcome it's summit cap, this mesa-topped high peak's big deterrent saves its surprise for the last hour before the weary adventurer approaches the high point—it's no wonder that one of my partners dubbed the peak both "Mount Masochistic" and "Manzanita Peak."

After fearlessly achieving the unthinkable—traversing across 0.75 mile of the thickest, most awful, most bushwhacky manzanita we'd ever encountered to the base of the final, technical summit cap—our legs were a blood-covered, pulpy mess. Pant legs in tatters, we tackled the summit cap, stepped onto the high point, and collectively vowed never to return. It seems that the consensus of the few who dare to climb all the way to the summit is that Mount Majestic is destined to *never* be considered a classic. It came as no surprise to us that there was no register on the highpoint. I'd say that Mount Majestic is a great peak, but I don't want to lie to you.

But there's good news: since my only visit to the mountain, a fire has burnt up most of the nasty brush, allowing a reasonably pleasant crossing of the plateau. Yay!

RT Mileage: 10-12
RT Elevation Gain: 3,000'
Time Required: 9-11 hours
Latitude: +37.2736
Longitude: -112.9623
FA: Unknown
Etymology: Stephen Johnson named the mountain in 1922 during an exploratory trip up Zion Canyon. The mountain is indeed majestic, though its close neighbor, Cathedral Mountain, steals most of the attention.
Star Rating: **

Route: Behunin Ridge (class 4+)

Follow the directions given for Sneak Peak to the footbridge over the shallow slot just northwest of Refrigerator Peak. Continue along the West Rim Trail to a pass between the northwest corner of Mount Majestic (on your left) and the West Rim (on your right). Here, the trail bends sharply right and begins to ascend to the rim. This is where you leave the trail.

From the pass, look for a good use trail through the brush that will drop down the other side of the pass and into upper Behunin Canyon. Follow it down and to the right, before it jogs to the left and dumps you off in the watercourse immediately below the impressive Behunin Canyon headwall and the canyoneering route that begins there.

Follow Behunin Canyon south for about 0.75 mile until it turns sharply left then abruptly comes to the first significant drop-off. At this point, and immediately to your left, you'll notice the steep slabs of lower Behunin Ridge heading northward. Leave the canyon and get onto the ridge. From the lower part of Behunin Ridge, follow it up, staying near the west side of the crest to avoid greater difficulties. Though exposed in places, the lower ridge goes at class 3-4. Staying on or near the west side of the crest, follow it northward past a couple of false summits until you come to the final, steep portion of the ridge that ultimately connects to Mount Majestic's summit mesa above. This is the steepest and most exposed portion of Behunin Ridge—and also the most exciting.

You'll notice a brushy gully to the right of the upper Behunin Ridge. Follow the brushy gully to its top to avoid difficulties and exposure. Traverse left (class 3) from the top of the gully onto the upper ridge. Follow the ridge crest to the summit mesa a short distance above. The going is mostly class 3 (with a couple of short class 4 sections) and staying in a crack just barely right of the crest should minimize difficulties. One section, near the top, is low 5th class (and extremely exposed), though it can be converted into 3rd class by crawling underneath a bush (awkward) immediately before a large tree root that you must crawl over (you should know it when you see it). This tree/root makes a fine belay spot if your partners need assistance getting past this crux of the ridge.

(By the way, I didn't mention it earlier, but one can get a good view of Behunin Ridge from the finger of land just to the west, accessible via a short, easy off-trail hike from the beaten path along the West Rim.)

You've made the mesa. A short distance to the north and northeast, you'll notice the north summit cap of Mount Majestic. It's reportedly 1-foot lower than the elusive south summit cap. Its summit is reached via a walk-up (class 2) on its south side.

The main (south) summit cap is about 0.75 mile south across the mesa. On the north side of the south summit cap is a series of minor weaknesses in the cliffs. The easiest sure thing involves a short amount (8 feet) of YDS 5.8+ face climbing, followed by a 12-foot awkward YDS 5.8 chimney then loose and crappy class 2-3 terrain leading to the highpoint a short distance away. Alternatively, the south cliffs of the south summit cap offer a class 4-5 weakness that I've not climbed (but only viewed while rappelling from the cap).

A 60m rope is recommended for the route.

Alternative descent option (Behunin Canyon: 3BIV, for the combo):
By dropping back down Behunin Ridge to Behunin Canyon, one may utilize the canyon for a splendid return route. The canyon features about 9 rappels up to 165 feet, and some downclimbs and swimming. The final drop is a free air rappel out of the canyon. After the last rappel, scurry down the bouldery wash until you can pick up the good trail that heads left and back to the Grotto.

Wetsuits are advisable in cooler weather. A canyoneering permit is required. Bring two 60m ropes.

Looking up Hook Canyon from the vicinity of Majestic Spur

Alternative descent option (Hook Canyon: 3AIV, for the combo):
From the vicinity of the south summit cap, head southeast to the col separating Mount Majestic from Cathedral Mountain (just to the east). Hook Canyon drains north from the col, while Spearhead Canyon drains south.

From the col, work to the head of Hook Canyon and look for a tree (with a sling around it) for the first rappel, which is about 90 feet. At the bottom of this rappel, continue down-canyon over loose terrain in the watercourse. Along the way, expect two more rappels (though both can be down-climbed by strong climbers). The first of these two rappels is a short one (about 12 feet) from a chockstone at its edge (or from any of the trees above). The final rappel is about 80 feet from a tree with a sling around it.

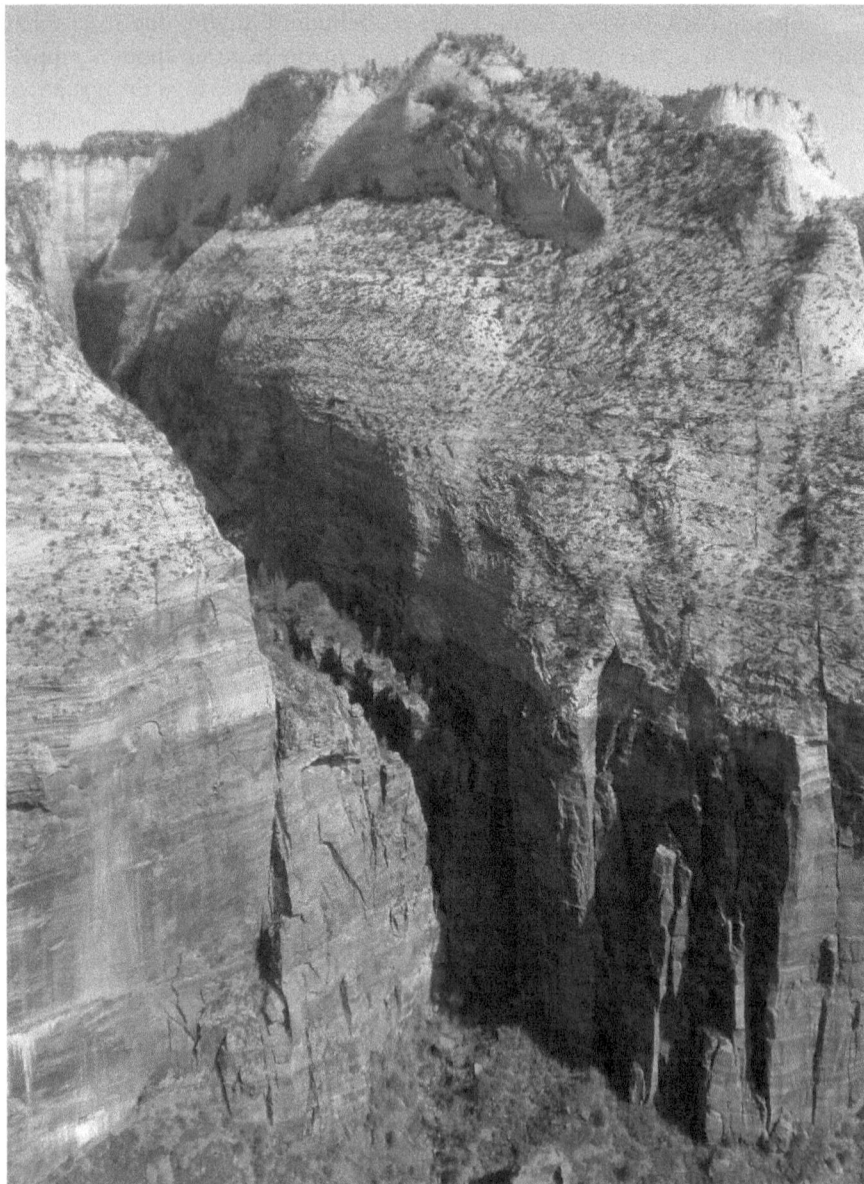

Behunin Canyon from the Lady Mountain massif

Continue down the watercourse a short distance more until you're out of the canyon. Once out of the canyon, you may note that you're less than 0.5 mile from the West Rim Trail. Continue down the watercourse, staying just left of and above it. Head northeast until you see that drainages are on both sides of you (the one on the right is the aforementioned watercourse draining down from Hook Canyon; the other one drains from the hilly features to your left). Follow this rib above the drainages as it continues east-northeast then heads north. If all goes well, you'll soon find yourself running into the West Rim Trail. Follow the West Rim Trail to the right and back to the tourist-laden, busy trailhead.

A 60m rope is recommended for this descent option.

According to Ram...

In 95°F temperatures one summer day many years ago, Ram and his partners made their way across the tedious, manzanita-choked summit plateau of Mount Majestic en route to the head of Spearhead Canyon. So fed up with the obnoxiousness of the intense brush continually tearing at their legs, they eventually donned their wetsuits, pulling them up to their waists, and continued their hot and sweaty romp to the canyon.

A bit drastic for such a hot, summer day? Not at all. He said he'd do it again! (I told you it used to be bad!)

"Imsleepy Peak" (6,258)

Imsleepy Peak is well-protected by Imlay Canyon, which runs along its north and east sides, Sleepy Hollow, which runs along its south side, and the massive cliffs of the West Rim, which tower to the west above the summit. I failed twice on attempts to climb this nicely hidden peak before eventually reaching the summit via a remarkably reasonable route. The route utilizes the Left Imlay Sneak Route to eventually access the peak's east face, which is reminiscent of a more benign version of the routes I describe for Aires Butte or Twin Brothers.

Despite being surrounded on all sides by impressive high cliffs and deep, technical canyons, the summit of Imsleepy Peak is a sweet and welcoming spot with several nice pine trees, the occasional manzanita, and some flat slickrock to lounge upon. I believe this is a peak I will return to time and again.

RT Mileage: 12
RT Elevation Gain: 4,000'
Time Required: 9-12 hours
Latitude: +37.317681
Longitude: -112.970288
FKA: Andy Archibald & Courtney Purcell (May 20, 2015)
Etymology: The name is derived from the peak's position above the confluence of Imlay Canyon and Sleepy Hollow, a magical place whispering legends indeed. The name is pronounced like "I'm Sleepy."
Star Rating: ***

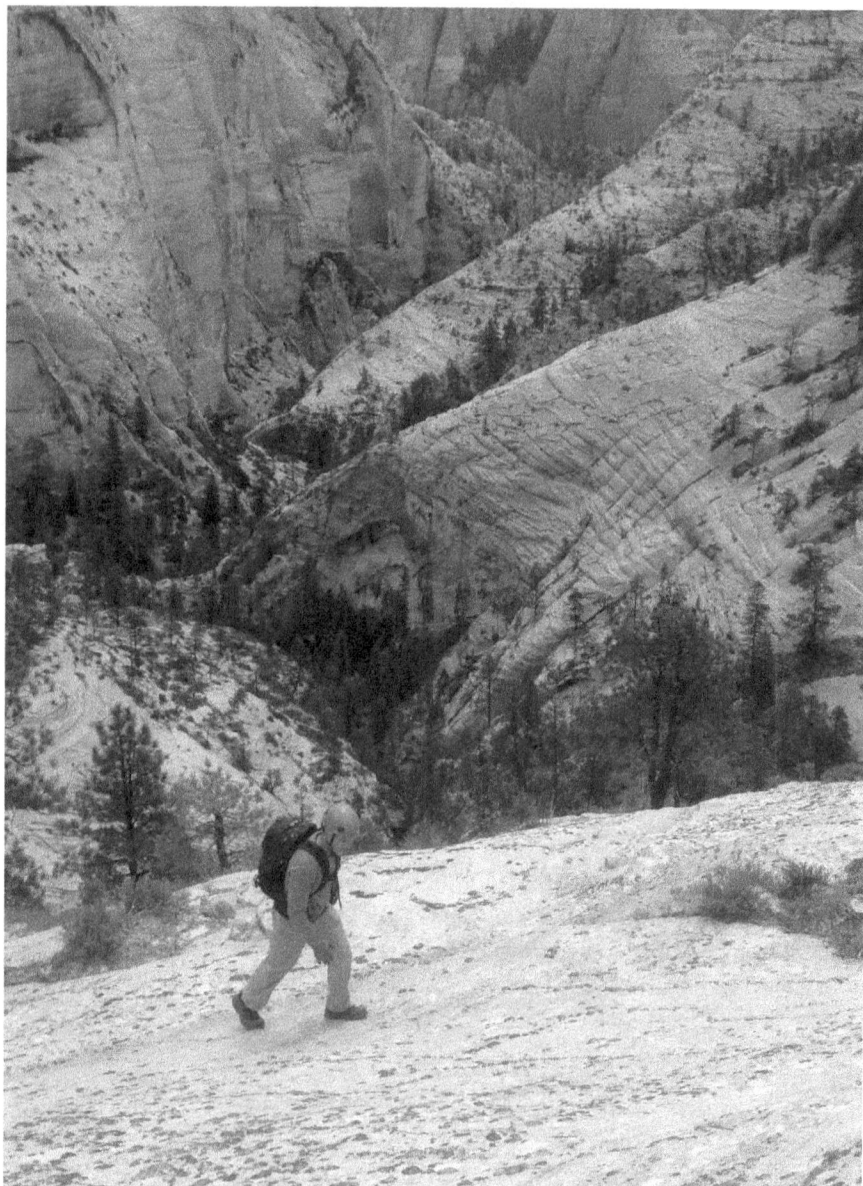

Andy Archibald ascending the east face of Imsleepy Peak

Route: East Face (class 3-4)

Follow the directions given for The Bodhisattva to the base of that peak's south buttress. Take the left fork and continue north up the canyon to the pass. This route is known as the "Left Imlay Sneak Route." (The "*Right* Imlay Sneak Route" parallels this one on the east side of The Bodhisattva. Both

Sneak Routes provide essentially non-technical canyon access to middle Imlay Canyon, though the Left Sneak Route has some steep terrain in its lower stretches that must be rappelled or carefully downclimbed.)

Descend the Left Sneak Route north from the pass to just before a significant drop in the canyon. The Left Sneak Route continues down the canyon. Here you will leave the canyon on the left (looking down-canyon) and ascend about 200 vertical feet via a rightward traverse across dirty slopes. You'll encounter a very steep chute that is accessed via a sketchy dead tree just below its head. Climb down the chute (class 3) for about 100 feet until you can cut left and begin traversing slabs and ledges to the north-northwest, maintaining a somewhat consistent elevation. These slabs and ledges eventually contour to the west above Imlay Canyon. Continue your traverse at about the same elevation, following vegetated ledges immediately below a prominent cliff band, to just before the point where the ledges meet Sleepy Hollow. Descend the most vegetated route (class 2) into the floor of Sleepy Hollow. (A steep class 3 slab to the right, which descends directly toward the Sleepy Hollow-Imlay Canyon confluence, also goes with proper route-finding.) Gain the base of the peak on its right side via class 4 ledges or on the left via a sweet class 2-3 sidewalk that angles back to the right. Zigzag up the face (class 3-4) to the summit.

Some parties may want a 30m rope for the route.

Cathedral Mountain (6,920)

Cathedral Mountain is the high, imposing, big-walled peak to the immediate west of the famous Angels Landing.

The first major formation climbed in Zion was Great White Throne, which saw its first ascent in 1927. The second major formation climbed was Cathedral Mountain, which was first overcome on August 31, 1931 by Walter Becker, Fritz Becker and Rudolph Weidner. I don't know which route they took (I suspect they ascended Hook Canyon), though it reportedly involved some tricky terrain and considerable physical challenge.

RT Mileage: 10-12
RT Elevation Gain: 3,000'
Time Required: 11-13 hours
Latitude: +37.2750
Longitude: -112.9582
FKA: Walter Becker, Fritz Becker and Rudolph Weidner (August 31, 1931)
Etymology: The peak was named by an early settler named Stephen Johnson in 1922 after the summit cap's resemblance to a cathedral.
Star Rating: **

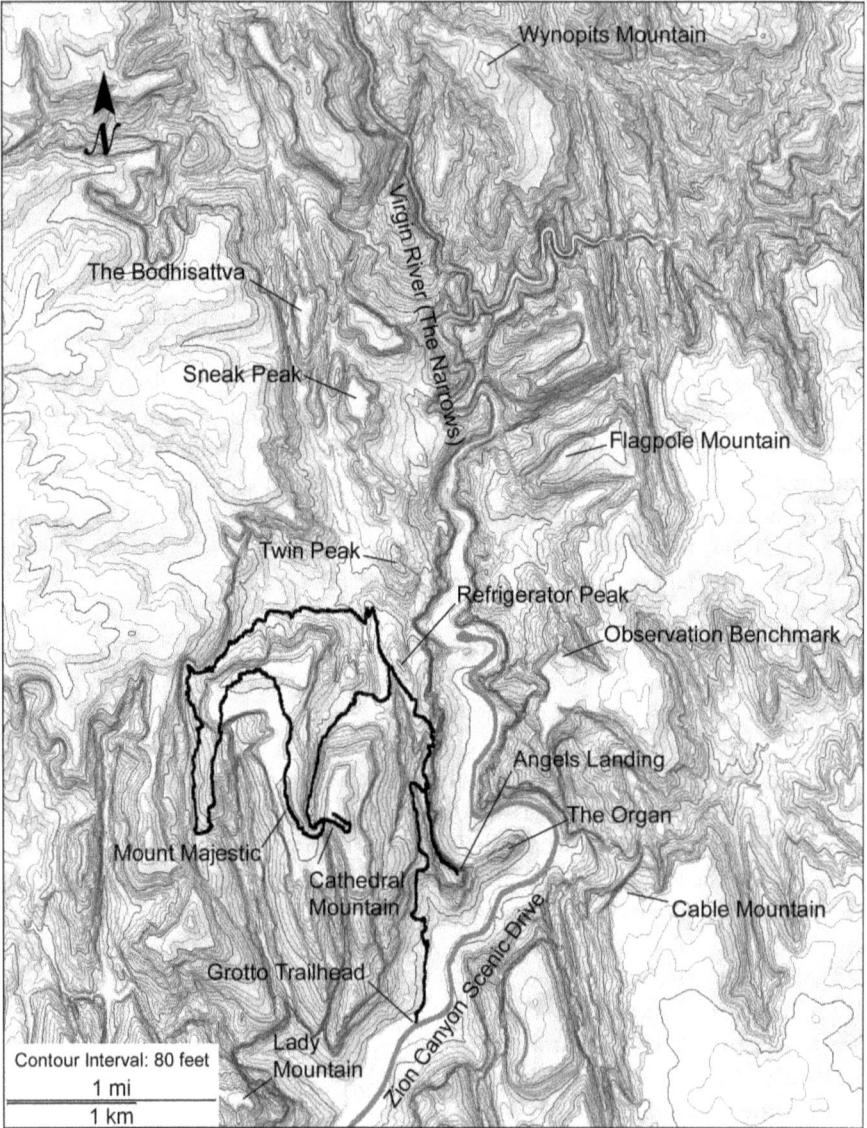

Map of the Cathedral Mountain area

Hiking in Zion

Route: Behunin Ridge (class 4)

Follow the directions given for Mount Majestic to the Mount Majestic-Cathedral Mountain col. From the col, bushwhack to the southwest corner of Cathedral Mountain's sprawling summit cap. Once there, traverse to the east along the south side of the cap below a magnificent overhanging wall reminiscent of Zion's well-known "Weeping Rock." As you approach the cap's southeast side, notice a class 4 weakness in the form of steep slabs and ledges to the left. Try those, or keep following the cap around a bit more. After about 50 feet more, you'll come to some exposed class 3 ledges that also provide a way up. Continuing yet another 50-75 feet, you'll come to the easiest way up you're going to find—class 2, over loose rock. Any of these options will work. From the top of the difficulties, bushwhack the summit cap northward to the indistinguishable highpoint, so representative of the many mesa-topped summits of Zion—great views on the approach; very little to see from the summit.

The easiest (and quickest) descent option is via Hook Canyon (see Mount Majestic for further information). As a matter of fact, this option is so highly recommended and obvious for its speed and efficiency that it would seem ludicrous to pursue the alternative, assuming one possesses the gear and know-how to safely descend the canyon.

Behunin Ridge, as seen from the plateau below Gunsight Point. Although the lower and middle sections of the ridge are quite reasonable, from this vantage point it's hard to imagine that the very steep-looking upper segment can be done ropeless (though some may feel more comfortable with one). It was a delight first visiting this area with two of my long-time mountain partners, though the day would be long, with us finishing up the rappels in Hook Canyon after dark and returning home hours past my standard 8 p.m. bedtime. Fortunately, my buddy kept me awake (but dreamy) repeatedly playing The Cure's "The Same Deep Water As You" for what seemed like most of the way home.

44. Twin Brothers	54. Stevensworth Peak	62. Lost Peak
45. Mountain of the Sun	55. Destination Peak	63. The Triplets
49. Deertrap Mountain	56. Gifford Peak	64. The Fin
50. Progeny Peak	57. Hepworth Peak	65. Nippletop
51. Ant Hill	58. Roof Peak	66. Separation Peak
52. Aires Butte	59. Red Jenny	67. Checkerboard Mesa
53. South Ariel Peak	60. Jenny Peak	79. The East Temple
	61. Little Jenny Peak	80. Crazy Quilt Mesa

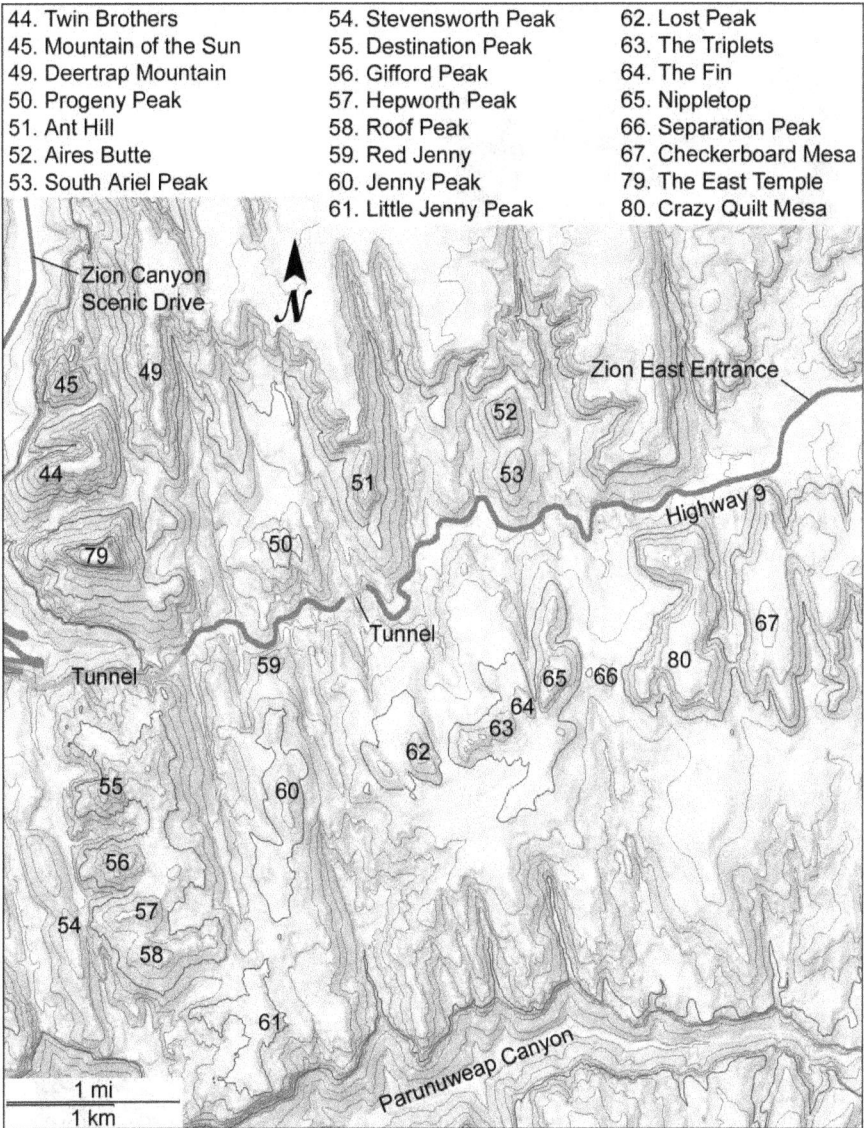

Map of Zion's East Side (aka Southeast Slickrock). The numbers utilized here are specific only to this map.

Bridge Mountain from the approach to The East Temple (Photo by Aron Ralston)

Shelf Point from Bighorn Peak

East Side

Zion National Park's east side is a special place of slot canyons, slickrock and funky hoodoos. It's also home to Checkerboard Mesa—one of the most photographed features in the entire park.

With UT-9 flowing at a relatively high elevation on this side of the park, most of the peaks accessed from here can be done rather quickly. There are lots and lots of quality, half-day ascents to be had.

The park's east entrance on UT-9 sits at an elevation of about 5,700 feet, which is roughly 1,700 feet above Zion Canyon.

Getting There:
From I-15 in St. George, Utah, follow signage north toward Zion National Park. Get off I-15 at exit 16 (UT-9) and follow UT-9 east toward the park. At 12.4 miles, UT-9 will turn right in La Verkin, Utah. Continuing on UT-9 for 30.3 miles from I-15, you'll soon reach the charming community of Springdale, Utah. Springdale likes just outside of the main park entrance. (Alternatively, from St. George you can follow I-15 north to exit 27 (UT-17). Exit, and take UT-17 six miles (through Toquerville) and then turn left onto UT-9 in La Verkin. Continue from there.)

Following UT-9 for 1.5 miles once inside the park, you will come to a junction. At the junction, UT-9 continues straight ahead toward the Zion-Mt.

Carmel Tunnel and a side road (Zion Canyon Scenic Drive) heads off to the left toward the Zion Lodge and a host of Zion goodies. Continuing 4.5 miles along UT-9, you will encounter several switchbacks that will soon lead you to and through the Zion-Mt. Carmel Tunnel and into the park's east side.

A massive waterfall in Gifford Canyon during a fall storm

Gifford Canyon Trailhead

Immediately east of the Zion-Mt. Carmel Tunnel is a small parking lot on the right. There are restrooms here and a little booth where the park staff hangs out when not directing traffic through the tunnel. If that spot is unavailable (as it usually is), continue 0.1 mile and park in a newly established parking area on the left.

The peaks in this subsection are roughly arranged from shortest-hike-from-the-trailhead to longest-hike-from-the-trailhead.

"Tunnel Knob" (5,270)

This is a fun time-killer while waiting for your buddy to get off the can at the Gifford Canyon Trailhead. It only takes 10 minutes car-to-car, the views are good, and the scrambling is enjoyable. Many will probably want a belay for the downclimb off the summit crag.

Not only is the summit block a fine spot for meditation, but for watching people and other forms of wildlife as well—it's common to see bighorn sheep and the tourists who gawk at them. I can't blame them—the sheep are majestic as they effortlessly stroll about steep slopes.

RT Mileage: 0.25
RT Elevation Gain: 150'
Time Required: A few minutes (!)
Latitude: +37.2133
Longitude: -112.9399
FA: O. Hellifino (date unknown)
Etymology: It's a knob-like summit next to the Big Tunnel.
Star Rating: **

Bridge Mountain from UT-9

Route: North Face (class 4)
From the parking area immediately east of the big tunnel, head east up the small, craggy lump adjacent to the parking area via class 2-3 terrain. The summit knob is climbed via 12 feet of exposed class 4 scrambling on its north side.

"Destination Point" (6,411)
This minor viewpoint just east-northeast of Destination Peak doesn't look much like a peak unless you're on Shelf Point. Still, it's an easy bag with swell views.

Destination Point (top-center; lame) and Destination Peak (top-right)
from the slabs above Canyon Overlook

RT Mileage: 4
RT Elevation Gain: 1,800'
Time Required: 3-5 hours
Latitude: +37.2036
Longitude: -112.9447

FA: Unknown
Etymology: Destination Point is merely a mellow, tree'd lump next to Destination Peak.
Star Rating: *

Route: West and Southwest Slopes (class 2)
Follow the directions given for Bridge Mountain to the sand and brush plateau just east of Gifford Peak and Destination Peak. From here, hike northwest toward the Destination Peak-Destination Point saddle then angle right over easy slopes leading to the top.

Although it doesn't make much sense to do so, I've also approached the summit from the convoluted plateau northwest of the peak via Hepworth Wash.

Destination Peak from the southeast

"Destination Peak" (6,631)

Originally eyeballing this obscure but easily accessible peak from Hepworth Peak, and then later exploring along the peak's west, north and east sides to find the way to the summit blocked by steep cliffs and loose, dangerous terrain, I thought this to be among the most challenging of the peaks on the park's east side. Then months later, while atop the closer perch of neighborly

Gifford Peak, I spotted a weakness on the peak's southeast face—a low angle chute that went nearly all the way to the summit. Hmmm!

Indeed, the peak is a reasonable ascent with fun scrambling, interesting terrain, and a ton of great scenery.

RT Mileage: 4
RT Elevation Gain: 2,000'
Time Required: 4-6 hours
Latitude: +37.2024
Longitude: -112.9488
FA: Unknown. When my partners and I reached this obscure summit, we found a register had been placed one month earlier by Joe French and Pearl Meadows.
Etymology: Although I'd considered dubbing the peak "Stevens Peak" after nearby Stevens Wash, one of my partners, Tanya Milligan, casually referred to this peak in a subsequent photo caption as our "destination peak." Seemed like a good name to me, and my partners agreed.
Star Rating: ***

Route: Southeast Chute (class 4)

Follow the directions given for Bridge Mountain to the sand and brush plateau just east of Gifford Peak and Destination Peak. From there, note a large and prominent chute running up the southeast face of Destination Peak. Near the top of the chute, it narrows considerably and bends to the northwest. You'll ultimately want to gain this chute.

Leave the sand and brush plateau and drop toward the slot on the west side, as if approaching Bridge Mountain. You can do so via a number of class 2-3 options, though some route-finding may be required to do so. Work your way toward the northern edge of the bowl below the plateau and aim for a prominent flat saddle of sorts that is immediately east of Destination Peak's southeast chute. The saddle is perhaps 100 vertical feet above the bottom of the slot between the two peaks. Reach the small saddle via steep slabs and small ledges then traverse easily into the south chute and head up. At first staying near the right (eastern) edge of the chute, continue up until it narrows considerably and becomes brushy. Pushing through a short bit of brush, you'll soon come to a short (10-foot), class 4 headwall. This is the route's crux.

Above the headwall, work your way easily to the top of the chute. Once there, hang a right and follow the ridge (or slightly easier terrain just right of it) to the base of the final summit crag. To attain the summit, a number of class 3 options are available. With loose rock in places, and some exposure here and there, work your way to the top.

"Gifford Peak" (6,600)

Gifford Peak is a fine peak. It is nestled between Destination Peak and Hepworth Peak (to the north and south, respectively) and Hepworth Wash and Gifford Canyon (to the west and east, respectively).

During my first climb of the peak, a storm hit as we began our descent. As the rain poured, the descent became interesting as countless small cascades began to materialize on the steep and exposed slabs above Gifford Canyon. In the process, a gigantic 1000-foot waterfall formed on the east side of the canyon and spilled down to the floor with terrific force. Gifford Canyon became Gifford *Creek* that day, as we struggled through whitewater back to our vehicles.

Gifford Peak from the plateau connecting it and Destination Peak

RT Mileage: 4
RT Elevation Gain: 2,000'
Time Required: 4-6 hours
Latitude: +37.1964
Longitude: -112.9483
FKA: Dow Williams, Mike Cressman, DB and Courtney Purcell (September 22, 2007)

Etymology: Nothing fancy about this one. The peak lies immediately west of Gifford Canyon.
Star Rating: ***

Destination Peak (center) and Gifford Peak (right) from G2

Route: Northeast Face (YDS 5.0)

Follow the directions given for Bridge Mountain to the sand and brush plateau just east of Gifford Peak and Destination Peak. From the plateau, hike toward the base of Gifford Peak's northeast face. As you approach the base, drop about 50 feet into a gully that parallels and runs directly north along the base of the face. An escape leading onto the ridge to your left presents itself. Climb easily onto the ridge then head south up the ridge until forced onto easier terrain in an adjacent chute on the immediate right. Following the chute south as it parallels the ridge, you'll soon reach a slot-like chimney. Either climb up the chimney, or bypass it by climbing up and left just before the bottom of the chimney. Continue climbing up the ridge until it eventually bends right, at which time you can climb class 2 terrain to the base of a 15-foot headwall. A dead tree lies against the headwall—this is the crux.

Climb the dead tree, step left onto the wall, and work small edges up to the top. The leader can belay others up from a healthy, living tree above the headwall. From the top of the crux, work right, easily route-finding your way to the summit.

For the descent of the crux, a tree near the edge and just barely east of the top of the headwall makes a fine rappel anchor.

A 50m rope is adequate for the route.

According to Bob…

Most will just go back the way they came, but those up for a little adventure may like to know that shortly after rapping the crux, one can leave the ridge and find a more direct and more challenging way back down. For this, one would want a 60m rope for a rappel, though it's noted that with care one can avoid that rappel, which appears just when you start to believe this way will go and far enough down that you will detest the idea of heading back up. This different way down lands one by the waterfall in Gifford Canyon a short distance "upwash" from where the canyon was left earlier to climb the peak, and it adds some nice scenery and variety to the day.

DB climbing the crux of Gifford Peak. (Photo by Dow Williams)

"Hepworth Peak" (6,548)

Hepworth Peak lies just west of Gifford Canyon, east of Hepworth Wash, and north of aesthetic Roof Peak. It is an easy peak to bag, and the views from the summit are incredible.

Oddly enough, even though I've talked to people who've enjoyed the peak, I've only been there once and have never felt the need to return. Maybe it's because of that snake I almost stepped on during my descent many years ago.

RT Mileage: 6
RT Elevation Gain: 2,000'
Time Required: 3-4 hours
Latitude: +37.1921
Longitude: -112.9447
FA: Unknown
Etymology: Nothing fancy about this one either. It lies just east of Hepworth Wash.
Star Rating: **

Route: South Face (class 1-3)

Follow the directions given for Roof Peak's north col route to the col. Walk west a short distance from the col until you can pick out a nice-looking line to follow up Hepworth Peak's south face. There are plenty of options available, from class 1-2 scree/talus to more scrambly terrain. Follow your nose to the top.

"Roof Peak" (6,553)

Roof Peak is one of the most impressive, obscure peaks in the backcountry of eastern Zion National Park. Its shape is reminiscent of North Guardian Angel. In addition to fantastic views of a bunch of obscure, breathtaking mountains (including Hepworth Peak, immediately to the north), Roof Peak's summit views also include Parunuweap Canyon to the south, Hepworth Wash to the west, and Gifford Canyon to the east.

The west summit is the highpoint.

RT Mileage: 6
RT Elevation Gain: 2,000'
Time Required: 3-6 hours
Latitude: +37.1886
Longitude: -112.9441
FA: Unknown
Etymology: The peak is named for a beautiful, large roof on its north face.
Star Rating: ***

Route: East Ridge (class 4)

Follow the directions given for Explorers Knoll to the Little Jenny Peak-Roof Peak saddle. From the saddle, get into a chute at the base of Roof Peak's east ridge. Scramble up the east ridge, pass over a false summit, step across a deep, narrow crack near a tree, and eventually encounter a steep slabby/ledgy face—this is the crux. One hundred feet of class 4 scrambling leads to easier ground. As you climb higher, either pass over the lower, east summit or bypass it on its north side then climb to the true summit. Enjoy the views; they are excellent.

Some parties may like to have a 60m rope for the route.

Route: North Col (class 3)

Follow the directions given for Explorers Knoll nearly to the head of Gifford Canyon. A short distance before the canyon's head you'll encounter a steep drainage coming down from the west from the col between Roof Peak and Hepworth Peak. Leave Gifford Canyon and scramble (class 2-3) into the drainage. After some initial steep stuff to work around, the terrain mellows out. Follow the intermittent slickrock/sandy wash west toward the col. (Watch out for snakes! I almost stepped on a rattlesnake here.)

Eventually the wash turns into a beautiful, slickrock bowl directly beneath the awe-inspiring "roof" of Roof Peak. Hepworth Peak also looks impressively down on you to your right. Scramble up class 2-3 slickrock and find your way to the top of the col. The right side gives itself up most easily.

Continue west from the col a short distance until you find class 2-3 slabs to climb onto Roof Peak's northwest face. As you ascend, the slabs give way to broken rock. Shortly before the top, hang a left and follow a broken slope straight to the highpoint.

The view to Zion Canyon from Stevensworth Peak

"Stevensworth Peak" (5,850)

In the elite company of Jenny Peak, South Guardian Angel and No Mans Mountain, Stevensworth Peak is among the most slickrock-laden peaks in Zion National Park. This whaleback of red sandstone is a low but striking feature. Once on the beautiful massif, the views down into both Hepworth and Stevens Washes (as well as to the neighboring peaks) while walking the ridge south to the summit are terrific.

This minor peak has a splendid backcountry vibe.

RT Mileage: 8
RT Elevation Gain: 2,000'
Time Required: 5-7 hours
Latitude: +37.1911
Longitude: -112.9530
FKA: Courtney Purcell & DB (March 29, 2008)
Etymology: The north-to-south-running peak is bordered by Stevens Wash on the west and Hepworth Wash on the east.
Star Rating: ***

Stevensworth Peak from G2

Route: Northeast Face (YDS 5.0)

Follow the approach to Bridge Mountain to the junction of the east-west canyon (between Gifford Peak and Destination Peak) and Hepworth Wash. From the junction, follow a use trail northwest for less than 0.25 mile to a point where you can climb west-southwest up a vegetated slope to the base of Stevensworth Peak's northeast face. Note that this point is southeast of a large, reddish crag northwest of Stevensworth Peak proper. The two are separated by a distinctive slickrock col. Depending on brush and other terrain obstructions, you may or may not be able to see the slickrock col that separates them.

G2 from Stevensworth Peak

Once at the base of the northeast face, look for a chute immediately east of the steep cliffs of the north face. Just west of this chute are reasonable (class 3-4) slabs that one can scramble for 75 feet to a 2-foot ledge heading east. Scramble the ledge east to a large bush. Step just past the bush and climb straight up the face, initially starting on a short (10-foot) arête of sorts. Above that, you'll be working slabs adjacent to a crack on your right.

After about 50 feet of steep scrambling (YDS 5.0), work right to a large flat area just below a short, heavily broken talus and dirt slope. Clamber up the short talus and dirt slope and head southwest up slabs until you gain the crest of the ridge. Once there, simply follow beautiful, red slickrock south toward the highpoint. As you approach it, work right for 40 feet and then scramble a couple of short class 3 sections leading to the highpoint.

A 50m rope is recommended for the route.

Route: East Face (class 2+)

Follow the approach to Bridge Mountain to the junction of the east-west canyon (between Gifford Peak and Destination Peak) and Hepworth Wash. From the junction, follow Hepworth Wash south for about 0.5 mile to its head at a 75-foot high dirt saddle. From the saddle, simply hang a right and work class 2-3 slabs up to the crest just south of Stevensworth Peak's summit. Class 2 scrambling will put you on the summit.

"Jenny Hill" (6,162)

CLOSED TO RECREATIONAL USE—RNA *(It appears from park maps that the east and northeast sides of the mountain are within an RNA, while the west and southwest sides are not.)*

Jenny Hill is a minor bump on the plateau connecting Jenny Peak and Little Jenny Peak. Were it not for its summit-like appearance from Shelf Point, I suppose one would never notice it. This is not an objective of its own; rather, a convenient "bonus" peak while traveling through the area.

RT Mileage: 5
RT Elevation Gain: 1,800'
Time Required: 2-4 hours
Latitude: +37.1951
Longitude: -112.9322
FA: Unknown
Etymology: Jenny Hill is a small hill on the plateau between Jenny Peak and Little Jenny Peak.
Star Rating: *

Route: From Jenny Peak

CLOSED TO RECREATIONAL USE—RNA

Route: From Gifford Canyon (class 3-4)

Follow the directions given for Explorers Knoll (via Gifford Canyon) to the plateau above the head of Gifford Canyon. Here, hike northeast then north to the summit of Jenny Hill.

I love the sounds of nature as much, if not more than, the average soul—but for what it's worth, the casual stroll across the beautiful and gentle slopes leading to the summit would be a fine place to don headphones and immerse yourself in some of Pink Floyd's *Live at Pompeii* performance from 1972—this epic stuff blends awesomely with the landscape.

"Little Jenny Peak" (6,239)

Little Jenny Peak is an uninspiring minor summit (320' of prominence) in the backcountry of eastern Zion National Park. Situated behind more prominent peaks south of UT-9, such as Jenny Peak and The Triplets, this peak is not readily seen from any road.

The reward for tackling Little Jenny Peak is a visit to seldom-explored country, and incredible views from the vegetated summit of Parunuweap Canyon (AKA the east fork of the Virgin River) and Shunesburg Mountain.

RT Mileage: 5-6
RT Elevation Gain: 2,000'
Time Required: 3-4 hours
Latitude: +37.1830
Longitude: -112.9316
FA: Unknown
Etymology: It's not only near Jenny Peak, but arguably a sub-peak of her.
Star Rating: *

Route: From Jenny Peak
CLOSED TO RECREATIONAL USE—RNA

Route: From Gifford Canyon (class 3-4)
Follow the directions given for Explorers Knoll (via Gifford Canyon) to the plateau above the head of Gifford Canyon. Here, hike south-southeast to the summit of Little Jenny Peak.

"Explorers Knoll" (5,560)

This peak is a classic, not so much for the aesthetics of the summit (or summit climb) itself but for the wonderful wilderness experience of the entire route. The views from the top of the obscure knoll are splendid and obscure. This is a stellar outing.

RT Mileage: 7
RT Elevation Gain: 2,400'
Time Required: 6-8 hours
Latitude: +37.1764
Longitude: -112.9442
FKA: Courtney Purcell (April 11, 2010)
Etymology: This is the most obscure peak on the east side of Zion. Only an insatiable peak-explorer would find the time to look for a way to the top of the thing.
Star Rating: ****

Impressive cliffs west of the summit of Explorers Knoll

Route: From Gifford Canyon (class 3-4)

Follow the directions given for Bridge Mountain into Gifford Canyon. Follow Gifford Canyon toward its head, bypassing on the right a large pour-off midway up. Just before the canyon slots up and soon ends at a 120-foot dryfall (and 100 feet past a pour-off where the shallow canyon separating Roof Peak and Hepworth Peak comes in on the right), leave the floor of Gifford Canyon and follow a use trail up a vegetated and loose ridge-like feature on the left (east).

Follow game trails along the ridge as it steepens and narrows. Soon, you'll encounter a couple of very steep, loose, sandy, highly exposed traverses. Fortunately, they are short and there's usually enough brush nearby to grab onto for confidence. Near the top of the ridge-like feature, it appears that it's about to cliff out as it becomes more of a ledge you're walking. As you're forced to start hugging the walls along the soon-to-be 3-foot wide ledge, you'll encounter a notch you can climb 8 feet down into to gain the top of a pour-off 20 feet north of a hidden slot coming in on the left.

Walk across the top of the pour-off (easy; 8+ feet wide here) and enter the short slot on the left. Thirty feet of class 3-4 scrambling up the sandy chimney on the right side of the slot's head puts you on terra firma above.

Meander over mellow terrain to the Little Jenny Peak-Roof Peak saddle. A lovely, slickrock canyon drains west-southwest from the saddle. Follow the canyon down for several hundred feet, scrambling down two beautiful class 3 slickrock bowls to gain the sandy wash at the mouth of the canyon. This is a beautiful area. Explorers Knoll should finally come into view for the first time.

Follow the wash as it bends left (south) until another wash comes in on the left a couple hundred yards later. From the confluence, head downstream for 100 feet and then scramble up easy dirt/vegetable terrain on the left to gain the manzanita-juniper woodland immediately north of Explorers Knoll. Head south to the base of the peak's north cliffs and steep slabs.

Rather than head up, hug the base of the cliffs as you work around the west side for a couple hundred yards until you come upon a 40-foot class 3-4 chimney on the left. The chimney tops out at a small notch. Scramble up the chimney to flattish ground, which you can follow easily north to the highpoint.

A 30m rope is recommended for the route.

The critical ramp one must find to head up the southeast face of Bridge Mountain. A friend of mine was once stalked by a mountain lion not far from here.

Bridge Mountain (6,814)

Sitting northeast of The Watchman and south-southwest of Mount Spry along the eastern rim of Zion Canyon, Bridge Mountain is the impressive peak one sees when gazing east from the Zion Canyon visitor center. Steep on all sides, there does not *appear* to be any non-technical routes to its summit, but...!

I remember years back when I first started looking at Bridge Mountain as an objective. I was gung-ho and even more naïve than I am today, and despite a days-long heavy downpour over Zion Canyon, I was resolute about going for the summit. Fortunately, reason prevailed, I decided to hold off, and I lived to climb it another day.

RT Mileage: 7-8
RT Elevation Gain: 3,000'
Time Required: 6-10 hours
Latitude: +37.2061
Longitude: -112.9661
FKA: Unknown party; 1965
Etymology: Named by pioneer William Crawford's wife for a large, aesthetic arch on the mountain's northwest side that can be seen from the park's visitor center. Prior to this, the mountain had been called Crawford Mountain.
Star Rating: ****

Route: Southeast Face (class 4)

From the parking lot just east of the Zion-Mt. Carmel Tunnel, follow a use trail next to the bridge into Pine Creek, the wash immediately south of the parking area. From the bottom of the wash, you want to get into Gifford Canyon, the wide canyon running south from the Pine Creek drainage. A use trail on the left side of Gifford Canyon, near the confluence of the two drainages, will take you above a vegetated cliff band near the mouth of Gifford Canyon.

Once in Gifford Canyon, follow it about 0.9 mile south toward its head. When you reach a point roughly due west of the summit of Jenny Peak (not visible, but above to the east), and just before the canyon makes a quick bend to the right at a high (50-foot) section of slabs and dry falls in the canyon floor, exit the canyon to the west on steep slabs. Heading up the slabs about 500 vertical feet (look for cairns), you'll soon come to a broken cliff band. Work through the cliffs, trending to the left (south). When done, continue up and slightly left until you come to a bowl. The bowl is large and apparent on the topo map, west-southwest of Jenny Peak's summit (and on the west side of Gifford Canyon). The bowl is slightly northeast of Gifford Peak.

At the top of the bowl is a flattish, plateau-like area of sand and brush that sits below the bases of Gifford Peak and Destination Peak. On the west side of the plateau between the two peaks is an unnamed canyon. Work your way to the base of the canyon's head, bypassing a dry waterfall there on its right side (as you look down-canyon). This will require a bit of route-finding to accomplish, but it is best done by working around to the southeast side of Destination Peak, where you can pick up an exposed ledge system that leads to a rock rib. On the west side of the rib, a steep chute can be followed down into the east-west canyon just below its head.

Once in the canyon, follow it easily to its end at Hepworth Wash. Head north in Hepworth Wash, following your nose and/or the occasional use trail to a point just southeast of Bridge Mountain. Cross-country it (either via a small, side wash or via a low ridge on your left) to the base of Bridge Mountain's southeast face. It is a steep, intimidating sight!

Heading west into the small, unnamed canyon between Bridge Mountain (on the right) and G3 (on the left), just inside the mouth you'll come to the south-facing toe of a ramp system heading steeply up the southeast face of Bridge. The slabs of the ramp run directly north from the very bottom of the canyon. Follow the ramp until it ends at a band of cliffs high on the face of the mountain. You will likely be required to drop left into a steep, vegetated chute (class 3-4) adjacent to the ramp at one point to avoid very steep and exposed slabs.

Upon reaching the band of cliffs at the head of the ramp, look left to an exposed, narrow ledge system that works toward a prominent tree 30-40 feet away. Head to the tree. Once there, continue left another 15-20 feet then mantle up about 4 feet to another ledge. Follow this ledge system left for about another 25 feet then climb a short (10-12 feet) but very exposed broken face (class 4) to a ledge with a bush on it. Once the bushy ledge is gained, route-find your way left and drop slightly, before wandering along narrow ledges that ultimately work their way to the substantially easier ground above. It sounds more complicated than it is. Common sense, and seeking out the easiest route possible, should get the job done. It only takes about 5-10 minutes to work from the top of the ramp to the easier ground above the ledge system.

Upon gaining the easier ground above the ledge system, head up, following cairns and/or your nose. You'll soon reach the base of the southeast face of the steep summit block. Scramble up (class 3) then meander to the summit. The views from there are astonishing.

Fortunately for the descent, cairns are plentiful—it would be easy to get off-route (and find yourself in a bad position on difficult terrain) on the return to the top of the ramp. Choose your route carefully—down-climbing poor, supremely exposed 5th class rock is not fun.

A 50m rope is recommended for the route.

According to Ram...

On an exploratory of Bridge Mountain long before I ever set foot on the peak, Ram found himself wandering up the very same ramp that I would later take up the southeast face. Although I was solo and able to negotiate the gritty and unnerving terrain above the ledges beyond the top of the ramp without a rope, Ram felt I must have been inspired that day to keep the route class 4.

Bridge Mountain

"G3" (6,274)

G3 is a small peak nestled between G2 and Bridge Mountain, both of which are classics; this one is not.

RT Mileage: 8
RT Elevation Gain: 2,700'
Time Required: 7-10 hours
Latitude: +37.2019
Longitude: -112.9644

FA: Unknown, though one of my partners found an arrowhead just below the summit of neighboring G2 the same day. We found no signs of prior ascent of this peak, and built a tree cairn on the summit.

Etymology: The peak immediately south of this one is called G2, while a peak south-southwest of G2 is called G1. G3 seemed about right for this feature.

Star Rating: *

Route: South Face – West Gully (class 2+)
Follow either of the approaches given for G2 to the south face of G3. There are two gullies on the south face. The west one is the easier of the two. Follow it to the summit area.

Route: South Face – East Gully (class 3+)
Follow either of the approaches given for G2 to the south face of G3. Of the two gullies on the south face, the east one is more difficult. Anticipate a 12-foot class 3-4 section on the ridge above the gully, as one traverses west to the summit.

The south face of Bridge Mountain from the slopes below the summit of G2

"G2" (6,602)
G2 is a backcountry classic. With a long and stunning approach featuring interesting route-finding and scenery, coupled with challenging scrambling and easy climbing, the G2 experience culminates with what I believe to be among the best summit views in all of Zion.

RT Mileage: 8
RT Elevation Gain: 3,000'
Time Required: 8-12 hours
Latitude: +37.1986
Longitude: -112.9655
FKA: Joe French and Zach Lee (February 2008) via a technical route from Zion Canyon
Etymology: Brody and Jared Greer climbed an unnamed peak to the south-southwest of G2 via a technical route from Zion Canyon and dubbed it G1. After French and Lee later climbed G1's northern and arguably more impressive neighbor, they dubbed it G2.
Star Rating: ****

James Hiebert just below the summit of G2

Route: Northwest Face via Hepworth Wash (YDS 5.3)

This is the easier of the two routes detailed here (shorter than the distance/time estimates given above, and with fewer technical challenges).

Follow the directions given for Bridge Mountain to the ramp at the base of that peak's southeast face. Instead of heading up the ramp, continue up the canyon to the col at its head. It is easily gained via a talus slope. Hike south from the col for 0.25 mile to the base of G2's northwest face. Route-find your way up the face via a number of class 3-4 possibilities until you come to a cliff band with few options. Look around for a high-angle slab angling up and right toward a medium-sized pine tree above. Climb the slab (YDS 5.3) then step left near the top to gain a ledge next to a pine. Once above the slab, continue up class 2-3 terrain to the summit and its expansive views.

Some parties may find a 30m rope useful for this route.

Route: Northwest Face via Stevens Wash (YDS 5.3)

Follow the directions given for Bridge Mountain to a point near that peak's southeast face. Before you get there, hike south into Stevens Wash. Continue down the wash for less than 0.25 mile then look for access onto a steep and slabby ramp system that heads directly up toward the col immediately north of G2. A number of options are available, though you might anticipate a bit of exposed class 4-5 scrambling, depending on your choice.

Once on the ramp system, head up to the col. More class 3-4 scrambling should be anticipated in a couple of spots. From the col, drop down the other side and contour around to the base of G2's northwest face. Once there, follow the directions given for the route above up the northwest face.

Some parties may find a 50m rope useful for this route.

"The Annex" (6,000)

This easily overlooked, little red peak sits conspicuously on the east rim of Zion Canyon immediately north of Bridge Mountain. Its summit views are fantastic. While you're in the area, it would seem foolish not to take the time to visit nearby Crawford Arch (AKA Bridge Mountain Arch), just to the south. With a studying eye, this awesome arch is visible from the Zion Canyon floor near the visitor center.

RT Mileage: 8
RT Elevation Gain: 2,500'
Time Required: 8-12 hours
Latitude: +37.2106
Longitude: -112.9671
FA: Unknown
Etymology: Under circumstances I no longer recall, I once heard this small peak referred to as The Annex. I've not since heard it referred to as such.
Star Rating: ****

Route: East Slope via Hepworth Wash (YDS 5.4)

Follow the directions given for Bridge Mountain to a point in Hepworth Wash east or southeast of Bridge Mountain. Leave Hepworth Wash and head northwest to a prominent notch between Bridge Mountain and the craggy terrain just to its right (northeast). From the top of this notch, head down the north side until you can cut left to cross a short, exposed slab. Just around the corner is the crux of the route—a short but funky face leading to a 30-foot chimney (YDS 5.4) that can be safely (albeit awkwardly) squeezed to flattish ground above. Continue up then walk a narrow ledge, mantle a ledge next to a large tree, and find yourself working ledges and slabs rightward to an easy downclimb to a magnificent sandy, treed area near the Bridge Mountain-Annex saddle. A talus slope leads west to the top of The Annex.

A 30m rope is recommended for the route.

The east face of The East Temple

The East Temple (7,709)

The East Temple is one of the most sought-after climbing objectives in Zion. It is a stunning and dominating mountain by any definition. In the last few years, the peak has gone from relative climbing obscurity to almost-popular, thanks in no small part to a new, bolted variation near the route I describe below. I've not done the variation, and can't speak to its specifics. In any case, this is a big, serious mountain.

The East Temple has 1,749' of prominence.

RT Mileage: 4

RT Elevation Gain: 2,200'
Time Required: 5-12 hours
Latitude: +37.2208
Longitude: -112.9508
FKA: A Sierra Club group led by Glen Dawson (1938)
Etymology: According to Steve Allen's *Utah's Canyon Country Place Names, Volume 1*, Clarence Dutton of the Powell Survey named the peak: "Just behind them [Temples *(sic)* of the Virgin], rising a thousand feet higher, is the East Temple, crowned with a cylindric dome of white sandstone."
Star Rating: ****

Route: The Casual Route (YDS 5.7)

Buzz Burrell first brought this route to my attention. I believe it was he who dubbed this route up the upper west face of the mountain "The Casual Route."

From the east end of the big tunnel, follow the crowds for 0.5 mile up the Canyon Overlook Trail. From near trail's end, gain the slabs to the north and start an upward traverse northwest to near the top of a huge V-feature in the southwest face of The East Temple. This V-feature is obvious from the switchbacks below the big tunnel. Get into the V-feature, drop a bit, and eventually gain a steep chute on the other side that starts out mellow but becomes steeper near the top. A number of short, class 5 obstacles in the chute will need to be negotiated. Soon, a troublesome dryfall is encountered. Here, work a steep slab below loose blocks and brush to reach a short but steep traverse on thin edges. Work through the traverse and climb a short stair-step pitch to a belay at a large pine.

Traverse left below some hoodoos and then drop a hundred feet to contour around to a weakness on the other side of the hoodoos. Steep ledges then lead easily upward. Soon, find yourself on a flattish spot below the upper west face, which allows reasonable upward progress. Head up the face to a suitable belay at a small pine. The next pitch is a bit steeper, with monstrous exposure into Spry Canyon far below. Above this pitch is easy scrambling leading to a short ridge scramble, and then, the summit plateau.

Now only 100 feet below the summit, walk northeast through a beautiful patch of ponderosa on the summit cap's north side and past a lovely orange-red alcove toward the northeast corner. Just past here, a low-angle ramp breaks through the summit cap. Easy hiking up a talus slope and a vegetated ramp leads to a single short step that takes one to the flattish summit area. It's just a short walk west from there to the summit.

Two 60m ropes are recommended for the route. Bring several long slings, several biners, and maybe a set of quick draws (in case you find the bolted variation).

Upper Pine Creek Trailhead

Continue east on UT-9 for 0.25 mile past the east end of the big tunnel to a small pull-out (big enough for two cars) on the left.

The peaks in this subsection are roughly arranged from shortest-hike-from-the-trailhead to longest-hike-from-the-trailhead.

The East Temple from the summit of Mount Spry

"Mind's Eye" (5,634)

With barely enough prominence to even be considered a "summit," Mind's Eye is more of a *viewpoint* of the upper Pine Creek, Progeny Peak, East Temple, Jenny Peak, and Shelf Canyon portion of Zion National Park's east side.

Shelf Canyon is the tiny, narrow canyon immediately west of Mind's Eye. The short canyon drains south to UT-9 and is a favorite hangout for the East Side's bighorn sheep population. Shelf Canyon is not a canyoneering destination; rather, a pleasant little drainage with some narrow walls and nice scenery. It's worth taking a short stroll into it from any of the nearby parking areas.

Although the south ridge of Mind's Eye is a feasible and pleasant route to the top, I recommend the north ridge for its highly enjoyable slickrock aesthetics. Or do a loop, which is nearly always more satisfying than a lame out-and-back. A really nice way to piece together a short-ish but beautiful outing is to traverse Mind's Eye south-to-north, then continue to Bighorn Peak and Shelf Point, returning via Canyon Overlook.

RT Mileage: 1
RT Elevation Gain: 500'
Time Required: 1-2 hours
Latitude: +37.2185
Longitude: -113.9391
FA: Unknown
Etymology: Named for the trippy and beautiful, psychedelic patterns I found in a natural depression in the summit block.
Star Rating: *

Route: North Ridge (class 2)

From the trailhead, follow a use trail down into upper Pine Creek. Follow the pleasant drainage north until you can exit left (class 2) onto the slabs above. From here, walk south-southwest toward the head of Shelf Canyon. A short hike south from here puts you on the summit.

Route: South Ridge (class 3)

Walk west from the trailhead to the base of the south ridge then scramble north to the summit, bypassing difficulties on the east side of the crest.

Above Shelf Canyon, while heading to Bighorn Peak from Mind's Eye (at center)

"Bighorn Peak" (6,205)

A minor peak with awesome slickrock and astonishing views of The East Temple's east face. A loop of the southeast face and north ridge makes for a highly rewarding, short day out in the mountains.

The southwest summit (with a dead tree) appears to be the highpoint.

RT Mileage: 2.5
RT Elevation Gain: 1,100'
Time Required: 2-4 hours
Latitude: +37.2235
Longitude: -113.9438
FA: Unknown. We found no signs of prior visitation on top. My partner built a tree cairn on the south summit.
Etymology: Named for the 24 (!) bighorn sheep we saw on the mountain's slopes the day we climbed it.
Star Rating: ***

Route: Southeast Face (class 2-3)

Follow the directions given for the north ridge route to Mind's Eye to the head of Shelf Canyon. Cut west around the very head of the canyon on a convenient ledge then scramble northwest up Bighorn Peak's southeast face. Although harder lines exist, keeping a watchful eye on the route can keep the difficulty class 2-3.

Route: North Ridge (class 2-3)

Follow the directions given for Mind's Eye to the exit from upper Pine Creek. Wander northwest from here into the slickrock bowl that forms at the toe of Deertrap Mountain's south buttress. Eventually exit north out of the bowl to gain the lovely Deertrap Mountain-Bighorn Peak saddle. A short hike up Bighorn Peak's north ridge (class 2) leads to the summit.

Route: Southwest Ridge (class 3)

The southwest ridge can be followed from the summit to the charming col at the head of the south fork of Spry Canyon. The ridge is class 2, except for a 6-foot class 3 step. From here, it's easy to scramble south and then east into the bowl below the south face of Bighorn Peak.

"Shelf Point" (6,150)

Shelf Point is south-southeast of Bighorn Peak and west of Mind's Eye. The very minor summit of this lovely dome visible from UT-9 at the southwestern base of Progeny Peak offers a neat view down the length of Gifford Canyon. Shelf Canyon runs along the eastern base of the dome, separating it from

Mind's Eye (whose summit is 500 feet below the top of the dome). Shelf Point's south face has an interesting appearance when viewed from Gifford Canyon.

Courtney Purcell descending the slabs above Canyon Overlook on the return from Shelf Point. Bridge Mountain beckons. (Photo by DB)

RT Mileage: 2
RT Elevation Gain: 1,000'
Time Required: 2-4 hours
Latitude: +37.2185
Longitude: -112.9416
FA: Unknown
Etymology: This striking viewpoint hovers majestically over Shelf Canyon.
Star Rating: **

Route: West Slope via Northwest Slabs (class 2-3)
Follow the directions given for the southeast face route on Bighorn Peak to the head of Shelf Canyon. From here, hike west up the bowl until you can angle left and scramble class 2-3 slabs up to the crest above. A short hike east leads to the minor summit of the dome.

Route: West Slope via Canyon Overlook (class 3)
Follow the Gifford Canyon Trailhead, follow the Canyon Overlook Trail for 0.5 mile to its end. Gain the slabs northeast of the overlook and follow lots of cairns north-northeast up steep slabs (class 3) to the East Temple-Shelf Point saddle. Wander easily east to the minor summit of the dome.

The summit cairn on Progeny Peak nicely frames Bridge Mountain

"Progeny Peak" (6,288)

Lying a mere half-mile off of the Zion-Mt. Carmel Highway (UT-9) on the east side of Zion National Park, Progeny Peak is a fine and often overlooked peak that offers absolutely stunning views of The East Temple, Bridge Mountain, Twin Brothers, and many other beautiful officially unnamed peaks.

Progeny Peak is the first significant peak east of The East Temple, an astonishing and imposing spectacle of a mountain on the east rim of Zion Canyon. The East Temple and Progeny Peak are separated by Pine Creek.

Progeny Peak holds a special place in my heart, as it was the first of my Zion exploratories.

RT Mileage: 1
RT Elevation Gain: 1,000'
Time Required: 2-3 hours
Latitude: +37.22170
Longitude: -112.9307
FA: Unknown
Etymology: Photographer extraordinaire Joe Braun wanted to name an arch on the peak "Progeny" because of its similarity to the large arch on nearby Bridge Mountain. When Tanya Milligan and Bo Beck later learned the arch had already been given a local name ("Two Pines Arch"), the two dubbed the peak "Progeny" instead.
Star Rating: ***

Route: Southwest Face (Direct) – YDS 5.2

From UT-9 immediately east of upper Pine Creek, follow a small drainage northeast toward the base of the peak. Route-finding is not difficult as the mountain is directly in front of you. Once the base of the mountain is gained, the drainage forks somewhat and tends to continue to the left and more northerly. The right fork, though less prominent, initially goes east then leads north when cliffs are encountered. This is the most direct approach to the summit.

Take the right fork and work up class 2-4 slabs and ledges until you top out at a sort of notch. There is a large dead tree at this notch. From the notch, you can either down-climb class 3-4 terrain (which ultimately leads back to the slabs above the left fork just mentioned) or you can 10-15 feet climb up an exposed YDS 5.2 wide crack to a ledge above.

From the flat ledge atop the crack, continue straight up over class 2-4 terrain, choosing the path of preferred resistance and head toward the false summit above. Soon enough, you will find yourself only a few hundred feet below the summit on a wide ledgy area with a series of narrow sandstone steps leading you upward. In warm, dry months, this is straightforward class

2-3 scrambling; however, in cold, wet months these steps are ridiculously iced over and downright treacherous (though the frozen cascades and icicles are beautiful). Assuming the terrain is passable and dry, head up the steps, which will eventually turn back into wider ledges, and ultimately cruise on up to the summit. The views from the top are phenomenal.

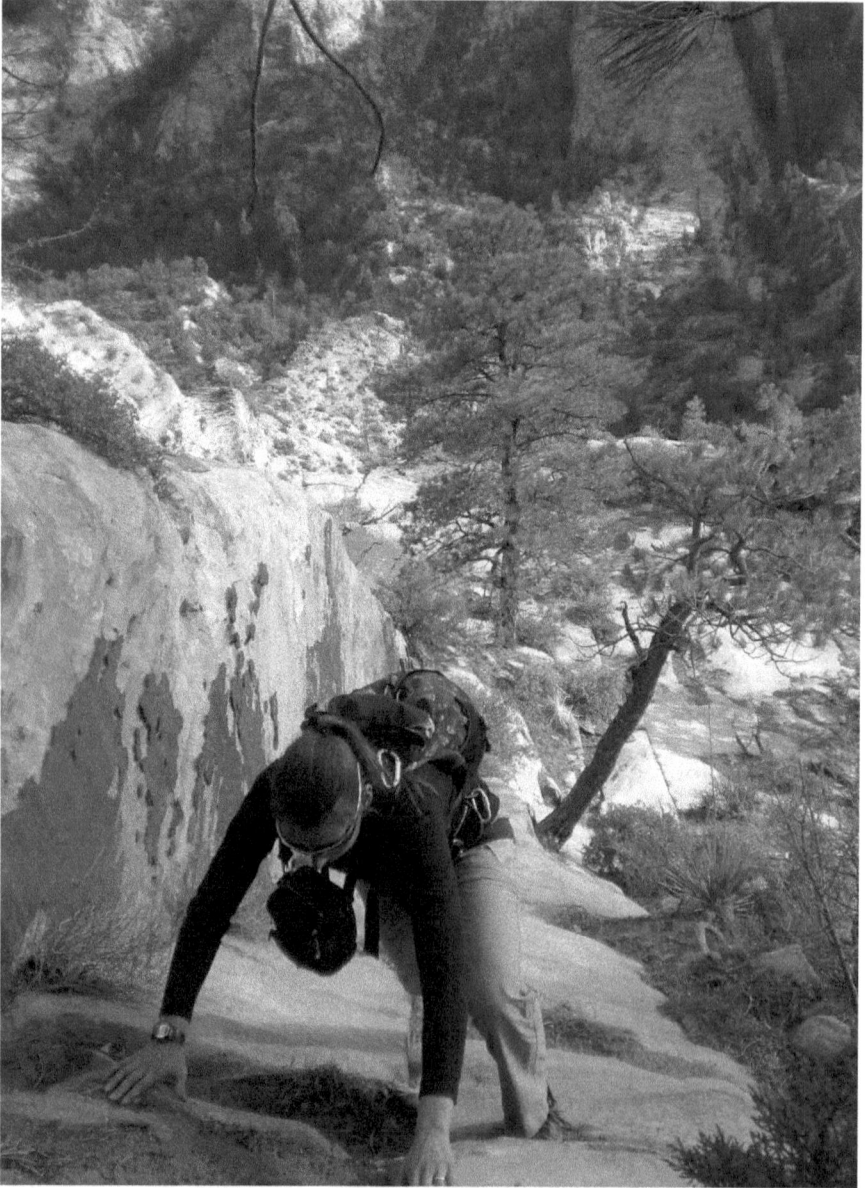

Sarah Meiser scrambling the southwest face of Progeny Peak

Route: Southwest Face (Indirect) – class 3

Follow the directions given for the direct route to the fork in the drainage near the base of the mountain. Rather than go right (as for the direct route), take the left fork and aim for one of the ramp systems leading upward toward the west ridge above. The second one from the right seems easiest. Follow class 2-3 ramps and ledges upward until the crest of the mountain's west ridge is gained.

From the ridge crest, head east until you find yourself only a few hundred feet below the summit on a wide ledgy area with a series of narrow sandstone steps leading you upward. In warm, dry months this is straightforward class 2-3 hiking/scrambling; however, in cold, wet months these steps can be ridiculously iced over and downright treacherous. Assuming the terrain is passable and dry, head up the steps, which will eventually turn back into wider ledges, and ultimately head to the summit.

Progeny Peak (dome at upper-left) from the upper south buttress of Deertrap Mountain

"Jenny Peak" (6,322)
CLOSED TO RECREATIONAL USE—RNA

Jenny Peak features some of the finest slickrock scenery in all of Zion National Park. Its elegant northwest ridge heads down from the summit to UT-9 as it passes through the east side of the park. It is a gorgeous peak that catches the eyes of many.

Just south of the summit are "Jenny's Nipples," a pair of impressive crags with an interesting appearance when viewed from points along the plateau west of Gifford Canyon.

Latitude: +37.2019
Longitude: -112.9300
Etymology: Named after a University of Indiana student who, in climbing the peak in the 1990's, was inspired enough in the process to change the course of her life and to seek a greater vision.

Jenny Peak from Deertrap Mountain

"Aeolian Point" (6,040)

It's time for a short story:

I'm far from the fastest person in the backcountry, but I'm equally far from the slowest. I've often tried to explain to the slower, less motivated members of the species that thrilling feeling of *living* that one feels when moving quickly and efficiently over uneven terrain, gliding across a sublime desert landscape.

So it was day-three of a long weekend in Zion. DB and I had bagged an improbable summit two days earlier, jogged through hail in an effort to beat out an in-moving storm while returning from another the day before, and now I set out alone at a quick pace, with temperatures in the low-forties. I cruised up upper Pine Creek, bounced over the pass, and race down Lodge Canyon to a point northeast of the peak. I moved quickly up slabs then traversed south to the summit and its extraordinary views. I was breathing hard, my chest was pounding—and I was *loving* it. I built a cairn, studied the map, then raced down the south face slabs, slipping once on some wet lichen I'd failed to notice. I hung a right and bushwhacked to the head of a short canyon, just to see what was there. I found a tick on my leg and brushed it off.

Returning down-canyon, I came upon a deep and dark slot full of log jams. And decided against it. So I was to go back up to the summit and retrace my steps, or find another way. I liked the idea of finding another way. Class 4-5 slabs on the south-southeast face did the trick, dumping me out near the mouth of that short but deep and dark, dangerous slot. So I went back up-canyon to check it out. Soon, it became very dark. There's a hidden chunk of canyon you can't just go into, though one could rappel into it from the top…and maybe get stuck. Not a good situation. Folks should stay out of this little canyon.

So I turned around and cruised back toward the car, back up Lodge, over the pass, raced down that beautiful orange slickrock past the petroglyphs and then zoomed down upper Pine Creek—terrain I was so familiar with, that I'd been exploring for years, in search of peaks and canyons, wildlife and artifacts.

I greeted DB 2 hours and 35 minutes after kissing her goodbye and saying I'd miss her but would see her soon. It is a wonderful feeling, however temporary, to be young and improbably healthy.

RT Mileage: 6
RT Elevation Gain: 1,500'
Time Required: 3-5 hours
Latitude: +37.23837
Longitude: -112.95194
FKA: Courtney Purcell (October 31, 2010)
Etymology: The name relates to the feeling of flowing effortlessly like the wind.
Star Rating: ***

Route: North Ridge (class 2-3)
Follow the directions given for Mountain of the Sun into Lodge Canyon. Continue north down the pretty canyon to a point where you can easily gain the slabs on the left leading to the north ridge of the objective. Hike easily to the un-prominent summit and its outrageous views up and across Zion Canyon.

The Sentinel from the summit of Aeolian Point

Route: South-southeast Face (class 4-5)

Although I used this route on my descent, as an ascent route one would essentially follow Lodge Canyon to its confluence with a minor canyon draining east from the Mountain of the Sun-Aeolian Point saddle. Before the minor canyon narrows and gets serious, scramble up class 4-5 slabs on the south-southeast face of our objective then hike easily to the summit.

Mountain of the Sun (6,723)

Mountain of the Sun is one of the high, majestic peaks lying along the eastern rim of Zion Canyon. Like most of its neighbors, this big-walled, imposing bad boy is begging for attention. Its name alone sounds cool and makes you want to climb it.

There exists a single non-technical route up the mountain. The route ascends the peak from its east side above the locally named Lodge Canyon (AKA: Employee Canyon). It is supremely enjoyable (and obnoxiously aesthetic).

RT Mileage: 6
RT Elevation Gain: 2,300'
Time Required: 5-7 hours
Latitude: +37.2349

Longitude: -112.9534

FA: Unknown, though petroglyphs located not far from the base of the mountain would indicate that Native American ascents are possible.

Etymology: Prior to becoming known by its current name, the mountain was known as one of the "Three Brothers," with the current "Twin Brothers" being the other two brothers. In 1917, William Wylie constructed what came to be known as Wylie Retreat, southeast of the Zion Lodge. He proposed that the mountain be named Mountain of the Sun because it was the first place the morning light could be seen from Wylie Retreat, which was the first place offering overnight accommodations in Zion Canyon.

Star Rating: ****

Mountain of the Sun from Deertrap Mountain

Route: East Face via Lodge Canyon (class 4+)

Follow the directions given for Mount Spry to the saddle between Deertrap Mountain and Bighorn Peak. From the saddle, you will have your first view of what lies ahead, though Mountain of the Sun itself has yet to come into view. Facing west from the saddle, The East Temple is on the left, the awesome Twin Brothers is in front of you on the right, and Deertrap Mountain is to the far right (and almost behind you). There is a prominent canyon in front of you and to the left, lying between The East Temple and Twin Brothers. That is Spry Canyon; it is not where you head. Work down surprisingly rugged class 3 terrain to the bowl below you. You'll notice a narrow canyon heading off to the north between Twin Brothers and Deertrap Mountain. Make your way north along the shallow drainage along the eastern base of Twin Brothers, over a narrow pass, and then drop down into the forested canyon—this is Lodge Canyon.

Head north down the canyon for about 0.5 mile over class 2-3 terrain. The steep walls of the canyon start to mellow out on the left; this occurs just before the canyon starts to open up. This mellowing out soon evolves into a slickrock ramp system that heads up and to the south. Get onto this ramp as soon as you feel comfortable and scramble south up and out of the canyon. With some minor route-finding, you should be able to find your way up to gentler terrain and to a col above. This col connects Mountain of the Sun (on the right) and Twin Brothers (on the left).

A couple of notes on route-finding on the ramp: One would assume that route-finding on the ramp would be straightforward (and it can be), but beware of the exposure on the steep slabs. I would suggest liberal placement of cairns on your way from the bottom of the canyon to the col above. Also, about halfway up the ramp, you should notice that a sort of chute branches off to the right. Heading up this chute requires a short amount (10 feet) of enjoyable class 4-5 climbing. This appears to me to be the safer bet when compared to the steep and evermore-exposed slabs on the ramp itself. Either option will work, though.

As an alternative to the ramp described, one can continue north down the canyon until another (more gentle) ramp appears on the left. Although I've not used this ramp, it appears to be easier (and potentially safer) than the ramp I described.

From the col, aim for a short, cliffy band on the southeast corner of Mountain of the Sun. Class 3-4 scrambling leads one to a prominent gully/ramp system above. Look carefully to stay on the route. Get into this north-trending gully/ramp system and work up over varying terrain. Follow the system not quite to its head. About 20 feet before the head, you will notice a steep chute branching off left and heading upward. There is a live tree and a large fallen tree branch at the entrance to this chute. Head up it. Once above (about 25 feet), follow loose and sandy terrain to the summit.

Some may find a 30m rope useful for this route.

Mount Spry (5,823)

Though Mount Spry is one of the lower peaks of Zion National Park, don't scratch this one off the list just yet—this scrawny but aesthetic peak is a totally worthwhile objective. Near the main entrance to Zion National Park, and diminutively sitting on the east rim of Zion Canyon next to giants like The East Temple and Twin Brothers, this inconspicuous little guy is a treasure waiting to be found.

I'd first heard of Mount Spry when inquiring many years ago at the park's backcountry desk about "reasonable" summit scrambles or climbs to be found in the park (other than the obvious one—Angels Landing). The ranger told me that Mount Spry goes at YDS 5.6 by its easiest route. Okay, fine. But sometimes later, I found this information to be inaccurate—it turns out that mere class 4-5 scrambling can get you to the top of this beautiful sandstone peak.

There exists a couple of interesting routes to the summit of Mount Spry via Spry Canyon, the steep canyon draining west from between The East Temple and Twin Brothers before bending south and dumping directly into the bottom of lower Pine Creek Canyon between Mount Spry and The East Temple.

With about nine rappels (and the option of perhaps four more) and cold-water wading and swimming in slots, coupled with unbelievable scenery in the canyon and on the peak itself—not to mention great scrambling in a stunning setting—the full-package Mount Spry-Spry Canyon combo is one of the best of the best in Zion National Park.

Like all technical canyoneering routes here, Spry Canyon requires a canyoneering permit.

Aron Ralston descends the photogenic north ridge of Mount Spry. This was Day Two of a fantastic long weekend we enjoyed in the park. Here, we were both a little groggy, having just woken from a stellar nap on the summit. If you've never enjoyed a summit nap, believe me when I say that it's never too late to start the habit—I only picked it up a few years ago.

RT Mileage: 5 (if doing the Spry Canyon descent option)
RT Elevation Gain: 1,200 feet (if doing the Spry Canyon descent option)
Time Required: 5-7 hours (if just doing the peak)
Latitude: +37.2208
Longitude: -112.9638
FKA: Unknown party; 1970
Etymology: The peak was named in honor of William Spry, the governor of Utah from 1909-1917.
Star Rating: ****

Route: North Ridge via Spry Canyon (class 4+)

Among other things, this route has the distinction of having a trailhead higher than the summit of the mountain. It is not an appropriate route for those having little or no experience (or at least lacking the company of someone having adequate experience) in rappelling.

From wherever you parked, drop easily into upper Pine Creek via a use trail found on the north side of the highway. Head north up the cnayon for 0.5 mile until you see a high, vertical dry fall on your right (east). Just past this fall, look for a class 3 slickrock exit from the canyon on the left. Head up and out there. Continue up (but not too high) on level-ish ground heading toward the northwest on class 2-3 slabs and ledges. It won't be long before the impressive south buttress of Deertrap Mountain comes into view in front of you to the north. Aim for the left side of the buttress. As you approach the vicinity of the buttress, make your way to the left and up the steepening slabs of a bowl, ultimately working to a saddle that will soon come into view. The saddle connects Deertrap Mountain and Bighorn Peak. Getting to the saddle itself allegedly requires class 4 climbing; however, there are many variations possible that keep the scrambling in the class 3 realm.

From the saddle, you will have your first view of what lies ahead. Facing west from the saddle, The East Temple is on the left, the awesome Twin Brothers is in front of you on the right, and Deertrap Mountain is way far over your right shoulder. In the distance between The East Temple and Twin Brothers, can be seen the ultra-sweet West Temple and Mount Kinesava. In the not-so-far distance between The East Temple and Twin Brothers is Mount Spry—your objective. In front of it all is a beautiful slickrock and brush bowl. There is also a prominent canyon in front of you and to the left, lying between The East Temple and Twin Brothers. This is Spry Canyon.

Work down surprisingly rugged class 3 terrain into the bowl below you. From there, you should have little difficulty finding a wash that you can follow toward the head of Spry Canyon. Head down the canyon for a short while until you come to your first obstacle—a 165-foot low angle rappel.

There is a two-bolt anchor on the left. At the bottom of the rappel is a seasonal pool. Either rappel into it, or look for a 2-inch wide ledge near the bottom—the ledge can be traversed north for 20 feet to avoid getting wet.

(If you choose to retrace your steps back to the car after doing the peak, rather than finish up thru Spry Canyon, be sure to leave a fixed rope at the 165-foot rappel. You will need to jumar, prussik or Batman back up it to get out.)

Continue down-canyon for a little over 0.25 mile to your next obstacle. On your immediate left, you should notice a slot canyon forming. To stay true to the canyoneering route, at this point you would get ready for the next rap—this one from a tree anchor into the slot. However, this slot canyon happens to mark your exit point from the canyon. It's time to head for the peak!

From the top of the 2nd rappel, head up and to the right on a use trail. Although the use trail starts to spider web a bit, work your way up and over a rocky rib in front of you. You should be able to get to the other side of the rib via class 3 terrain. From there, Mount Spry is apparent as the little red peak in the near-distance. It looks very close, but the complex terrain to come will chew up some time.

Rather than dropping back from the rib into the seemingly easier terrain in the canyon bottom below, try to stay fairly high, crossing another rib, while traversing rugged terrain to the saddle between Mount Spry and Twin Brothers. After crossing the second rib, you will need to drop a few hundred feet over class 3-4 terrain into a brushy wash. Follow the wash north-ish for a short distance (less than 0.25 mile) until you arrive at the saddle.

From the saddle, note a ridge that runs south directly toward Mount Spry. Cruising this mostly class 2-3 (occasionally class 4-5) ridge is fun and will take you all the way to the base of Mount Spry's summit pyramid. Along the way, you'll encounter a short knife-edge section. Once at the base of the summit pyramid, look for the path of least resistance to the top. The north side seems easiest (class 3-4).

From the summit, retrace your steps back to the wash below the Mount Spry/Twin Brothers saddle. Once there, you have a few options: 1) retrace your steps all the way back to the rappel that you bypassed to head for the peak and do the entire Spry Canyon (3BIII) experience (which involves a few additional rappels than option 2); 2) having left a fixed rope at the first rappel, Batman out and retrace your steps back to the car; or 3) follow the wash in a southerly direction toward the gap between Mount Spry and The East Temple.

Following option #3, the wash will dump you off at the top of nasty terrain above the slot portion of Spry Canyon. As you approach this section, traverse left and back up-canyon a short distance until you come to a portion of the watercourse allowing walk-in access to the tightening canyon. Get into the watercourse and follow it down a short distance to your next obstacle—an 80-foot rappel into a slot. A 2-bolt anchor is on the left. There may or may not be swimming required at the bottom of this slot. From the bottom of this 2nd rappel of the day, head down-canyon a hundred feet or so to the next rappel. Again, here you have two options: 1) rappel about 45 feet from a slung chockstone into the slot on your right, followed by another rappel into the canyon-bottom, or 2) walk up and left for 15-20 feet past the chockstone anchor and look for a tree anchor. From there, you can rappel about 75 feet down to the canyon-bottom. Again, getting wet may be necessary. Once at the bottom of the canyon again, you'll immediately come to another couple of short drops off of a bolted anchor. The first drops about 25 feet into a bowl, followed by a shorter drop of about 10 feet. As you follow the canyon to the right, you'll see a two-bolt anchor on your right. Rappel 40 feet into a pool of water in a slot. Deal with the pool, then rappel or down-climb 10-12 feet of steep slickrock to another pool—this one is deep. After disconnecting from the rappel just above the pool, swim the 20-foot pool to its exit—a tight notch. Just before this notch, on a 4-foot long narrow section of dry rock, clip into a two-bolt anchor in a shallow alcove on your left. Rappel 65 feet into a bowl below you. Climb up slightly and out of the bowl to the left and look for a tree anchor. Rappel 70 feet to the bouldery wash below. Follow the boulder wash down-canyon for a bit until you cliff out. Another tree anchor allows a stunning 95-foot rappel (most of it free-hanging) into the wash below. With the day's rappels done, continue down the wash until you reach a junction of two drainages. Hang a right and follow the wash (admiring the lovely pools of Pine Creek) for 0.5 mile to the bridge and the waiting car that you remembered to spot that morning.

Two 60m ropes are recommended for the route. In addition to standard technical canyoneering equipment if doing the full Spry Canyon, a wetsuit is appropriate during the cooler months.

Route: East Face via Spry Canyon (YDS 5.4)
Following the approach directions given for Mount Spry's north ridge route, do the 165-foot rappel and hike down the watercourse until you come to the next drop. The drop can be rappelled via a tree on the ridge (looking down-canyon) or downclimbed by strong climbers. Drop into the slot and continue down-canyon, negotiating a few short drops (rappels and/or downclimbs) until you come to a 15-20 foot over-hanging drop that will require a rappel. After doing the rappel, hike down-canyon for another 50 feet until you can exit on the right via class 2 terrain. From there, dropping in and out of a couple of washes and climbing over a couple of ribs, make for the east face of Mount Spry.

Study the face above, looking for zig-zagging weaknesses that allow access to the upper mountain. A number of options are present. Anticipate class 2-3 terrain and a crux slab near the top of the southern end of the face that will require YDS 5.3-5.5 climbing (depending on the line taken) for 20-30 feet to gain easier ground above. Follow class 2 terrain west toward the red summit pyramid ahead. Class 3-4 scrambling on the north side of the pyramid leads to the summit.

For the descent, either retrace your steps back down the east face and into the Spry Canyon drainage below the 15-20 foot over-hanging drop or descend Mount Spry's north ridge via the directions provided above.

The gear recommendations for the other route are also applicable here.

Twin Brothers (right) and The East Temple (center) from Deertrap Mountain

According to Ram...

Before he'd ever approached Mount Spry or Twin Brothers from upper Spry Canyon, Ram pieced together a very steep YDS 5.4 route up to them from the Pine Creek Bridge at the first switchback on UT-9. Working his way up the Spry Canyon drainage, he swung left around the final, 95-foot free rappel, and continued up boulders to the bottom of the second-to-last rappel (70-feet, from a tree). Climbing out to the right, he worked across a face up and right to a 50-foot vertical section (YDS 5.4) leading to a class 3-4 chimney above. At the top, Ram went over a small pass that led him to the platform next to the chockstone above the narrow swimmer slot in the middle-lower portion of the canyon. From there, he walked a thin, slanted ledge just right of the chockstone, made a right turn up a slabby, dirty gully in which bushes *could* be slung for protection. From the top, he walked left a few yards, jumped across a narrow slot and found himself on scrambling terrain on the slabs below the Mount Spry-Twin Brothers col.

Twin Brothers (6,850)

Quite prominently standing above the east rim of Zion Canyon (just to the south of Mountain of the Sun and just to the north of Mount Spry and The East Temple, and directly across the canyon from The Sentinel), this big walled monster of a mountain sees relatively few visitors. Twin Brothers does not have any non-technical routes to its summit. The easiest route on the mountain is a steep and exposed, fabulously improbable YDS 5.3 route up the mountain's impressive and slabby southwest face. Ram called it "delightful." Despite meager roundtrip numbers, this route is a full-day, serious endeavor, with dire consequences in the event of a mistake.

RT Mileage: 6
RT Elevation Gain: 2,500'
Time Required: 9-11 hours (if just doing the peak)
Latitude: +37.2276
Longitude: -112.9553
FKA: Unknown party; 1968
Etymology: This peak, with its twin ramparts, was once, coupled with its third rampart to the north (which is now called Mountain of the Sun), known as two of the Three Brothers.
Star Rating: ****

Route: Southwest Face (YDS 5.3)

Follow the directions given for Mount Spry's north ridge route to the top of the 2nd rappel in Spry Canyon.

(If returning to your car the way you came, rather than descending the remainder of beautiful Spry Canyon (3BIII), you'll need to leave a rope to ascend the steep slabs of the 165-foot rappel.)

From the top of the 2nd rappel, head up and to the right on a use trail. Although the use trail starts to spider web a bit, hike up and over a rocky rib in front of you. You should be able to get to the other side of the rib via class 3 terrain. Rather than drop all the way back from the rib into the seemingly easier terrain in the canyon bottom below, try to stay fairly high and traverse to the next rib to the west. Cross the next rib and make your way a bit further west until you can pick up the red slabs at the base of Twin Brothers' southwest face.

You can thank me now for cairning the heck out of the route from here. This gesture will cut down considerable time on both the ascent and descent, as well as make the route safer. In case the cairns aren't there to assist you, follow the path of least resistance upward on the red slabs. Mostly class 2-3, the route begins to steepen as the red slabs soon start to transition into yellow slabs. As this transition starts to occur, you should note a shallow groove near the western edge of the southwest face. Somehow, you need to get into this groove. We managed to find a somewhat vegetated mini-ledge that allowed us, after donning our rock shoes, to gingerly head over on tiny edges.

Once in the shallow groove, head up this first crux (YDS 5.3) a short distance until you can get on the slabs just west of the groove (this required a zig-zag; right-then-left). Following these will lead you into a vegetated portion of the upper groove. The vegetation, consisting primarily of small bushes, provides fantastic psychological pro as well as tentative handholds. Continue up ever-steepening, loose slabs, zig-zagging back and forth to utilize small weaknesses. Although impossible to describe the route in great detail, we found that trending slightly left seemed to be more productive than right.

You will eventually come to a more broken portion of the face, characterized by an increased amount of small vegetation, as well as some sporadic healthy pines. As the route-finding issues relent somewhat and the steepness lets up some, continue toward a prominent, steep, stair-steppy chute just left of a conspicuous headwall on the upper mountain. The chute has a craggy ridge on its left side, and a large pine at its head. Reaching the chute and follow the line of least resistance (YDS 5.3) to the tree at the top. If someone can solo this section, the tree makes a fine spot from which to belay others. From the tree at the top of the chute, head through the notch just north of it. Once on the other side of the notch, you should be able to clearly make out a sheep trail working weaknesses northeast up along ledges. Follow the class 3 ledge system a short distance to the mesa at the top of the mountain. The highpoint is a boulder protruding from the far western edge of the flattish mesa.

To descend, carefully retrace your steps to the base of the mountain, then either a) retrace your steps back to your starting point, climbing the fixed rope at the 165-rappel on the way out, or b) follow the directions below for the Spry Canyon descent option. Two 60m ropes are recommended for either option.

Spry Canyon Descent Option (3BIII):
This option is not recommended for a single-day effort, simply because of the time issues involved. Only super-fast parties already familiar with the route

could expect to escape a bivy situation in a dark and wet, technical slot canyon. This option is inappropriate for those having little or no experience (or at least lacking the company of someone having adequate experience) in rappelling and technical canyoneering.

From the summit, carefully retrace your steps to the base of the mountain. Once there, you have a couple of options: 1) retrace your steps all the way back to the rappel that you bypassed to head for the peak, and do the entire Spry Canyon experience (it involves four additional rappels than option 2), or 2) follow the wash in a southwesterly direction toward the gap between Mount Spry and The East Temple.

Following option #2, the wash will dump you off at the top of nasty terrain above the slot portion of Spry Canyon. As you approach this section, traverse left and back up-canyon a short distance until you come to a point in the watercourse allowing walk-in access to the canyon. Get into the watercourse and follow it down a short distance to your next obstacle—an 80-foot rappel into a slot. A two-bolt anchor is on the left. From here, follow the directions given for the portion of Spry Canyon starting at the 80-foot rappel in Mount Spry's north ridge description.

In addition to standard technical canyoneering equipment, a wetsuit is appropriate during the cooler months.

According to Ram...

If one were to approach the southwest face of Twin Brothers from directly below, there's a steep and tricky YDS 5.3 spot right in the shallow groove where the red rock meets the white. Careful! Continuing up to near the top of the face, the final chute (YDS 5.3; sandy and insecure) below the traverse around to the summit plateau can be avoided by climbing onto the ridge on the left. The ridge (YDS 5.3) has better rock and is "stellar."

Swinging around to the other side of the mountain, Ram shared beta on a route he'd once done from the Mountain of the Sun-Twin Brothers col. From the col, he walked slickrock west toward Zion Canyon. Climbing up left onto a ridge (class 3) that parallels back east toward the col, he stayed right of the ridge and worked through vegetation to a notch. Continuing up, he ascended a steep section, traversing up and left for 15 feet (YDS 5.6) around a blind corner with big exposure. Once around the corner, he continued up shallow grooves, trending left occasionally (YDS 5.3), soon reaching the sub-cap. Several short, gymnastic 5th class options with minimal exposure allowed him and his partner to gain the summit plateau through cliffs. From there, a walk led to the summit. Ram did caution that this route, while "stellar and pristine," is not appropriate for poor weather/conditions. He climbed it in a storm, and didn't think you should do the same.

Heading up the southeast face of Lost Peak on a snowy morning

Red Jenny Trailhead

Drive east from the big tunnel on UT-9 for 0.8 mile to a one-car pull-out on the south side of UT-9. The pull-out is next to a large rock outcropping.

"Red Jenny" (5,850)

CLOSED TO RECREATIONAL USE—RNA

Red Jenny is a striking, red sub-peak of Jenny Peak that proudly guards the south side of UT-9 just north of Jenny Peak. The bold and beautiful arms of its northeast and northwest ridges seem to embrace the highway as it crosses the peak's bosom.

Latitude: +37.2121
Longitude: -112.9319
FA: Unknown
Etymology: A major sub-peak of Jenny Peak, Red Jenny is readily recognized by its bold coloration.

Lost Peak Trailhead

Once through the Zion-Mt. Carmel Tunnel, continue east to a second tunnel, this one much shorter. Once through the second tunnel, continue for 0.5 mile to a point where an unnamed, prominent drainage with a slickrock pour-off (sometimes dry; sometimes wet; usually just seeping) comes down from a point approximately north of The Triplets' westernmost summit. There is a parking pull-out just northwest of the pour-off. The two are separated by Clear Creek.

The peaks in this subsection are roughly arranged from shortest-hike-from-the-trailhead to longest-hike-from-the-trailhead.

"Lost Peak" (6,460)

Lost Peak is a fantastic stroll through a slickrock wonderland. Located just inside the backcountry on the east side of the park, this once-obscure but now-popular little mountain sits between The Triplets and Jenny Peak, about a mile south of UT-9.

The summits views, like those from any of the peaks in this part of the park, are stunning.

RT Mileage: 2
RT Elevation Gain: 1,000'
Time Required: 2-3 hours
Latitude: +37.2050
Longitude: -112.9167
FA: Unknown

Etymology: Pathetic to say, but I dubbed this peak "Lost Peak" for purely sentimental reasons; I'd just ended a long relationship and felt a sense of loss about it.
Star Rating: **

On the snowy summit of Lost Peak one cold November morning

Route: North Ridge (class 2)

From wherever you park, drop into Clear Creek, which is the east-west wash that runs parallel to UT-9 on its south side. Climbing back out of Clear Creek, your goal is to get into the drainage that runs south up toward The Triplets. Your first obstacle, the slickrock pour-off mentioned in the trailhead directions, can be bypassed via slabs on its left side. Once in the drainage proper, head south until you can exit easily onto the slickrock (and occasionally brushy) terrain northwest of The Triplets. Lost Peak will be just off to the right.

Work over beautiful slickrock terrain toward the slabby north ridge of Lost Peak. Gain the north ridge and simply follow the easiest line of ascent to the summit above. Great, rewardingly aesthetic stuff. This is an awesome part of the park, with so many generally short but fun things like this to do.

Route: Southeast Ridge (class 2-3)

Follow the wash just northeast of the peak to the Lost Peak-Triplets saddle then walk to the base of the peak's southeast ridge. Scramble the slabby ridge to the summit.

A chilly January morning on the summit of Lost Teton

"Lost Teton" (6,266)

Lost Teton is a minor backcountry summit with good views of Jenny Peak and Lost Peak.

RT Mileage: 2
RT Elevation Gain: 1,000'
Time Required: 2-4 hours
Latitude: +37.2035
Longitude: -112.9198
FA: Unknown; we found no signs of prior visitation. DB built a cairn on the summit.
Etymology: An obscure reference to the small peak's position between Lost Peak and Jenny's Nipples.
Star Rating: **

Route: East Ridge (class 2)

Follow the directions given for Lost Peak to the base of that peak's north ridge. Easily traverse southwest to the Lost Peak-Lost Teton saddle then hike west to the highpoint.

The Triplets in winter

"The Triplets" (6,531)
The Triplets is a largely hidden gem of a peak. Visible from one short stretch of UT-9 as it winds through the eastern portion of the park, despite the name The Triplets actually consists of *four* peaklets, each of them interesting and worthy of ascent.

RT Mileage: 3
RT Elevation Gain: 1,500'
Time Required: 4-6 hours
Latitude: +37.2069
Longitude: -112.9077
FKA: Steve Ramras (May 1996)
Etymology: Steve Ramras gave the name to me a few years ago. Not sure where he got it. Maybe it's because the feature has *four* summits! (Okay, three prominent ones and a very minor fourth one.)
Star Rating: ****

Route: West-to-East Traverse (class 4)
Some parties may wish to bring a 30m rope for the traverse of the four summits.

Follow the directions given for Lost Peak to the slickrock terrain northwest of the main summit of The Triplets. For efficiency of communication, I'll now label the four summits of The Triplets as peaklets #1, 2, 3 and 4 (west-to-east):

Peaklet #1:
There are a couple of steep, dirty chutes that head up the northwest corner of The Triplets, ultimately ending in the saddle between the westernmost peaklet (#1) and its sister to the east (#2). Follow one of them, or scramble up class 3 slabs and ledges on the right (west) side of the westernmost chute. From the saddle, hang a right to bag peaklet #1. There's a great tree growing right out of the summit rocks.

Peaklet #2:
Drop back to the saddle between peaklet #1 and peaklet #2 then head east toward peaklet #2. The going is straightforward, with a few trivial route-finding issues.

Peaklet #3:
This is the most challenging of the four peaklets.

Drop east from peaklet #2, cross a saddle, then make your way to the southwest face of peaklet #3. From there, look for a funky chimney (dirty class 4) and climb it. Once through the chimney, wander to the summit.

Peaklet #4:

This peaklet is the highest.

Work your way off of peaklet #3 by heading east, looking for dirty ledges that will allow you to drop to the next saddle. Once down, cross the saddle and scramble up a few class 3 difficulties to gentler terrain above. I found that the northwestern edge of peaklet #4's lower section above the saddle appeared to be the easiest option.

To descend, work dirty ledges to the east-northeast of peaklet #4, aiming for the saddle between The Triplets and The Fin, to the northeast. Once at the saddle, drop north then cross-country it back toward the drainage from whence you originally came.

"The Fin" (6,434)

The Fin is an aesthetic narrow ridge situated between The Triplets and Nippletop. Steep-to-vertical on all sides, the only reasonable weakness is found on the mountain's class 4 north ridge.

Although the peak is entirely overshadowed by the higher, more striking mountains on either side, The Fin is a worthwhile endeavor with neat views and the standard exposed scrambling over horrifyingly sketchy rock.

RT Mileage: 2
RT Elevation Gain: 1,000'
Time Required: 2-3 hours
Latitude: +37.2085
Longitude: -112.9050
FKA: Courtney Purcell & Mark Beauchamp (May 27, 2006)
Etymology: This small and easily overlooked but visually appealing peak is a narrow fin of crumbly rock.
Star Rating: ***

Route: North Ridge (class 4)

Follow the directions given for Lost Peak to the slickrock terrain northwest of the main summit of The Triplets. From there, hike east across gentle terrain toward the northwestern foot of The Fin, which appears tiny between the larger Triplets and Nippletop. Gain the north ridge of The Fin and scramble to the top. The crux (class 4) is a 12-15 foot open book-like feature just above a left-leading, dirty ledge, perhaps halfway up the ridge. Once the narrow crest is gained, walk carefully south to the highpoint.

Some may wish to bring a 30m rope for the route.

For an alternative approach, one can start at the Petroglyph Canyon Trailhead and wander south up gentle slopes to the base of the peak's north ridge.

Views toward Ant Hill (right) from the southwest ridge of Bighorn Peak

"Ant Hill" (6,641)

Ant Hill is one of the more visible and impressive of the park's east side peaks. First climbing the peak many years ago, I found the south buttress route (despite its modest class 4 rating) to be steep and imposing, though not as severe as it appears from the road. It offered good scrambling on slabs, followed by a steep headwall at the very top. Taking the north ridge on the descent, I found it to be very loose, exposed in places, and somewhat unpleasant. Regardless, together they made for an adventurous loop. A 30m rope is suggested.

RT Mileage: 2-3
RT Elevation Gain: 1,400'
Time Required: 5-7 hours
Latitude: +37.2266
Longitude: -112.9221
FA: Unknown
Etymology: Ram told me he got the name from the Black Book, the old route book one can find at the park's backcountry desk. In there, an early (first?) ascent party dubbed the peak "Ant Hill." I can't help but think the

name has everything to do with all of the biting ants we encountered (and dealt with) while climbing the south buttress.
Star Rating: ***

Route: South Buttress (class 4)
More than one adventurous and talented party has balked at this route. It's a little spooky to look at.

Climb onto Ant Hill's southern protrusion via any number of possible lines and route-find your way to the base of the peak's south buttress. To gain the south buttress, scramble up a talus slope just west of the southern end of the buttress. When you reach steep terrain near the top of the slope, gain the south buttress via class 4 slabs (with little exposure) on the right. Working further right to gain the crest of the now-exposed, slabby buttress, scramble up the path of least resistance. Mostly class 2-3, some may find the steeper portions of the buttress intimidating.

Soon enough, the terrain will have you working right to traverse a ledge system just east of the crest of the buttress. Just beyond, passing over the head of an exposed, steep chute, scramble up loose and dirty, steep terrain to the base of a headwall just below Ant Hill's summit mesa. Be careful here. Climb the 30-foot class 4 headwall to the top.

Route: North Ridge (YDS 5.2)
With significant exposure in spots and plenty of bad rock, this route can be dangerous.

This route is best approached from the pull-out just west of the second tunnel. Scramble north up the canyon separating Ant Hill (right) from Progeny Peak (left). With only minor obstacles along the way, exit the canyon about 0.75 mile up and hike northeast to Ant Hill's north col. Gaining the col, the crux of the route is immediately encountered—a crack of sorts (YDS 5.2; with poor protection) that runs up about 10 feet from just above the col. Fortunately, the exposure isn't bad. Continuing along above the crux, scramble through a variety of obstacles (mostly class 2-3), staying on or near the crest of the loose ridge. Soon enough, the summit plateau is gained via a final, short class 3 scramble.

"Parunuweap Peak" (5,935)
Parunuweap Peak is a minor summit with terrifically obscure views of places like Crawford Wash and Dennett Canyon. The journey to get there is a highly enjoyable one through a slickrock wonderland.

RT Mileage: 4
RT Elevation Gain: 1,800'
Time Required: 3-5 hours

Latitude: +37.1915
Longitude: -112.9152
FA: Unknown; we found no signs of prior visitation. I built a cairn on the summit.
Etymology: The summit affords incredible views of the Parunuweap area.
Star Rating: ***

Route: Northeast Ridge (class 2)

Follow the directions given for Lost Teton to the Lost Peak-Lost Teton saddle. From the saddle, aim southeast toward the indistinct start of Parunuweap Peak's northeast ridge.

Alternatively (and more aesthetically), one can drop into the slickrock bowl at the head of the east fork of Crawford Wash and follow that wash to the first dryfall (at a point north of the summit) then leave the drainage and scramble south to gain Parunuweap Peak's northeast ridge just before the top. (It appears that the upper portion of this wash is CLOSED TO RECREATIONAL USE—RNA.)

Either way you approach it, gain the ridge and follow it to the summit. Breathe in the terrific views of Dennett Canyon, Parunuweap Canyon, Crawford Wash and the massive slickrock splendor of Jenny Peak.

Many Pools Trailhead

Once through the Zion-Mt. Carmel Tunnel, continue east to a second tunnel, this one much shorter. Once through the second tunnel, continue for 0.9 mile to a pull-out on the right, opposite a small drainage on the north side of UT-9.

The peaks in this subsection are roughly arranged from shortest-hike-from-the-trailhead to longest-hike-from-the-trailhead.

"The Scarlet Begonia" (6,965)

This is a backcountry hike to a minor summit with good views of the east side of Zion, including Nippletop, Aires Butte, The East Temple, G2 and Roof Peak. As much as I love climbing the bigger, more impressive peaks of the park, there's something equally (yet subtly) powerful about a casual hike across plateau and through forest to clifftop perches like this.

The Scarlet Begonia has 395' of prominence.

RT Mileage: 7
RT Elevation Gain: 1,800'
Time Required: 5-7 hours
Latitude: +37.23593
Longitude: -112.92461

FA: Unknown; we found no signs of prior visitation. I built a cairn on the summit.

Etymology: Just my fanciful name for an obscure, pleasant mountain. If you care to dig a little deeper, check out the Dead's 1974 album *From the Mars Hotel.*

Star Rating: *

Views from the summit of The Scarlet Begonia

Route: North Slope via Many Pools (class 3-4)
Follow the directions given for Cable Mountain via Many Pools (class 3-4) to the Deertrap Mountain Trail. Walk west on the trail to where it bends left near the head of Hidden Canyon. Just before the trail switchbacks up a short outcropping, head south through an open meadow just northwest of the peak. With careful route-finding, the summit is reached with little or no bushwhacking.

The massive north face of Cable Mountain

Cable Mountain (6,798)

Cable Mountain is an imposing presence above the Weeping Rock Trailhead in Zion Canyon. Curiously enough, the "summit" of this impressive feature is actually a level point a couple hundred feet lower than the highpoint of the connected plateau to the south. Regardless, Cable Mountain is a fine point from which to view Zion Canyon, Angels Landing, The Organ, Observation Point, Echo Canyon, and even the yellow, hoodoo'd summit of Great White Throne. Not only that, but the summit features the old cable works that was used in the early 20th century to lower timber from the summit plateau to Zion Canyon, some 2,500 vertical feet below. The cable works can be seen from the Weeping Rock Trailhead—cool stuff.

Although not covered in any detail in this guide, maintained and signed trails lead to the summit of Cable Mountain from the Observation Point Trailhead (in Zion Canyon), the East Rim Trailhead (just west of the park's east entrance), and the Stave Spring Trailhead (the shortest trail route to Cable Mountain; off North Fork Road).

Here, I'll be sharing some more adventurous ways to enjoy Cable Mountain.

RT Mileage: 8
RT Elevation Gain: 2,000'
Time Required: 6-8 hours
Latitude: +37.2680
Longitude: -112.9335
FA: Unknown
Etymology: Named for the cable works on the summit that was used from 1900-1926 to lower timber from the forested summit plateau to Zion Canyon.
Star Rating: **

Route: Via Many Pools (class 3+)

From the parking area, note a pair of parallel canyons that run north from UT-9 toward the rim above. The canyons are immediately east of Ant Hill. On the map, the canyons bear a striking resemblance to the roots of one's teeth, hence them being locally known as the "Root Canals."

Hike up the eastern of the two canyons, which is known as "Many Pools." Enjoy the pretty slickrock terrain and many small potholes (beautiful just after a rain), until after about two miles and a bit of bushwhacking in the upper canyon you climb through a couple of short class 3-4 steps in the watercourse and eventually gain the rim above. Walk north across the plateau for 200 yards until you stumble upon the Deertrap Mountain Trail. Follow the trail northeast for about 0.25 mile to the signed junction of the Cable Mountain Trail. Follow the lovely Cable Mountain Trail left for about 1.5 miles to the cable works at the "summit." This is a pretty fascinating place with interesting history. The view down into the canyon from here is spectacular—you get to see what birds see.

Alternative descent option #1 (Hidden Canyon: 3AIII):

With a canyoneering permit, a 60-meter rope, some webbing, a helmet, harness, rappel device, and the means to return to your vehicle from another trailhead, this otherwise mundane peak can be turned into a fine day out in the wilderness.

From the summit of Cable Mountain, retrace your steps to the junction of the Cable Mountain-Deertrap Mountain trails. Get on the Deertrap Mountain Trail and head southwest and then west for about a mile to a point where the trail bends sharply southwest as it works around a large cliff band above the head of Hidden Canyon. Leave the trail and hike west-southwest for 5-10 minutes to the very head of the canyon. The canyon drains north along the east side of Great White Throne, offering a pleasing view into an otherwise mellow landscape.

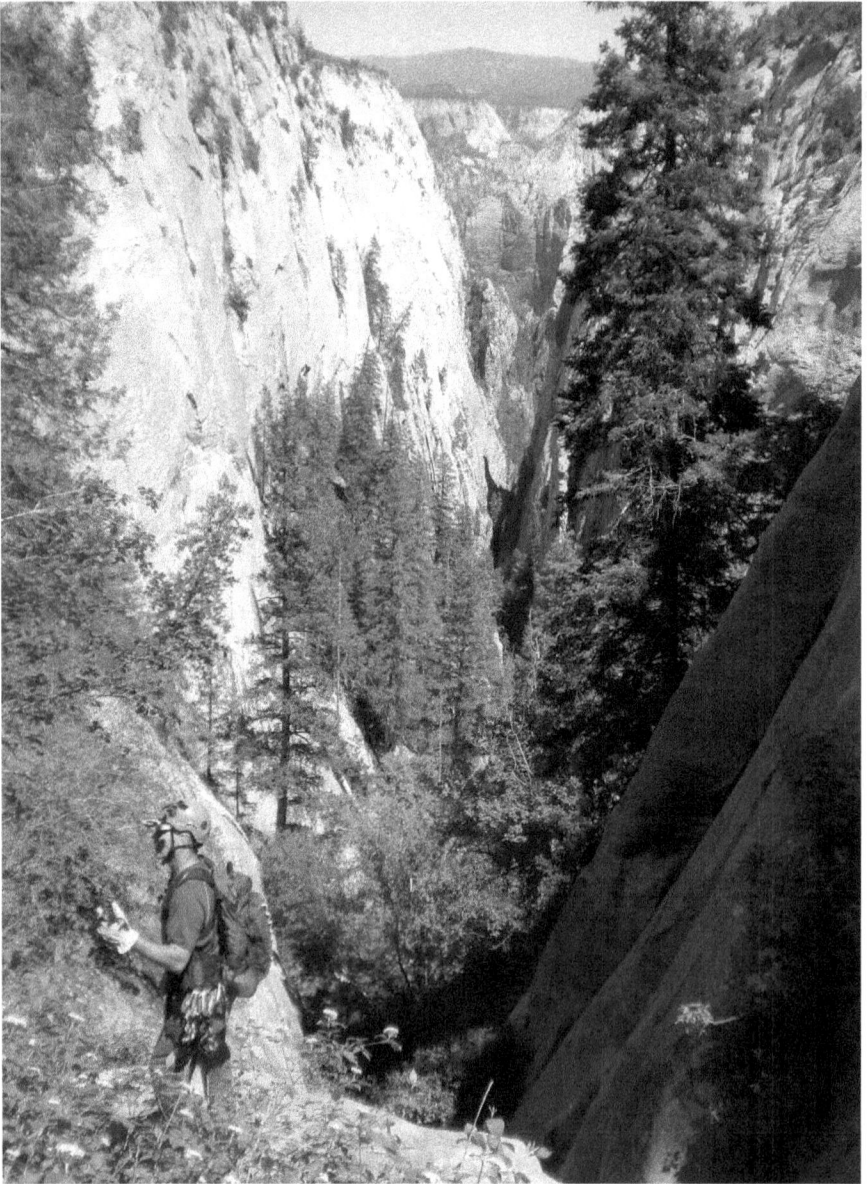

Double-A near the head of Hidden Canyon

The loose and sandy terrain gets steep as you drop down to the large pine (rappel slings present) at the apex of the head. Drop into the canyon and negotiate a number of rappels (up to 100 feet, some with awkward starts) and downclimbs until you eventually find yourself on the signed and maintained Hidden Canyon Trail near the mouth of the canyon. Follow the trail to the junction of the Observation Point Trail, where you hang a left and hike down to the Weeping Rock Trailhead in Zion Canyon.

Alternative descent option #2 (North Ridge):
Work east from the summit to gain the peak's north ridge. With careful route-finding, the descent of the ridge is essentially a stiff, dirty scramble, except for a 160-foot rappel mid-way down. Many may wish to make another 30-foot rappel below that. From the base of the ridge, easily cross Echo Canyon and follow the Observation Point Trail west to the Weeping Rock Trailhead in Zion Canyon.

Two 60m ropes are recommended for this route.

Deertrap Mountain (6,910)
Deertrap Mountain is a minor summit atop a sprawling plateau with absolutely fantastic views of much of Zion Canyon, including close-ups of Mountain of the Sun and Twin Brothers.

Although the mountain is most commonly ascended via a long (17-mile roundtrip) class 1 trail from the East Rim Trailhead near the park's east entrance on UT-9, those will some skills (and a tolerance for steep scrambling on extremely loose rock over massive exposure) will likely find the 3-mile roundtrip South Buttress route award-winning.

Although not covered in any detail in this guide, maintained trails lead to the summit of Deertrap Mountain from:

-Weeping Rock Trailhead in Zion Canyon. This route is very long;

-Stave Spring (Cable Mountain) Trailhead (off of North Fork Road, east of the park's east entrance). This is the shortest trail route.

-East Rim Trailhead (just west of the park's east entrance).

RT Mileage: 3 (South Buttress)
RT Elevation Gain: 2,000' (South Buttress)
Time Required: 4-6 hours (South Buttress)
Latitude: +37.2356
Longitude: -112.9444
FA: Unknown
Etymology: The mountain was named after early pioneers learned that the Paiutes would herd mule deer onto the mesa of the mountaintop in order to trap them for food.

Star Rating: ***

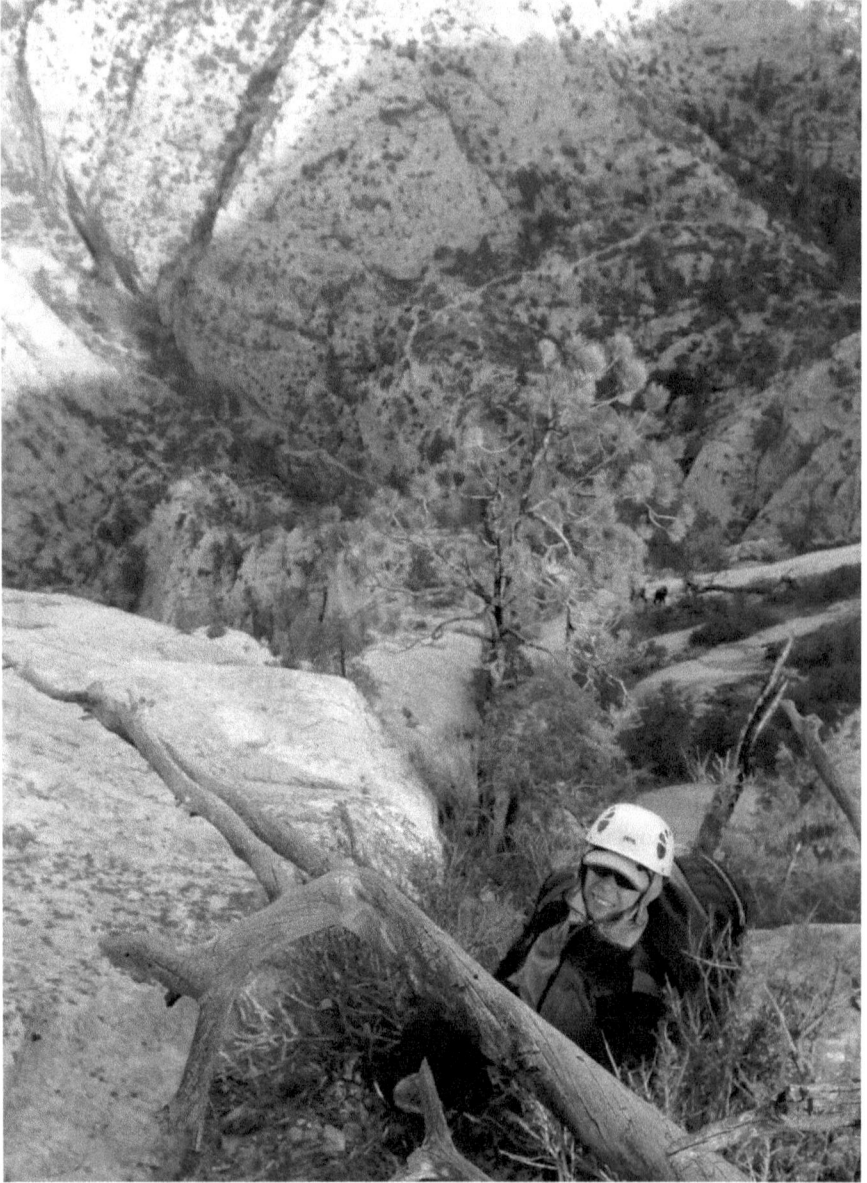

DB descends the steep north ridge of Cable Mountain. Ram first brought this route to my attention many years earlier when he speculated about whether it could be used for an ascent of Cable Mountain. DB and I eventually made an attempt but were turned back by an impenetrable cliff midway up. Fortunately, the ridge works beautifully as an adventurous descent route though.

Deertrap Mountain and its aesthetic south buttress from the southeast

Route: South Buttress (class 4-5)

Follow the directions given for Mind's Eye to the exit from upper Pine Creek. Wander northwest from here into the slickrock bowl that forms at the toe of Deertrap Mountain's south buttress. Aim for the left side of the toe of the buttress. Here, it can most easily be gained via class 3-4 slabs. Head up class 3-4 slabs for a few hundred feet until the terrain mellows considerably and becomes rather vegetated with lots of manzanita. Continue up a bit more then steer left around the steepening, narrowing ridge forming above. Ledges lead to a shallow saddle on a knife edge just below the steepest part of the route.

From here, continue up, trending toward the right side of the ridge crest (and never actually on it once the initial knife-edge is crossed), via ledges and faces, following the easiest line. Be careful here, as some of the loosest rock and biggest exposure is found along this part of the route.

Soon, a 5-foot mantle followed by 5-foot face through brush eventually leads to the summit plateau. An easy level walk north for 0.25 mile leads to a short, class 2 scramble to the highpoint via its east side.

Many parties will wish to rappel portions of the return. Reliable anchors could be a challenge to establish in spots. A 60m rope is recommended for the route.

Route: Via Many Pools (class 3-4)

While this semi-wild route is much more casual than the South Buttress route, it is probably five miles longer on the roundtrip. DB and I once found some interesting Indian ceremonial "stuff" scattered on the slickrock slabs at Many Pools.

Follow the directions given for Cable Mountain via Many Pools (class 3-4) to the Deertrap Mountain Trail. Hike west on the trail to near the east rim of Zion Canyon then cut left and walk south to the base of the summit cap, which is a short, class 2 scramble on its east side.

Approaching The Center of the Universe, the southeast face route is just out of sight behind the right skyline

Petroglyph Canyon Trailhead

Once through the Zion-Mt. Carmel Tunnel, continue east to a second tunnel, this one much shorter. Once through the second tunnel, continue east for 1.4 miles to a parking area on the right side of the road. The pull-out will be just as the road bends sharply right, having just passed by the prominent canyon that runs north immediately west of Aires Butte and South Ariel Peak. You'll see a wooden fence along the parking area. The pull-out is 2.6 miles west of the park's east entrance.

"Aires Butte" (6,492)

Aires Butte appears at a glance to be mostly unclimbable via any of its faces. With that said, the small peak's southeast face harbors a very reasonable technical line ("Led by Sheep") up the thing. The line happens to be Zion's only "easy" multi-pitch "sport" route. Consisting of four pitches of mostly class 3-4 scrambling (with several 5th class sections up to about YDS 5.5) the bolt- and piton-protected route is surprisingly fun and aesthetic. I've done it numerous times.

RT Mileage: 2
RT Elevation Gain: 1,200'
Time Required: 5-7 hours
Latitude: +37.2325
Longitude: -112.9076
FKA: David Littman & Jeffery Herrick (summer 2005)
Etymology: Though the origin of the name is not clear, some have heard this peak called both Aires Butte and Mount Ariel. Bo Beck climbed it prior to my initial ascent and saw that whoever placed the register at the time had called it Aires Butte.
Star Rating: ****

Route: Southeast Face (AKA: Led by Sheep) - YDS 5.5

From the parking area, head for the prominent canyon (Petroglyph Canyon) on the north side of the highway. Drop into the canyon via a beaten use trail on the east side of the drainage and wander north for 0.25 mile until you can angle east up steep slickrock slabs (class 4-5) that lead to the col between Aires Butte (to the north) and South Ariel Peak (to the south).

The col is a surreal landscape of arcing sandstone some stoned teenager in Springdale referred to as "The Center of the Universe" some years back. From The Center of the Universe, work up to the southeast side of Aires Butte above a small area of trees and bushes next to a small depression on the left. Moving beyond the vegetation, contour north along the southeast face and look for two bushes alone amongst the white/yellow slabs immediately above the small depression. Just beyond the bushes (perhaps 30 feet to the north) is a piton about 25 feet up the face. The route starts below the piton.

Head up for four bolt- and piton-protected pitches. The belays are established. At the top of the last pitch, you'll find the belay slightly around the corner to the left amidst talus and some brush. From there, scramble 40 feet to the summit via loose class 2 terrain.

Two 60-meter ropes are needed for the route. Watch for rockfall, particularly on the upper pitch. Bring five quick draws.

Steve Newell at the Center of the Universe

Alternative descent option (Full Keyhole Canyon: 3BII):

In addition to the technical gear you'll already have with you, this descent option will require a canyoneering permit and a wetsuit. It is terrific—beautiful and subterranean, wet and wonderful. I've done Keyhole Canyon about 10 times.

Once back at the Aires Butte-South Ariel Peak col, drop to the obvious bench southeast of Aires Butte via class 2-3 slabs then hike east across gentle terrain until you can scramble down into upper Keyhole Canyon. (Did you notice the sweet jug handle arch up high on the left as you strolled across the bench?)

Heading down-canyon, you'll encounter some wading and a few fun downclimbs. After 0.25 mile, you'll reach middle Keyhole Canyon, where the canyon bends right, becomes more entrenched, and the fun picks up a tad. After a hundred yards of fun in middle Keyhole Canyon, the canyon opens up to a sandy wash with a large tree on the right. Looking to your left from the tree, you'll see a two-bolt anchor above a slot. Drop into the slot via a 20-foot rappel and continue down the deep, dark, cold and wet canyon, negotiating a few more short rappels, some slippery downclimbs, and a long swim through a narrow, cold channel. Just after the swim, a bit more wading and downclimbing leads you out into the sun and UT-9. Walk the road 0.5 mile west to your car.

Rappelling the upper pitch on Aires Butte's southeast face

Keyhole Canyon Trailhead

Once through the Zion-Mt. Carmel Tunnel, continue east to a second tunnel, this one much shorter. Once through the second tunnel, continue for 1.9 mile to a pull-off on the south side of the road. The pull-off is immediately opposite a minor canyon coming in from the north. The canyon is a sweet technical slot known as Keyhole Canyon. South Ariel Peak will be immediately to the northwest, towering above the road in glorious slickrock splendor and easily identified by the presence of tourists constantly photographing each other on its lower slopes. This pull-off is 2.1 miles west of the park's east entrance.

The peaks in this subsection are roughly arranged from shortest-hike-from-the-trailhead to longest-hike-from-the-trailhead.

"South Ariel Peak" (6,251)

Though a minor summit, South Ariel Peak is a splendid scramble with phenomenal views from its top. The mountain's slickrock slopes beckon the photographer to photograph it, and the hiker/scrambler to climb it. Absurd summit etchings, a gift from modern man, adorn the highest rocks of this small peak.

DB and Jenn enjoying Keyhole Canyon

RT Mileage: 1.5
RT Elevation Gain: 700'
Time Required: 2-3 hours
Latitude: +37.2272
Longitude: -112.9067
FA: Unknown. Dozens of names have been scratched into the summit rocks over the years. In that respect, it's the only summit of its kind in Zion.
Etymology: There's a bit of confusion in some minds as to the naming of this peak. It all stems from the mistaken belief that the more prominent summit to the north (Aires Butte) was called Mount Ariel or Ariel Peak. And so South Ariel Peak was born!
Star Rating: **

Route: Southeast Face (class 4)

From the pull-off, walk across the highway and start up the slickrock of South Ariel's southeast face. You are ultimately aiming for the highest point visible above you. Route-finding the beginning of the route is not difficult but as you ascend the terrain becomes steeper and more convoluted. Not far below the top (perhaps 200-250 feet) you'll encounter the crux of the route—a class 4 section of steep slabs. The crux is perhaps 100 feet, and at times intimidating.

Weaving back and forth a bit to find latent ledges and weaknesses, work up the steep slabs to easier, broken ground. Once the easier terrain is gained, continue to a minor saddle. Hang a left at the saddle and scramble up class 2-3 terrain to the highpoint and its etchings. Please don't add your dopey name to the others.

Route: South Slope (class 2+)
The appeal of the south slope route on this peak is that 1) it sure beats having to down-climb the steep, exposed 4th class slabs on the southeast face on the descent, and 2) there exists a completely unlikely, brilliant hidden ledge system that makes this route feasible and entertaining.

From the parking area, walk west on the highway for less than 100 yards then scramble onto the slickrock near the eastern edge of South Ariel's lower south slope. Follow the easiest line upward toward the visible highpoint above. After several hundred feet of class 2-3 scrambling you'll come to near-vertical terrain near the base of the summit mass. Look to the left (west) and pick up a funky, sandy, and occasionally vegetated ledge system that works its way nearly horizontally north below the summit cliffs above and the steep slabs and cliffs below. Quite pleasingly, the route goes.

As you work north a bit, ignore the occasional chute or lower-angle terrain that materializes—they seem to lead to dead ends. Instead, continue around to the northwest side of the peak until the terrain leads to the minor saddle above. This is the same minor saddle encountered near the top of the southeast face route. A touch of class 3 scrambling on poor rock may be required to get up to the saddle. From the saddle, hang a right and follow class 2-3 terrain to the highpoint.

"Separation Peak" (6,111)
Separation Peak is a minor peak located at the head of Separation Canyon, a locally-named canyon nestled in between Nippletop and Crazy Quilt Mesa. A short, scenic hike from the road, Separation Peak offers a fun class 3 final scramble up to the summit block and its hefty views into Parunuweap.

RT Mileage: 2
RT Elevation Gain: 700'
Time Required: 2-4 hours
Latitude: +37.2110
Longitude: -112.8967
FA: Unknown
Etymology: After spying a nice-looking canyon from the summit of South Ariel Peak one day, Bo Beck and Tanya Milligan decided to explore it. Doing so, they eventually came to a fork in the shallow canyon. Continuing up one

of the forks, they soon found themselves atop a small, crumbly peak. Bo dubbed the peak "Separation Peak" and the canyon "Separation Canyon."
Star Rating: *

Route: Northwest Slope (class 3)

Follow the directions given for either route to Nippletop to the saddle-like area at the top of the slickrock watercourse below that peak. Continue south for 0.25 mile until you can pick up the white slickrock that takes you to the summit of Separation Peak. Several sketchy class 2-3 moves over crumbly, exposed sandstone are required to reach the tippy-top.

Alternative Approach (Separation Canyon):

One can also approach the peak directly from UT-9 via Separation Canyon. Walk east on UT-9 from the parking area and look around until you find a suitable place to gain the canyon. Once in Separation Canyon, follow it toward its head. The peak will be just west of the head of the shallow canyon. There, either cut west at a likely-looking spot to gain the class 2 white slickrock at the base of the peak's northwest slope or work directly up the northeast face (class 3) to the base of the steep summit block.

DB preparing to descend the steep and exposed summit block of Separation Peak

"Nippletop" (6,715)

Nippletop is the high, vegetated summit just east of The Fin and The Triplets. It can be clearly seen from UT-9 as one travels through the eastern portion of Zion. The peak sits directly south of UT-9, south-southeast of South Ariel Peak. The summit views are among the best in the park.

RT Mileage: 3
RT Elevation Gain: 1,500'
Time Required: 3-4 hours
Latitude: +37.2108
Longitude: -112.9022
FA: Unknown
Etymology: When viewed from nearby summits such as Aires Butte, the perfectly-positioned summit boulder of this peak resembles a well-centered nipple on a breast.
Star Rating: ***

Route: North Ridge (class 2+)

From the parking area, drop into the wash on the south side of the highway and follow it shortly west and then south toward the base of Nippletop's north ridge. East of the north ridge is a prominent slickrock watercourse running down to meet the wash you're in. Scramble up into the watercourse and follow it up to a sort of saddle at the top. At the saddle, short cliffs along the base of the north ridge prevent easy access onto it. Traverse north (and down) along the base of the cliffs for 50-75 vertical feet until you reach a large tree leaning against the cliffs. Fifteen feet beyond the tree is a narrow ledge that allows class 2-3 access to the north ridge proper.

Once the north ridge is gained, head south up to the false summit. From the false summit, drop a bit and continue south along a narrowing ridge. The true summit can be seen in the distance. As you pass through the narrowest portion of the ridge, it begins to widen and a use trail develops in the sand. Follow it. Climbing steeply up the sandy use trail toward the summit above, you'll soon encounter a short cliff band. Many class 2-3 opportunities to climb through it present themselves. Once above the short cliff band, head south and up for a few minutes to the summit. Class 2 scrambling will get you onto the highpoint. The views are enormous and inspiring.

Route: North Saddle (class 2+)

Follow the directions given for the north ridge route to the saddle at the top of the slickrock watercourse. At the saddle, short cliffs along the base of the north ridge prevent easy access onto it. Traversing south along the base of the cliffs, you'll soon come to a shallow slickrock drainage coming in from the west. This drainage separates the true summit from the false (north) summit.

Head west up the drainage, climb onto the slickrock, and start making your way up to the north ridge above you. The north ridge proper can be readily gained (class 2) by heading right (north) as you climb higher. From here, continue to the summit along the north ridge route described above.

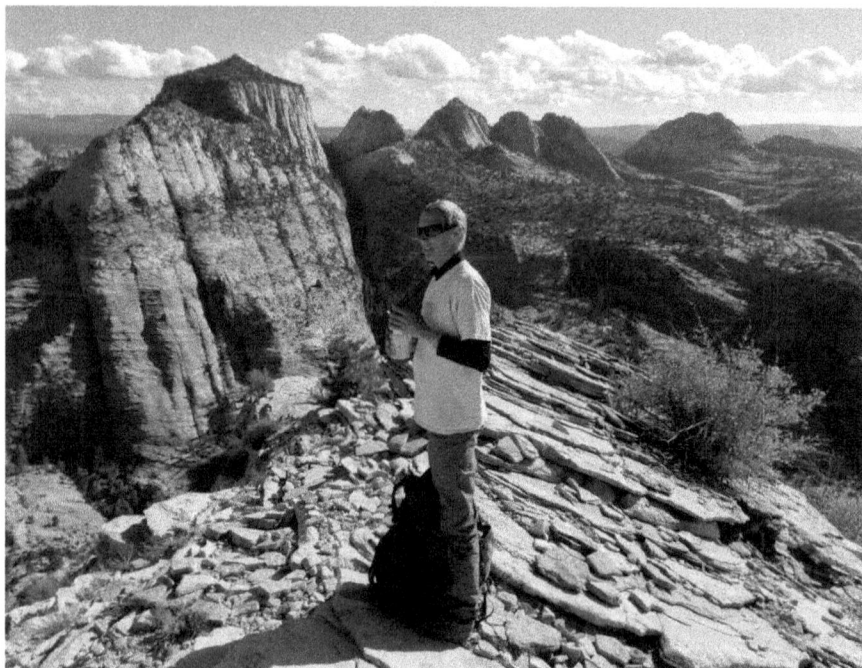

Our pal Andy Mac on the summit of South Ariel Peak. Nippletop (left), The Fin, The Triplets and Lost Peak (right) are visible in the background.

"Point of Compassion" (6,266)

Point of Compassion is a short, easy hike to a nice viewpoint of Antler Point and The Triplets. The summit provides a close-up view of the seldom-climbed Fin. A short walk to the northwest also allows one to peer into the canyon draining north from the narrow Nippletop-Fin col.

RT Mileage: 4
RT Elevation Gain: 800'
Time Required: 2-4 hours
Latitude: +37.2065
Longitude: -112.9014
FA: Unknown; we found no signs of prior visitation. I built a cairn on the summit.

Etymology: Just seemed appropriate.
Star Rating: **

Route: From Separation Canyon (class 2-3)
Follow the directions given for Antler Point to the area of the Crazy Quilt Mesa-Separation Peak saddle. Rather than go all the way to the saddle, cut southwest over slickrock (class 2-4, depending on line taken) to gain the Nippletop-Separation Peak col. From there, drop 50 feet south into a small slickrock bowl above the impressive canyon whose head is the Nippletop-Point of Compassion saddle. Rather than get into the canyon, traverse initially southwest on lovely slickrock (an area reminiscent of The Center of the Universe) and then hike up to the Nippletop-Point of Compassion saddle. Hang a left and wander to the summit.

"Antler Point" (6,161)

This is a fine backcountry hike to a small summit with interesting views of the red slickrock of the east side. This is slickrock paradise!

RT Mileage: 5
RT Elevation Gain: 1,000'
Time Required: 3-5 hours
Latitude: +37.1999
Longitude: -112.8851
FA: Unknown; but I know that our friend Jeff Branin was here a couple of years before me.
Etymology: Jeff Branin found some deer antlers near the summit and placed them amongst the highest rocks. In 2010, I built a cairn around the antlers. I wonder if they're still there.
Star Rating: **

Route: From Separation Canyon (class 2-3)
Follow the directions given for Separation Peak until you can easily angle left to the Crazy Quilt Mesa-Separation Peak saddle.

Alternatively, one can follow Clear Creek east from the pull-off for about 0.25 mile to where it meets Separation Canyon. About 0.25 mile east of that, look for a good use trail that leads onto the slickrock bench above (and just slightly northeast of) Separation Canyon. From there, follow the shallow canyon south past several potholes (easy walk-arounds) to the saddle.

From the saddle, bushwhack south to slickrock and then cross-country it to the gentle north slope of Antler Point, which is immediately south of Crazy Quilt Mesa. A touch of class 2-3 scrambling leads to the loose and semi-exposed summit ridge.

"Crazy Quilt Mesa" (6,760)
CLOSED TO RECREATIONAL USE—RNA

Crazy Quilt Mesa is the local name for the tall, high-walled mesa nestled between Nippletop and Checkerboard Mesa on the east side of the park. Just below the summit cap on the northwest corner route is a substantial arch (about 10 feet wide and 40-50 feet high), which Jeff Branin dubbed Crazy Quilt Arch.

RT Mileage: 3
RT Elevation Gain: 1,800'
Time Required: 2-5 hours
Latitude: +37.2120
Longitude: -112.8889
FA: Unknown
Etymology: Unknown
Star Rating: **

Route: Northwest Corner (class 4-5)
Follow the directions given for Separation Peak to the northeastern base of that peak. Next, work to the northwest corner of the arm of Crazy Quilt Mesa immediately east of Separation Peak. Fight brush up a reasonable weakness to a short class 4-5 step with easier going above. Once through, scramble higher to reach lovely forested ground below the summit cap. From here, study the landscape to piece together a meandering section of broken terrain that ultimately leads to a chimney, an exposed catwalk, and then, a final short off-width flake problem just below the top of the cliff. The broken terrain goes easily, the chimney is trivial, and the exposed catwalk is a bit wider than it appears from below. The off-width flake is dangerous—so proceed with caution. Above that, a short rock step is easily bypassed. The RNA begins at the mesa-top. As such, the true summit is closed to recreational use.

Route variation: Southwest Gully (class 2-3)
The prominent south-draining gully southwest of the summit can be used as a means to access the upper mountain. This variation intersections the northwest corner route at a point west-southwest of the summit. The RNA begins at the mesa-top. As such, the true summit is closed to recreational use.

Checkerboard Pass Trailhead
From the park's east entrance, travel west on UT-9 for about 0.75 mile to a parking pull-out on the right. A trail heads up a small sand dune on the south side of the highway then wanders into the canyon between Checkerboard Mesa and Crazy Quilt Mesa.

This is the view north from Artifact Arch Peak. The bloating of the cliffs is not a distortion of the image—it really looks like that. The namesake arch can be seen in the upper left skyline. Someday I'll have to get up to that arch, which seems to be easily accessed from the backside.

"Artifact Arch Peak" (6,142)

This is a pleasant peak with excellent views. Three hundred yards north of the summit is a striking arch on the rim of Artifact Mesa.

RT Mileage: 6
RT Elevation Gain: 1,500'
Time Required: 3-5 hours
Latitude: +37.20932
Longitude: -112.87292
FKA: Courtney Purcell (April 3, 2015)
Etymology: This minor summit is immediately south of Artifact Mesa (and southeast of Checkerboard Mesa). The summit affords a cool view of a neat arch on Artifact Mesa.
Star Rating: **

Route: Southeast Face (class 2)
From the trailhead, hike a use trail south up the canyon separating Checkerboard Mesa (to the east) and Crazy Quilt Mesa (to the west). Pass over the col (Checkerboard Pass) between the two peaks then descend the trail as it leaves the canyon and bends southeast around the toe of Checkerboard Mesa. Continue east along the trail to a point near the southeastern base of our objective. Leave the trail and head for the mountain, which is ascended via rubbly class 2 slopes on the southeast face. Reach the southwest ridge then walk easily to the highpoint.

Once on the summit, it is worth walking 50 feet to the north to get a good look at the arch, the gnarly face below the arch, and the otherwordly slickrock col separating our peak from Artifact Mesa.

Checkerboard Mesa Trailhead

Continue east from the Keyhole Canyon Trailhead for 1.7 miles to the signed Checkerboard Mesa viewpoint and parking area. Checkerboard Mesa is the prominent aesthetic feature south-southwest of the viewpoint. The parking area is 0.4 mile west of the park's east entrance.

The peaks in this subsection are roughly arranged from shortest-hike-from-the-trailhead to longest-hike-from-the-trailhead.

"Artifact Mesa" (6,570)

This is a minor summit on the mesa immediately east of Checkerboard Mesa. Native American artifacts have been found on the sprawling and undulating mesa. If you should be so fortunate, please consider leaving them where you found them.

DB and the author enjoying another classic day on the East Side. (Photo by Aron Ralston)

RT Mileage: 1
RT Elevation Gain: 800'
Time Required: 2-4 hours
Latitude: +37.2178

Longitude: -112.8744
FA: Unknown; Native American artifacts have been found on the summit mesa.
Etymology: The inspiration for the name should be apparent.
Star Rating: *

Route: West Col (class 2)

Follow the directions given for Checkerboard Mesa to that peak's east col. From the col, scramble east to the plateau above and then work south to the rocky outcropping that is the summit. Enjoy the occasional views and your efforts to spot artifacts as you wander the mesa.

Checkerboard Mesa (6,670)

Checkerboard Mesa is one of the most famous landmarks in all of Zion National Park, perhaps second only to Zion Canyon's massive Great White Throne, which is the largest monolith in the world. Checkerboard Mesa's funky, crisscrossed, meshy north face, a result of weathering and erosion of the imperfect vertical and horizontal fissures in the Navajo Formation, has graced countless postcards. On the east side of the park, where the mountain is located, there is a pull-out and viewpoint for the popular feature, and the visitor center is full of picture books and assorted souvenir paraphernalia flashing Checkerboard Mesa's bright smile.

Although technical climbing routes have been established on the Mesa, including Wheat Chex (YDS 5.8+ PG13; 5 pitches) on the north face, there also exists a hike/scramble to the summit via its east col.

Native American artifacts have been found in the area. If you are lucky enough to find anything cool, please leave it for others to enjoy.

RT Mileage: 1
RT Elevation Gain: 1,000'
Time Required: 2-4 hours
Latitude: +37.2155
Longitude: -112.8801
FA: Native Americans, to be sure.
Etymology: Originally known as Rock Candy Mountain (a name I really like), in 1938 park superintendent Preston Patraw renamed it Checkerboard Mesa. According to Steve Allen's *Utah's Canyon Country Place Names, Volume 1*, the mountain is also called Quilted Mountain.
Star Rating: *

Route: East Col (class 2)

From the Checkerboard Mesa viewpoint, walk down the road a short distance (0.1 mile) until you can drop onto the slickrock on the northeast corner of the mountain. From the slickrock, you can see a forested canyon heading south along the east side of the mountain. Head that way.

Either staying in the watercourse at the eastern base of the mountain (more fun and more challenging) or picking up a use trail that starts a little to the east but eventually finds itself in and around the watercourse, head up-canyon toward the col above. (Fun class 3-4 scrambling can be found if one stays in the watercourse for the duration; however, it can also be avoided and this part of the route kept at class 1-2, if one stays on the trail.)

Anyway, find your way to the col above. From the col, hang a right (go west) and scramble up to the summit mesa. Once on the treed summit mesa, follow your nose south-southwest to the highpoint. It's also worth it to wander north along the mesa to get a view.

East Entrance Trailhead

Continue east from the Keyhole Canyon Trailhead for 2.1 miles to the park's east entrance. You can park here or at the park entrance monument a bit further east.

The East Rim Trailhead is off a short spur road heading north from UT-9, just west of the east entrance. This trailhead also has parking.

Excellent views from the top of Misery Peak

"Misery Peak" (6,628)

This is the easternmost peak on the south side of UT-9 in Zion National Park. Although the north face route is very short (less than a mile to the summit), it is steep, loose and dangerous. An outstanding view of Misery Canyon can be enjoyed from a point just south of the summit.

RT Mileage: 2
RT Elevation Gain: 1,000'
Time Required: 2-4 hours
Latitude: +37.2254
Longitude: -112.8656
FA: Unknown
Etymology: The peak sits at the head of Misery canyon.
Star Rating: *

Looking south into the Misery Canyon complex from the summit of Misery Peak

Route: North Face (class 4)

Just east of the east entrance to the park, park in the pull-out adjacent to the large Zion National Park welcome monument. Note a tongue of sandstone immediately south protruding from the north face of Misery Peak. Hike up the tongue until you can cut over into the prominent, steep gully immediately west. Ascend the gully (class 4; loose and steep) all the way to its head, where the going suddenly becomes super-mellow as you wander the mesa top to its summit to the south-southwest. A 5-minute walk south from the summit gives up an outstanding (and seldom seen) view of Misery Canyon, which is a wonderful technical canyon that doesn't require a permit.

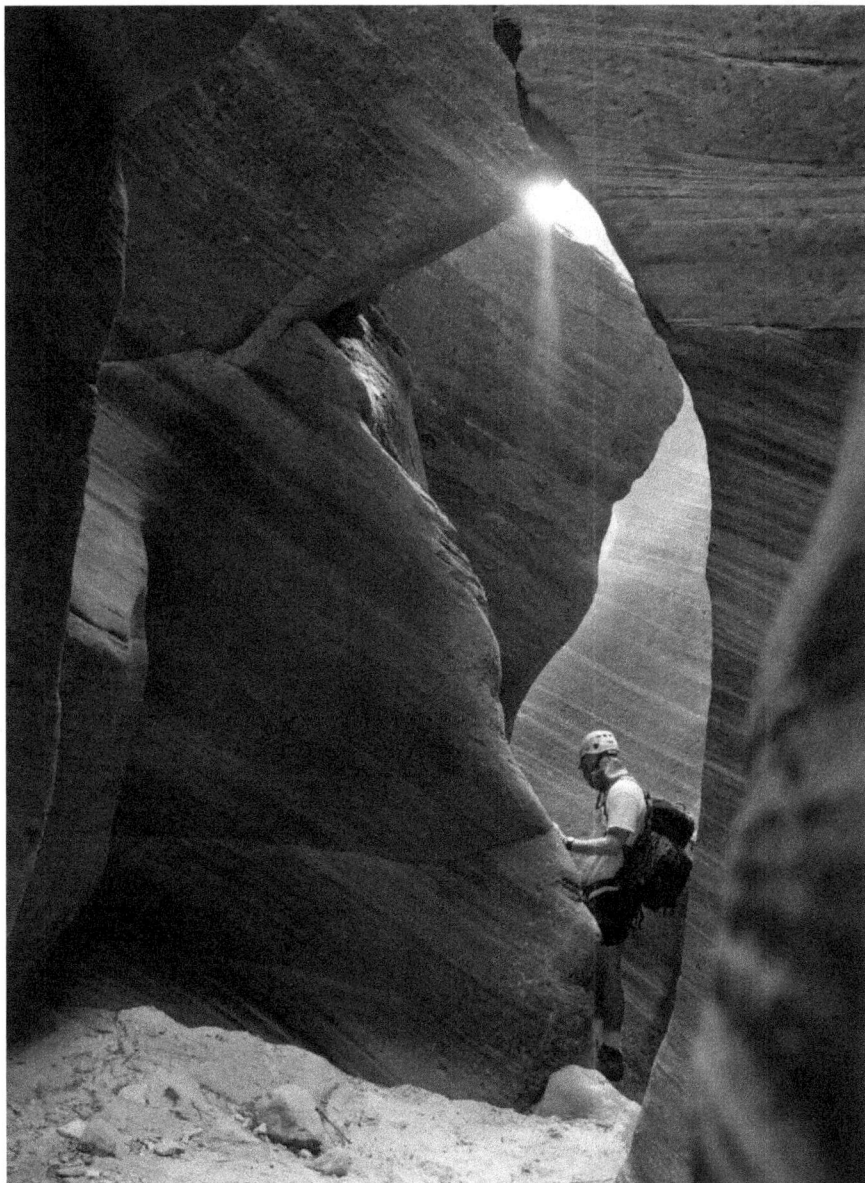

The author in Misery Canyon (Photo by Bryan Long)

To descend, you can retrace your steps (not recommended) or wander class 1-2 terrain southwest to the Misery Peak-Artifact Mesa saddle. From there, head west to the Artifact Mesa-Checkerboard Mesa saddle then descend the steep and rugged "trail" north to the road.

Backcountry views in Zion

Scattered

The peaks in this section are scattered widely around the greater Zion area.

Guacamole Trailhead

From I-15 in St. George, Utah, follow signage north toward Zion National Park. Getting off I-15 at exit 16 (UT-9), follow UT-9 east toward the park. At 12.4 miles, UT-9 will turn right in La Verkin, Utah. Continuing on UT-9, you'll pass through the small community of Virgin. Just past it, at mile marker 20, turn left onto the signed Dalton Wash road.

(Alternatively, from St. George, you can follow I-15 north to exit 27 (UT-17). Exit and take UT-17 six miles (passing through charming, little Toquerville along the way) and then turn left onto UT-9 in La Verkin. Continue from there.)

Follow the dirt Dalton Wash Road for 1.8 miles to a Y-junction. Veering left, continue up the road for another 1.6 miles to a junction with a good dirt road on the left. Staying straight on the main road, continue 0.5 mile up the narrowing Dalton Wash to where the head of the wash meets the plateau above. Once there, go another 0.5 mile (staying on the main road; ignoring minor dirt roads) to the "Guacamole Trailhead." The trailhead is unsigned but found at a parking area at road's end at the park boundary.

The peaks in this subsection are roughly arranged from shortest-hike-from-the-trailhead to longest-hike-from-the-trailhead.

Crater Hill (5,207)

A volcanic feature atop a seldom-visited plateau on the southwest corner of the park, Crater Hill offers interesting views of nearby Cougar Mountain, as well as The West Temple, Towers of the Virgin and Smithsonian Butte.

Once, after me and some friends returned to the Guacamole Trailhead from a semi-rigorous outing to The Little Altar, we challenged one of my speedy partners to see how quickly he could run up Crater Hill as a bonus peak. I don't remember precisely how long it took, but his roundtrip time was something like 20 minutes—something impressive like that.

RT Mileage: 2
RT Elevation Gain: 700'
Time Required: 1-2 hours
Latitude: +37.2104
Longitude: -113.1026
FA: Unknown
Etymology: The cinder cone is named for the eroded crater easily made out while looking south from the summit.
Star Rating: *

Route: West Slope (class 1)
From the trailhead, walk through the park gate on the east side of the parking area and follow the fence line south. Approach the west side of Crater Hill then pick a line and head up. Be prepared for loose gravel on steep slopes.

Evening on The West Temple from Guacamole Trailhead

"Moon-Eye Point" (5,503)
Only the hardcore lover of the Zion backcountry will take the time to hike up this nice, little peak. A mellow endeavor, the final narrow summit ridge leads surprisingly to a small, red sand summit with excellent views of the nearby towering Cougar Mountain.

RT Mileage: 5
RT Elevation Gain: 1,000'
Time Required: 3-5 hours
Latitude: +37.2456
Longitude: -113.0941
FA: Unknown; we found no signs of prior human visitation. I built a cairn on the summit.
Etymology: A nod to Edward Abbey, while thinking of the horse that had wandered onto park land and hung out with us near the head of Dalton Wash the day we climbed this small peak.

Star Rating: **

Route: From Guacamole Trailhead (class 2-4)
From the trailhead, enter the park through the gate and follow the fence line north past lots of petrified wood until you intersect Dalton Wash. Follow the wash northeast toward its head, looking for your choice of at least two breaks in the 50-foot cliff bands above you. I've climbed through two of them (one was class 4; the other was class 2 or so). Above the cliffs, gain the south ridge of Moon-Eye Point and follow it to the narrow summit.

DB climbing the summit block of Coalpits Peak

"Coalpits Peak (4,768)
Spotting the woodsy crest of this small peak from the Guacamole Trailhead one morning, I set off alone to bag a "sure thing." As I got within 50 feet of the top, I realized that the otherwise trivial ascent was suddenly complicated by a summit crag that was hugely overhung on one side and was a steep and exposed technical slab on the other. With my tail between my legs, I returned to my vehicle defeated...but returned with partners to try again the next day! With some funky creativity (and a touch of nerve), we tagged the virgin top.

RT Mileage: 6
RT Elevation Gain: 1,300'

Time Required: 3-5 hours
Latitude: +37.2108
Longitude: -113.0693
FKA: Courtney Purcell, DB, Sarah Meiser & Kevin Baker (November 15, 2009)
Etymology: The small peak splits Coalpits Wash from Scoggins Wash. Coalpits was a cooler name.
Star Rating: **

The Little Altar (upper-right) on a stormy day during my first (failed) attempt of Coalpits Peak

Route: Northwest Slope (class 2, with YDS 5.4 summit block)

From the Guacamole Trailhead, follow the trail east for 300 yards until it disappears into a shallow wash that drains to Coalpits Wash. Follow the shallow wash easily to Coalpits Wash, either downclimbing an 8-foot dryfall just before the confluence or bypassing it on either side with a little scrambling. Once at Coalpits Wash, work around a hill to the east and then hike up steep but easy slopes to the south (highest) summit of Coalpits Peak. The highpoint is a large, overhung boulder just off the crest. The boulder can be ascended via 40 feet of YDS 5.4 climbing (no protection) on its backside. We used a 50m rope *and* a 30m rope to ascend and descend the crag safely. Don't be afraid to get creative.

Matthew and Dwight approaching the summit of The Little Altar

"The Little Altar" (6,310)

The Little Altar is an amazing peak that separates upper Coalpits Wash from upper Scoggins Wash and lies immediately west of the Towers of the Virgin. The route to its excellent summit is an exercise in route-finding and tolerance for loose rock. I failed on my first attempt of this peak with Bo Beck two or three years before my eventual November 2009 success with several other friends.

The Little Altar has 610' of prominence.

RT Mileage: 8
RT Elevation Gain: 3,000'
Time Required: 8-10 hours
Latitude: +37.2218
Longitude: -113.0429
FA: Unknown; we found a fallen-over cairn on the highest block.
Etymology: So named for its minor (but spectacular) stature amongst hovering giants like The West Temple, Altar of Sacrifice and the Towers of the Virgin.
Star Rating: ****

The Bishopric massif (left) from the summit of The Little Altar

Route: Southwest Ridge via West Face (class 3+)

Follow the directions given for Coalpits Peak into Coalpits Wash. Once at Coalpits Wash, head up the wash to a bit past the oil well ruins shown on the map. Once in this area, start looking for a clean (albeit steep, loose and sandy) line up the pinyon-juniper slopes to an apparent weakness in the lower west face of the peak above. It would be ridiculous for me to try to explain the intricacies of the route from here, but I'll offer some clues:

Gain the face via class 2 terrain then follow ramps and chimneys through brushy, loose and steep class 2-3 terrain slightly east before you angle back west and step around a corner (class 3) onto the west face at the base of the steeper cliffs below the southwest ridge. A short traverse south allows you to step around another corner and begin working up to gain the crest of the actual southwest ridge. Follow the crest of the southwest ridge until you reach an obvious impasse. Don't give up! Backtrack 50 feet and then drop 100 feet (class 2) off the left (north) side of the ridge and look for a steep and very dirty (and loose) chimney/weakness (class 3-4) that can be followed back up to the crest. Fifty feet along the crest, you'll encounter a funky step-across move past a tree at the base of another significant cliff. Follow a ledge along the left (north) base of the cliff to gain a chute leading to a broken section (class 3) that dumps you out a mere five minutes from the summit. The highest block requires a touch of class 3 scrambling to surmount.

View north to The Bishopric from the summit of Avalokiteshvara Temple

"Avalokiteshvara Temple" (7,285)

This high peak of the Towers of the Virgin is sandwiched between Altar of Sacrifice and Meridian Tower. Despite its height and commanding position, it is not readily visible from any road. The very summit of the mountain can be seen from a very short stretch of UT-9 in Springdale. It's a fleeting glimpse requiring a trained and studying eye.

The peak has 665' of prominence.

I once had a curious encounter with a lizard and a snake just below the summit: This area is so seldom visited that when I happened upon first a lizard then shortly thereafter a snake, I swear they were both shocked virtually frozen, caught completely off-guard by the presence of a human being. I could see it in their eyes—unmistakable—it was like I was the first person they'd ever seen.

RT Mileage: 22
RT Elevation Gain: 4,000'
Time Required: 11-14 hours
Latitude: +37.2338
Longitude: -113.0093
FKA: Courtney Purcell (May 1, 2015)

Etymology: This high peak is named for the Buddhist bodhisattva of compassion. Sometimes spelled "Avalokitesvara," the bodhisattva is known to Tibetans as Chenrezig. She is one of the most revered bodhisattvas in Buddhism.

Star Rating: **

The Three Marys from the Towers of the Virgin

Route: South Gully (class 4)

Follow the directions given for Coalpits Peak into Coalpits Wash. Hike generally northeast up Coalpits Wash to its obscure confluence with the significant canyon draining north from the saddle between Altar of Sacrifice and Avalokiteshvara Temple. About 0.5 mile before this point, you will need to find and follow an elk trail out of the wash to the right. The trail, which bypasses a waterfall in a constriction in Coalpits Wash, meanders high above the canyon wall before dumping you back in the wash at a lovely slickrock area next to a waterfall.

From the confluence of Coalpits Wash and the canyon leading to the aforementioned saddle, leave Coalpits Wash and hike southeast up this lesser wash. The going is generally easy, and convenient elk trails on the left twice avoid brush and/or problematic stretches. Eventually, the wash tightens into a canyon and much dirty scrambling is encountered. The going here is generally class 2-3. The crux of the route is an exposed 7-foot class 4 chimney-like feature on the left wall mid-way up.

From the saddle at the head of the canyon, hike left for 100 feet to cliffs barring further progress. Skirt left for 100 feet along the base of the cliffs then scramble up a break to locate a convenient class 3-4 ramp on the right allowing access through the cliffs and onto the easier ground above. Here, make an upward traverse east, crossing a couple of washes, until you can get into the peak's south gully, whose head is 50 feet west of the summit. Follow the brush and the mellow yellow slabs and sand of the class 2 gully north to near its head, where you can cut right then scramble up a short but steep class 3 block leading to the summit.

Stave Spring Trailhead

A high-clearance vehicle is recommended in good conditions. In poor conditions, the final few miles to the trailhead may not be passable.

Head east on UT-9 from the park's east entrance for 2.4 miles to the signed North Fork Road on the left. Turning left onto the paved road, follow it 5.1 miles to the Zion Ponderosa Ranch (on the left). Turn into Zion Ponderosa Ranch and go straight (ignoring a cluster of cabins and the main resort buildings to the left) and soon pass a nice cabin on your left. The road then turns to dirt. At 0.4 mile from the ranch entrance, go right at a Y-junction. Go left at the next junction and follow signs for Cable Mountain. The trailhead is just inside the park boundary.

Dow Williams descending the south face of Great White Throne

Great White Throne (6,744)

Great White Throne is one of the most famous landmarks in Zion National Park—its huge, blocky bust grabs the eye of virtually everyone at the Grotto or Weeping Rock. The story of the first ascent (and the subsequent rescue of that fellow) has become almost legend. In brief, the story tells of a fearless daredevil climber carrying only a short bit of rope who soloed up the route we rope up for today but fell on his descent, leading to an epic rescue effort.

I'll tell another, slightly longer story—a boring one about me:

I'd eyeballed this thing for years—it beckoned me. And it intimidated me. Then it got worse—I was about to pull the trigger on the mountain via a south face route Jonathan and Brian Smoot put up and declared "improbable and classic." I was stoked, so I got hold of Brian and we spoke a bit on the phone one afternoon. He said the route, which he called the South Face Diagonal, *could* be a classic, but the bolts might need a fix'n. He offered to mail me a topo he'd drawn up. Great!

Then a friend of mine, a hardcore climber-dude from Virgin who had spent years putting up really nice (too hard for me) lines all over Zion's big walls, told me about *his* climb of Brian's route on Great White Throne shortly after moving to the area. Though *only* YDS 5.8 A0, this 5.11-ish free climber said the route was super run-out, had sketchy bolts (with only one natural gear placement), and freakishly traversed huge slabs of steep, brittle sandstone. It terrified him.

And so I put it away. I forgot about it. Peaks like Goose Creek Knoll and Blew By Peak suddenly sounded like fun.

Then while climbing The East Temple one morning with my friend Aron, by sheer, unlikely chance we bumped into a couple of speed climbers descending our route. They introduced themselves to us as Coloradoans Bill Wright and Homie Prater. As Aron belayed me up a spicy, loose YDS 5.7 pitch on the big mountain's face, our intimate group made small talk and I asked Bill what else they'd been doing in the park. He told me that he and Homie had climbed Great White Throne the day before.

"Oh yeah! How was it???"

"The bolts were great," he said. In six pitches of "fun and easy" climbing, he and Homie encountered only a single wiggly bolt. Alright, man!

The rest is history...

A year later, I found the route to be terrifically fun, very run-out though quite easy—with only one thing I think Brian's topo should have included (though maybe it did and I just don't remember it): there's no mention of the technical summit block, one-half mile away across the plateau at the top of the climbing route proper. I understand that Brian probably didn't care about some dopey summit block, but we peakbagger types yearn for the tippy top. And so I'll tell you a little bit about the route...

Descending the south face of Great White Throne

RT Mileage: 10
RT Elevation Gain: 2,000'
Time Required: 8-12 hours
Latitude: +37.2611
Longitude: -112.9411

FKA: William H. Evans (June 27, 1927) via the south face, though a human skull was found on the summit plateau three days later during the second ascent.

Etymology: In *Utah's Canyon Country Place Names, Volume 1*, Steve Allen writes that the mountain was named in 1916 by Dr. Frederick Vining Fischer, who wrote: "Never have I seen such a sight before. It is by all odds America's masterpiece. Boys, I have looked for this mountain all my life but I never expected to find it in this world. This mountain is the Great White Throne."

Star Rating: ****

Route: South Face Diagonal (YDS 5.8 A0)

The base of the route is about 2.5 hours from the Stave Spring Trailhead, or slightly longer via Many Pools or the south buttress of Deertrap Mountain.

From the trailhead, follow the trail initially west then south toward Stave Spring. At the Deertrap Mountain Trail junction, follow that trail west to a rise of land just southwest of the head of Hidden Canyon. Leave the trail and hike north to the head of the big gully that drains northwest toward the base of Great White Throne's big south face. The gully is easily descended (class 2) to the tree'd valley between Great White Throne and the rim.

The South Face Diagonal is six pitches (5.6, 5.6, 5.8, 5.8, 5.7 A0 & 5.7), each pitch about 160 feet in length. Bring five draws and a 1.5" Friend to protect the ascent.

In summary, the route starts at a lone pine just west of the center of the south face then angles sharply up and right to top out near the eastern edge of the top of the south face. Each pitch features extremely run-out but generally easy climbing. It's often hard to spot where to go, so look carefully for your next bolt before proceeding.

Specifically, the route starts immediately above a big, single pine left of center on the south face and immediately west of a very steep section at the base of the face. The first bolt (about 40' feet up) cannot be seen from the bottom of the pitch but the climbing begins at the most obvious point one can get onto the face (YDS 5.4). The vast majority of this slab route is YDS 5.4 or easier, and the harder sections consist of single moves or very short sequences. The route traverses up and right much more than you might expect, finishing the 6th pitch near a black, water-streaked section of rock in the vicinity of the upper-right side of the face. Near the end of the 5th pitch, you'll step right and pull on a piton to aid through a slick section of slab. Bolts (though few on the route) were in good shape (as of spring 2009). From the top of the 6th pitch, scramble up class 3-4 slabs to gain the beautiful tree'd, heavily cacti'd, grassy plateau. Walk 0.5 mile to the base of the highpoint crag, a large yellow protrusion with an orange top. A few spicy class 4-5 moves put you on the highpoint from the west, north or east sides. Due to the highpoint's position in the center of a fairly large, flat plateau, the summit views are not great.

Rappel the route with two 50-meter ropes.

The south face of Great White Throne

East Mesa Trailhead

A high-clearance vehicle is recommended in good conditions. In poor conditions, the final few miles to the trailhead may not be passable.

Head east on UT-9 from the park's east entrance for 2.4 miles to the signed North Fork Road on the left. Turning left onto the paved road, follow it 5.1 miles to the Zion Ponderosa Ranch (on the left). Turn into Zion Ponderosa Ranch and go straight (ignoring a cluster of cabins and the main resort buildings to the left) and soon pass a nice cabin on your left. The road then turns to dirt. At 0.4 mile from the ranch entrance, go right at a Y-junction. At 0.7 mile, go right at a T-junction that may be signed for either Observation Point or Twin Knolls Road. At 1.5 miles, go right at a T-junction. At 2.3 miles, go straight as Fir Road comes in. At 2.6 miles, the road becomes very rocky as it heads slightly downhill. Low clearance vehicles may wish to park just above this point. At 2.9 miles, go left at a Y-junction. The road soon ends at the park boundary (3.0 miles from the ranch entrance). There are several places to park amongst the trees.

The peaks in this subsection are roughly arranged from shortest-hike-from-the-trailhead to longest-hike-from-the-trailhead.

"Blew By Peak" (6,840)

One walks right over this bump on the way out to the rim to drop over to Flagpole Mountain. It's a short and easy bag from Observation Point or Observation Benchmark. The highpoint, only a quick walk from the trail, is in a burnt out area.

Despite the fact that it has 320' of prominence (and is therefore considered a "ranked" peak by some), Blew By Peak is so insignificant that I'd already "bagged" it twice before realizing it was a "peak."

RT Mileage: 5 (East Mesa Trailhead) / 8 (Weeping Rock Trailhead)
RT Elevation Gain: 150' (East Mesa Trailhead); 2,100' (Weeping Rock Trailhead)
Time Required: 2-3 hours (East Mesa Trailhead); 4-6 hours (Weeping Rock Trailhead)
Latitude: +37.2897
Longitude: -112.9327
FA: Unknown
Etymology: Twice I *blew by* this one on the way to Flagpole Mountain without realizing it was a "mountain."
Star Rating: *

Approach Option #1 (East Mesa Trailhead):

For a there-and-back hike, this is by far the fastest and easiest approach to the peak. A high-clearance vehicle is recommended in good conditions.

From the trailhead, enter the park via an open gate (50 feet left of the locked vehicle gate) and follow the East Mesa Trail for 2.2 miles to its junction with the well-used side trail on the right that leads to the apex of Mystery Canyon, some 40 feet away.

Approach Option #2 (Weeping Rock Trailhead):

Take the Zion Canyon Scenic Drive about 4.5 miles up-canyon from Canyon Junction to the Weeping Rock Trailhead. From the trailhead, head up the beautiful Observation Point Trail. Ignoring the popular side trail that leads to Hidden Canyon, the main trail will soon enter Echo Canyon. At another official trail junction, go left (remaining on the Observation Point Trail) and soon begin a series of switchbacks leading up to the east rim. Upon reaching the rim, follow the trail west to the Observation Point Trail-East Mesa Trail junction. From the junction of the two trails, take a right onto the East Mesa Trail and follow it another 20 minutes or so as it passes over a highpoint in the trail. Just beyond, look for a well-used side trail on the left that leads to the apex of Mystery Canyon, some 40 feet away.

Route: From the East Mesa Trail (class 1)
From the junction of the East Mesa Trail and the side trail leading to Mystery Canyon, head cross-country a short distance to the northwest through a burnt-out area to the semi-distinct highpoint. Congratulate yourself for this minor achievement.

Observation Benchmark (6,708)
Lying just north of the famed Observation Point, which provides awesome views of the southern portion of Zion Canyon, this minor summit provides fantastic views of the *northern* portion of Zion Canyon. Worth it!

Though Observation Benchmark boasts a commanding presence when viewed from the area of Twin Peak, it actually sports a very casual 188' of prominence.

RT Mileage: 6 (from either trailhead)
RT Elevation Gain: 200' (East Mesa Trailhead); 2,000' (Weeping Rock Trailhead)
Time Required: 2-3 hours (East Mesa Trailhead); 4-6 hours (Weeping Rock Trailhead)
Latitude: +37.2838
Longitude: -112.9388
FA: Unknown
Etymology: There's an 'Observation' benchmark on the summit. Nearby Observation Point was named by Stephen Johnson in 1922. Johnson would sometimes make the long hike up to the lookout point before the Echo Canyon Trail was constructed in 1928.
Star Rating: ***

Approach Option #1 (East Mesa Trailhead):
For a there-and-back hike to Observation Benchmark, this is (by far) the fastest (and easiest) approach.

From the trailhead, enter the park via an open gate (50 feet left of the locked vehicle gate) and follow the trail about 3 miles to the vicinity of the Observation Point Trail junction.

Approach Option #2 (Weeping Rock Trailhead):
Follow the directions given for Blew By Peak to the Observation Point Trail-East Mesa Trail junction.

Route: Southeast Slope (class 1)

From the vicinity of the trail junction, head cross-country for a hundred yards to the north-northwest, where several game trails lead to the top. A particularly fine viewpoint is found on a platform 20 feet west-northwest of the summit benchmark.

Alternative Descent Option (Echo Canyon: 3BII):

This descent option requires a canyoneering permit, 50 feet of rope, rappelling gear and full wetsuits. It is only recommended in mid-to-late summer, as it has several very cold swims (and deadly, lingering snow bridges can sometimes be found in the slot well into early summer). If starting from the East Mesa Trailhead, a car shuttle is needed (unless you want to slog all the way back uphill to the car).

Descending the Observation Point Trail to the official trail junction in Echo Canyon, go left toward Cable Mountain. In about 10 minutes, the trail crosses a minor canyon. Forty feet later, leave the trail on the right and follow a use trail along the rim of the minor canyon, soon entering it via a steep dirt slope.

Head down-canyon and negotiate four short rappels (be sure to check the anchors) and a possible keeper pothole that may require a partner assist to exit. Soon, the canyon opens up and you'll intersect the Observation Point Trail as it crosses through the watercourse. Assuming a return to Weeping Rock, hang a left and follow the Observation Point Trail down to civilization.

"Flagpole Mountain" (6,628)

Flagpole is an adventurers' mountain. Although it only features a nominal amount of class 4, the route to the summit requires a rappel on the *ascent* and offers four rappels on the *descent*. The summit is sublime, pristine and allows unbelievable views directly down into Zion Canyon, as well as close-up views of Mountain of Mystery.

The mountain's namesake 'flagpole' is a 40-foot tall pillar of yellow sandstone that can be seen just below the summit from portions of the West Rim Trail.

A 60m rope is recommended for any of the routes described.

RT Mileage: 7 (East Mesa Trailhead); 10 (Weeping Rock Trailhead)
RT Elevation Gain: 1,500' (East Mesa Trailhead); 3,500' (Weeping Rock Trailhead)
Time Required: 6-10 hours (East Mesa Trailhead); 9-13 hours (Weeping Rock Trailhead)
Latitude: +37.2966

Double-A at the namesake flagpole below the summit of Flagpole Mountain

Longitude: -112.9388
FKA: Courtney Purcell, DB and Andy Archibald (November 15, 2008)
Etymology: Tom Jones named the mountain for a flagpole-like pillar of rock that can be seen just below the summit from the West Rim Trail above Scout Lookout.
Star Rating: ***

Route: Via Blew By Peak (class 4)
Follow the directions given for Blew By Peak to the summit of that mountain. From there, continue north-northeast toward the Blew By Peak-Flagpole Mountain saddle. Although the going is initially easy, you'll soon encounter thick brush as you work toward the point where the rim meets the south end of the saddle. Mystery Canyon will loom just to the east.

Carefully approach the rim above the saddle and look for a 4-foot downclimb to a good pine on a small ledge immediately above the saddle. A 90-foot rappel (or 40', if one doesn't mind downclimbing very steep dirt) off the pine leads to flattish ground at the saddle. From the saddle, work north until you come to a 30-foot hidden cliff band. Along the way, you might notice a large arch ("Flagpole Arch") in the red sandstone immediately above (and south of) the saddle. A loose, rubbly break near the crest leads to a 10-foot class 3-4 downclimb. Continue on, aiming for the only apparent weakness through cliffs ahead. Here, a 12-foot class 4 chimney allows access to Flagpole Mountain.

Above the chimney, head cross-country through brushy terrain toward the yellow summit cap of Flagpole Mountain. Although there is a class 2 break on the east end of the cap, please avoid it, as there is significant brush and about an acre of cryptobiotic soil one must cross in order to reach the highpoint. Instead, I recommend that you work west below the south side of the summit cap until you come to one of a couple of class 3 breaks on the southwest side of the cap. Once there, scramble northeast a short distance to the summit.

Delightfully, the actual summit is a flat platform on the very edge that looks straight down into Zion Canyon! (On your way down from the southwest side of the cap, be sure to step around the western edge and visit the namesake 'flagpole'!)

On the descent, work back to the saddle. Here, I'll note three options:

1) The drainage west of the saddle is initially mellow and benign, but leads to Not Mystery Canyon, a serious area that has left folks stranded and needing rescue. By following the alternative return directions given for Freezer Point, it is possible to escape upper Not Mystery Canyon and return via Blew By Peak.

2) If you have ascending gear, and leave a fixed rope at the initial rappel from the mesa, you can re-ascend the rope and retrace your steps back to the car. This should be the fastest way to return.

3) To descend via Mystery Canyon, do a downward traverse north from the saddle (on the east side of the crest) until you come to a

large pine above a high-angle slab. Immediately above the large pine is a large, exposed root that should have a sling around it. Rappel 60 feet off the root to a large tree. Carefully downclimb eight feet of steep dirt and note another sling on an exposed root immediately below the large tree. Rappel 40 feet from the exposed root to a small ledge with a tree on it. From the tree, rappel 100 feet to a sandy gully of sorts. There, traverse south for 40 feet and then scramble 20 feet down to a small tree. From the small tree, rappel 90 feet into a dirty chute. Scramble down the dirty chute to the top of a pour-off. Step left 50 feet through trees to reach a rockslide. The rockslide can be followed down into the bottom of Mystery Canyon. Once in Mystery Canyon, head south *up-canyon*, bypassing two would-be rappels on their left sides, and follow the watercourse all the way up to the mesa. Once on the mesa, walk 40 feet south to intersect the East Mesa Trail. The East Mesa Trailhead will be 2.2 miles of trail to your left, while the Weeping Rock Trailhead will be about 3.5 miles of trail to your right.

DB and Double-A pose for a photograph on the summit of Flagpole Mountain. There is a lot of cryptobiotic soil around here, so please tread carefully and work hard to avoid stepping on (and thereby damaging) the slow-growing, critical crust.

Alternative Descent Option (Mystery Canyon: 3BIII):
This descent option requires a (usually hard-to-get) canyoneering permit, an additional 60m rope, and a shortee wetsuit (assuming summer conditions). If starting from the East Mesa Trailhead, a car shuttle is needed, as you'll end up at the Temple of Sinawava in Zion Canyon. Be prepared for a long day.

Following the directions given for the descent into the Mystery Canyon drainage, head *down-canyon*. Along the way, you'll encounter about 11 rappels (up to 120') and a swim at Mystery Spring. Be aware that the anchor for the 110' rappel into Mystery Spring is reached via an exposed slab traverse to your left. While on this rappel, be sure to first drop onto a boulder midway down before stepping right and completing the rappel into Mystery Spring. Be careful pulling your rope after this rappel, as the boulder can be a rope-grabber. The final 120-foot rappel is down a slippery, high-angle slab directly into the Zion Narrows. It is spectacular!

Once in the Zion Narrows, head south (down-canyon) for less than a half-mile to The Veranda, the point where the Riverside Walk meets the river. Depending on your time of arrival, there could be dozens of tourists there to greet you. Follow the paved Riverside Walk a mile to the Temple of Sinawava. From here, catch the shuttle, get into the car you spotted, or start walking back toward wherever you left a car.

The view south from the summit of Flagpole Mountain

"Freezer Point" (5,800)

This obscure summit within the confines of the Not Mystery watershed has awesome views of the area, including straight down into The Narrows. The peak has 240' of prominence.

Take note that although the peak has a class 2 rating, the approach features a 90' rappel and the return requires either several additional rappels or tricky route-finding through steep and exposed class 3-4 terrain.

RT Mileage: 8 (East Mesa Trailhead); 11 (Weeping Rock Trailhead)
RT Elevation Gain: 2,500' (East Mesa Trailhead); 4,500' (Weeping Rock Trailhead)
Time Required: 7-9 hours (East Mesa Trailhead); 10-12 hours (Weeping Rock Trailhead)
Latitude: +37.2882
Longitude: -112.9437
FKA: Courtney Purcell, DB & Andy Archibald (October 29, 2011)
Etymology: Named in keeping with the refrigerator theme from my recent ascent of Icebox Knoll. Additionally, Refrigerator Peak sits southwest across Zion Canyon from Freezer Point.
Star Rating: ***

Route: North Ridge (class 2)

Follow the directions given for Flagpole Mountain to the Blew By Peak-Flagpole Mountain saddle. From the saddle, scramble down the drainage to the west until you're at a point north of the summit of Freezer Point. From there, leave the drainage and follow the peak's north ridge to the summit.

For the return, one can head back to the Flagpole Mountain-Blew By Peak saddle and rappel into Mystery Canyon (as described under Flagpole Mountain). Alternatively, study the cliffs of Blew By Peak east of the summit of Freezer Point and note a weakness that allows access to the plateau above. Scramble to and through this weakness, which is steep, dirty and exposed class 3-4.

Mountain of Mystery (6,565)

Mountain of Mystery is a seldom-noticed but strikingly aesthetic mountain perched directly above the Zion Narrows near Mystery Falls. It is a serious and committing mountain.

Mountain of Mystery has 845' of prominence.

RT Mileage: 8-10
RT Elevation Gain: 3,000'
Time Required: 10-12 hours

Latitude: +37.3030
Longitude: -112.9391
FKA: Brian Cabe & Tom Jones (2001)
Etymology: According to Steve Allen's *Utah's Canyon Country Place Names, Volume 2*, in 1927 R.B. Gray wrote: "Farther up the canyon [the Narrows of Zion], apparently blocking it completely, rises a slender, ethereal cone of pink and white, a peak of such appealing symmetry and delicate tints that it always commands admiration. It is the Mountain of Mystery."
Star Rating: ***

Route: North Face (YDS 5.2)

The roundtrip numbers suggested above are assuming a start from the East Mesa Trailhead and a finish at the Temple of Sinawava. While this requires a car shuttle, it is a far faster option than starting from Weeping Rock.

This meandering route traverses five different sections of canyon. A wetsuit is suggested if it's not hot.

Follow the directions given for Blew By Peak to the side trail leading to the apex of Mystery Canyon. Descend Mystery Canyon (2AII, for the section you'll be in) until shortly before the first rappel, where it's possible to exit the slot on the right via a bushwhack. Traverse north above the slot to a mellow, vegetated saddle between Mountain of Mystery and what is essentially the east mesa. On the north side of the saddle, descend an uninteresting canyon known as Not Worth It (3AII) to its confluence with Orderville Canyon. (The canyon due north of this confluence is known as Kidee Canyon.) Turn left down Orderville Canyon but immediately cut left around the corner into Monolith Canyon (3AII), which parallels Not Worth It and also drains north into Orderville Canyon.

Monolith Canyon presents several interesting obstacles, including 1) a steep class 4-5 dirt slope for which many will wish a belay, 2) a very tight, awkward slot, and 3) a climb of a dead tree (YDS 5.2) wedged almost vertically in the canyon. Without this dead tree, upward progress is hopeless for non-superheroes like me, as it is crucial to overcoming a 30-foot overhung drop.

Near the head of Monolith Canyon, find an initially wide ledge system that leads out of the canyon and toward the mountain's north face. The wide ledge eventually peters out and dumps you out on the extremely dirt north face. Ascend the face, generally keeping to the brushiest parts, where things to grab are more available. The going is intense, dirty, and dangerous—extreme care is required. At the top of the face is a short but dirty YDS 5.0 pitch that leads to the summit plateau. A tree above the pitch can be used for convenient and secure protection.

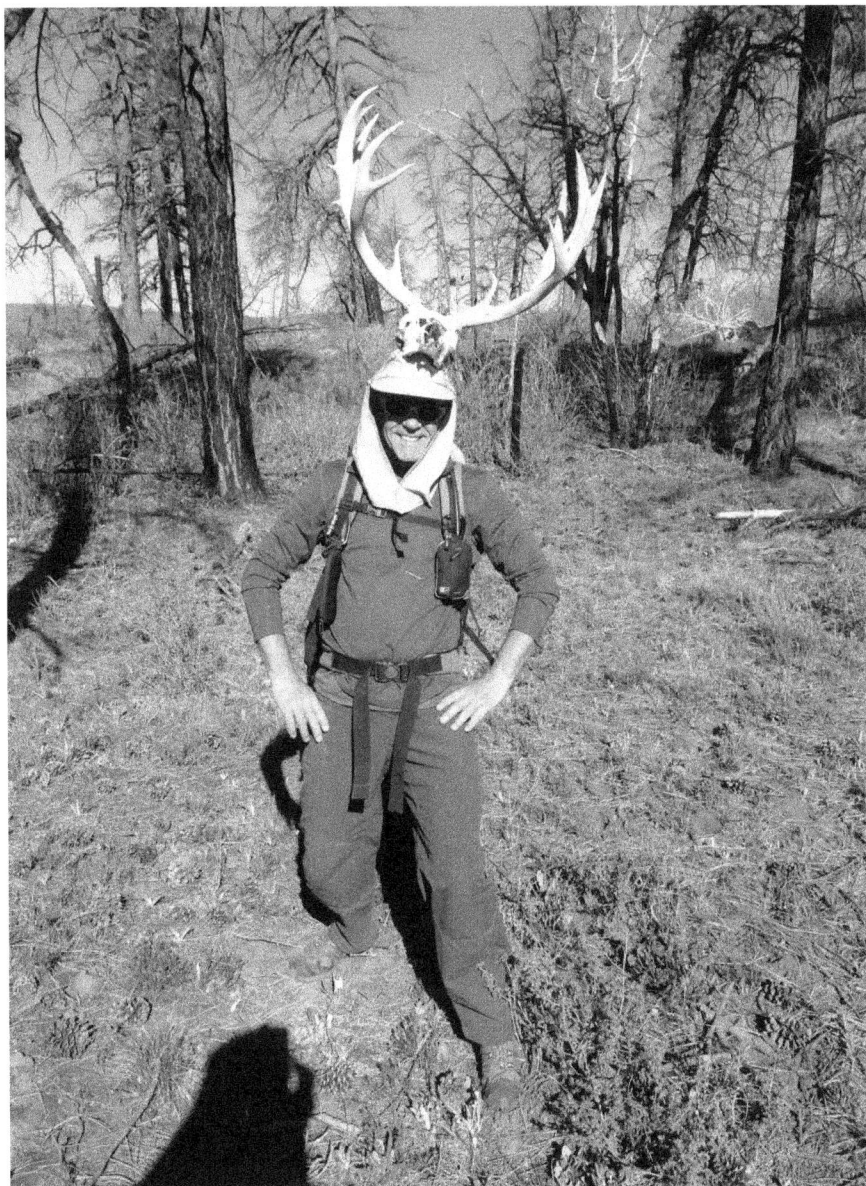

Once on the summit plateau, traverse south past the north summit to near the saddle between the two summits, where you'll encounter a highly exposed, nasty traverse. Beyond this, continue traversing south until you can cut around to the south side of the south summit cap. Here, a short YDS 5.0 slab leads to the summit.

Prepare to do a variety of rappels, perhaps from obscure or questionable anchors, on the return to the Monolith Canyon-Orderville Canyon confluence. From this confluence, head down Orderville Canyon (3BII) to its confluence with the Narrows (2BII), where you'll turn left and follow the river to the trail leading to Temple of Sinawava.

A 60m rope is recommended for the route.

Dakota Hill Trailhead

From the park's east entrance, continue east on UT-9 for 2.3 miles to the signed North Fork Road on the left. Turn left and follow the initially paved (turns to dirt after 5.4 miles) North Fork Road approx. 13.6 miles to a minor left fork in the road. Taking the left fork (roughly west of Point 7,804), follow the quickly deteriorating road (high clearance 4WD may be needed) as far as you're comfortable. It's best to park at the junction of BLM roads #92 and 92G, though a high clearance vehicle can be driven 0.4 mile further down BLM road #92. The road ends after about a mile and becomes a narrow dirt track leading toward the head of Walker Gulch.

The peaks in this subsection are roughly arranged from shortest-hike-from-the-trailhead to longest-hike-from-the-trailhead.

Dakota Hill (6,661)

Dakota Hill, with a mere 220' of prominence, is an uninspiring small point lying on BLM land near a seldom-visited portion of the park. In addition to guaranteed solitude, it offers interesting views of the nearby high country and the significant Orderville, Deep Creek and North Fork-Virgin River drainages.

This is one of those peaks that you eventually pass over a dozen times on your way to a million other, cooler places.

RT Mileage: 2 (if starting from road's end)
RT Elevation Gain: 200'
Time Required: 1-2 hours
Latitude: +37.3533
Longitude: -112.8854
FA: Unknown
Etymology: According to Steve Allen's *Utah's Canyon Country Place Names, Volume 1*, a topographical engineer for the USGS named R.T. Evans suggested the name "on account of its capping of Dakota conglomerate gravels."
Star Rating: *

Route: From the East (class 2)
From the junction of BLM roads #92 and #92G, walk road #92 for 0.8 mile until it turns left and begins to drop toward Walker Gulch. Just as it turns left, note a trail continuing straight on the ridge. Follow the trail to the summit of Dakota Hill.

"South Dakota Hill" (6,690)
This slightly higher neighbor lies just to the southwest of the officially named Dakota Hill. The views and required effort are similar.

RT Mileage: 2 (if starting from road's end)
RT Elevation Gain: 300'
Time Required: 2 hours
Latitude: +37.3491
Longitude: -112.8891
FA: Unknown
Etymology: This is the higher, south summit of Dakota Hill.
Star Rating: *

DB on the summit of South Dakota Hill. Don't be fooled into assuming DB's thinking she's chic with the cheesy posture she's assumed here—she was playfully mocking someone we'd recently seen "striking a pose."

Route: Northeast Ridge (class 2)
Follow the directions given for Dakota Hill to the summit of that peak. From there, simply drop south to the saddle then hike easily to the summit.

DB approaching the brush-choked summit of Chessboard Mountain

"Chessboard Mountain" (6,812)

This isolated mountain sitting at the head of Checkerboard Canyon is unremarkable. Only the truly obsessed Zion peakbagger will consider this lonely, brushy, viewless peak an objective worthy of an entire morning of hiking.

The peak has 452' of prominence.

RT Mileage: 10
RT Elevation Gain: 2,200'
Time Required: 4-6 hours
Latitude: +37.3552
Longitude: -112.9201
FA: Unknown
Etymology: The peak sits at the head of Checkerboard Canyon. Since we already have a feature in the park named Checkerboard, I thought perhaps Chessboard would work instead.

Star Rating: *

Route: East Ridge (class 1-2)
Follow the directions given for Dakota Hill to the summit of that mountain. From there, drop down the west ridge to pick up the long and meandering east ridge of Chessboard Mountain. Follow it to the summit. Most brush can be avoided along the route, until the last 10 minutes before the summit, when the going becomes obnoxious.

While the views along the ridge are pleasant, those from the summit are not memorable.

"Bulloch Peak" (6,396)
This obscurity has very nice views from its summit. We built a cairn atop the highest point. The peak has 276' of prominence.

RT Mileage: 8
RT Elevation Gain: 1,500'
Time Required: 6-8 hours
Latitude: +37.3185
Longitude: -112.9179
FKA: Courtney Purcell, DB & Andy Archibald (October 28, 2011)
Etymology: This minor peak sits above middle Bulloch Gulch.

Star Rating: **

Route: Northeast Ridge (class 3)

Follow the directions given for South Dakota Hill to the summit of that peak. From the summit, drop west and cut around the head of Esplin Gulch to gain the brushy plateau on the west side of the gulch. The plateau can be followed south-southwest to its terminus just northeast of Bulloch Peak. Scramble to the saddle northeast of the peak then cut around the left side of the peak's northeast ridge until you can scramble through cliff bands to easier terrain above. The summit is a short walk away.

Sarah Meiser on the summit of Upsilon Temple

Upsilon Temple (6,200)

Upsilon Temple is one of my very favorite summits in all of Zion, if only for its improbability. I'd long written this one off as out-of-my-league, until I spotted an unlikely possibility in the rim cliffs southeast of the summit. With minimal coaxing, I recruited some of my pals to join me for an attempt. And it went!

This super-obscure peak above the confluence of the Virgin River and Deep Creek has funky views into a part of the park almost no one has ever seen, though hundreds (thousands?) of people each year walk right below it.

Upsilon Temple has 320' of prominence.

RT Mileage: 14
RT Elevation Gain: 3,500'
Time Required: 8-10 hours
Latitude: +37.3586
Longitude: -112.9491
FKA: Courtney Purcell, Giles Wallace and Sarah & Dominic Meiser (November 30, 2013)
Etymology: Unknown
Star Rating: ***

Route: South Aspect (class 3)

Follow the directions given for Chessboard Mountain to the summit of that peak. From there, drop to the northwest to gain the open, Ponderosa pine plateau that leads west toward Upsilon Temple. Keep your eyes peeled for elk—I once saw a large herd just below the summit of Chessboard Mountain.

As you near the western end of the plateau, a shallow drainage will begin to form east-southeast of Upsilon Temple. Do not confuse this minor drainage with the much more substantial drainage immediately south, whose head is 0.5 mile west-northwest of the summit of Chessboard Mountain.

Follow the shallow drainage west until you reach a pour-off, where you'll angle left along the rim until you can piece together a class 3 way north-northwest down into the bottom of the drainage. (It may be beneficial to first walk the rim opposite this wall to eyeball a route.) Once there, follow the drainage down for a hundred yards or so until you can cut right across easy terrain to the base of the peak's southeast slope. Scramble northwest up the steep slope (class 2) until you can angle right to the summit.

"North Wynopits" (6,665)

CLOSED TO RECREATIONAL USE—RNA

North Wynopits is a forgettable summit sandwiched between almost-as-forgettable summits. The mountain is highly brushy and universally uninteresting. To the west, though, is an intriguing view into the yawning obscurity of Corral Hollow. The Virgin River glides below the peak in the depths of the Narrows.

North Wynopits has 465' of prominence.

Latitude: +37.3352
Longitude: -112.9437
Etymology: This summit is one mile north of Wynopits Mountain. Although it is a distinctly different mountain, it just sort of feels like a lesser, northern extension of the sprawling main peak.

Getting ready to rappel in Kidee Canyon

"Mount Kerouac" (6,580)
CLOSED TO RECREATIONAL USE—RNA

This peak, which has 300' of prominence, features a large shelter cave on its east face.

Latitude: +37.3398
Longitude: -112.9423
Etymology: A tribute to Jack Kerouac, the author of *On the Road*—a book that altered the course of my life.

"Kidee Point" (6,600)

CLOSED TO RECREATIONAL USE—RNA

Despite its minor stature, Kidee Point, which is southeast of North Wynopits and northeast of Wynopits Mountain, is an interesting peak deep in the Zion National Park backcountry.

Kidee Point has 240' of prominence.

Latitude: +37.3271
Longitude: -112.9371
Etymology: This minor peak sits a half mile north of the head of Kidee Canyon.

Wynopits Mountain (6,891)

CLOSED TO RECREATIONAL USE—RNA *(Although the summit itself is not closed to recreational use, much of the approach is closed. There is no known way to approach the summit without crossing closed land.)*

Wynopits Mountain is a commanding mountain buried in a hard-to-reach and obscure part of the park. The mountain is east of Corral Hollow Peak, though the two are separated by the cool depths of the Narrows and the glorious river snaking through it.

Wynopits Mountain has 831' of prominence.

Latitude: +37.3228
Longitude: -112.9452
Etymology: According to the USGS, Wynopits was a local Indian name for the Deity of Evil.

Shunes Hollow Trailhead

This ultra-obscure park trailhead is at road's end in a lovely, open area of Shunes Hollow, about a mile southeast of the summit of Transview Mountain. To get there requires a 4WD vehicle capable of handling about 10 miles of committing, deep sand.

To get there take UT-389 south from Hildale/Colorado City to the paved Rosy Canyon road toward Cane Beds. As the road enters Rosy Canyon it turns to graded dirt. Pass through the canyon until the road opens up again, looking for a lesser dirt road which leaves the main road north at a point south of Elephant Butte. Follow the main, well-traveled (though funky and sandy) road generally north, around the west sides of Elephant Butte and Sandstone Butte, and make your way to Shunes Hollow.

The peaks in this subsection are roughly arranged from shortest-hike-from-the-trailhead to longest-hike-from-the-trailhead.

"Dennett Peak" (6,082)

This so-so peak, which has 362' of prominence, is a mellow endeavor, in contrast to its wild and rugged brethren just to the west. The views from the top are nice.

RT Mileage: 4
RT Elevation Gain: 800'
Time Required: 1-2 hours
Latitude: +37.1615
Longitude: -112.8964
FA: Unknown
Etymology: The peak sits just east of Dennett Canyon. When I decided to call this Dennett Peak, I'd forgotten that I'd already dubbed another peak just to the northwest Dennett Mountain. Oh well.
Star Rating: *

Getting to the Mountain:

Follow the directions given for Shunesburg Mountain but park further east up Shunes Hollow at an obvious cluster of cool-looking sandstone hoodoos south of Dennett Peak.

Route: South Slope (class 1)

From wherever you park, wander easily north to the highpoint.

Transview Mountain (6,321)

While this is a breathtakingly wonderful, obscure part of Zion, don't let my five ascents of this mountain fool you into thinking it's particularly good. It's not. Surprisingly, I once found cell service on top and was able to order tickets to a 3-night Phish run in Denver. Score!

The peak has 681' of prominence.

RT Mileage: 4-5
RT Elevation Gain: 1,000'
Time Required: 2-3
Latitude: +37.1503
Longitude: -112.9204
FA: Unknown
Etymology: I suppose the name has something to do with the views, which stretch across a breathtaking panorama of Zion National Park and the Canaan Mountain area, as well as vast tracts of obscurity to the east and southeast. I dunno; I could be wrong.
Star Rating: **

Route: Southeast Slope (class 2)
From the trailhead, pass through the gate and follow a wash north into the slickrock bowl at the southern base of Transview Mountain. Scramble up the delightful bowl to its top then cruise northwest to the mountain's northwest summit.

"Dennett Mountain" (5,880)
This minor peak is west of Dennett Canyon and northeast of Transview Mountain. It has 240' of prominence.

RT Mileage: 6-8
RT Elevation Gain: 1,800'
Time Required: 4-6 hours
Latitude: +37.1680
Longitude: -112.9140
FKA: Courtney Purcell (June 4, 2011)
Etymology: The peak lies closely west of Dennett Canyon.
Star Rating: ***

Route: Southwest Face (class 4)
Follow the directions given for Transview Mountain to the top of the initial slickrock bowl then cut north across the plateau before dropping down a suitable line (class 2) leading to the flattish terrain northeast of Transview Mountain and southwest of Dennett Mountain. Once at the base of the southwest face of Dennett Mountain's southern rampart, scramble up steep terrain (class 4) then work north toward the highpoint. Downclimbing the final stretch of the southwest face on the return was memorable.

"The Sphinx" (5,872)
CLOSED TO RECREATIONAL USE—RNA
This peak is just west of Transview Mountain. The peak has 312' of prominence.

Latitude: +37.1525
Longitude: -112.9373
Etymology: I named it, but I can't remember for what.

"Ramp Peak" (5,960)
CLOSED TO RECREATIONAL USE—RNA
Ramp Peak is just northwest of The Sphinx and Transview Mountain in the obscure Shunes Hollow portion of Zion National Park. The mountain has 440' of prominence.

Latitude: +37.1586
Longitude: -112.9446
Etymology: Named for the graceful ramp on the east side of the peak

Shunesburg Mountain (5,960)
CLOSED TO RECREATIONAL USE—RNA

Shunesburg Mountain is west of Transview Mountain. It has 640' of prominence.

Latitude: +37.1564
Longitude: -112.9566
Etymology: Named after a Mormon townsite in the 1860s along the East Fork of the Virgin River, east of Rockville. Shunes was the name of an old Paiute chief.

"Shunes Hollow Peak" (5,720)
CLOSED TO RECREATIONAL USE—RNA

This little peak is west of Transview Mountain, and closely southwest of Shunesburg Mountain. Shunes Hollow Peak has 320' of prominence.

Latitude: +37.1540
Longitude: -112.9623
Etymology: Named after nearby Shunes Hollow

Outside the Park

The peaks in this subsection are scattered about and arranged here in no particular order.

Clear Creek Mountain (8,123)

Clear Creek Mountain is a mostly-pleasant hike with excellent views from the top. As one might imagine—given the high elevation—the gaze is far-reaching, giving one's eyes a taste of Zion's temples *and* plateaus.

The mountain has 623' of prominence.

RT Mileage: 4
RT Elevation Gain: 1,500'
Time Required: 3-4 hours
Latitude: +37.2938
Longitude: -112.8478
FA: Unknown
Etymology: Clear Creek, which runs west past Zion's east entrance before meeting Pine Creek at the east end of the big tunnel and flowing to its

confluence with the Virgin River in Zion Canyon, has its headwaters on Clear Creek Mountain.

Star Rating: **

The view to Zion Canyon from the summit of Smithsonian Butte

Getting to the Trailhead:

From the park's east entrance, continue east on UT-9 for 2.3 miles to the signed North Fork Road on the left. Turn left and follow the initially paved (turns to dirt after 5.4 miles) North Fork Road as it wraps around the west end of the mountain's southwest ridge. As it cuts along the north side of where the road crosses the ridge, look carefully for a trail on the right side of the road. Park in a pull-out (big enough for 1, maybe 2, cars) 100 feet past the trail.

Route: Southwest Ridge (class 1)

Hopefully you found the trail because the brush is otherwise awful and borderline impenetrable.

Anyhow—follow the shockingly good trail as it meanders up the ridge before petering out when it reaches an old road halfway up the mountain. Now the unpleasantness presents itself. Continue up the ridge, thrashing through nasty brush, until it finally eases off a few hundred feet below the summit. The views open and the going is pleasant and scenic.

Elephant Butte (6,812)

Elephant Butte and nearby Sandstone Butte, just to the north, make ideal bonus peaks while traveling to/from the sweet peaks of the Shunes Hollow area of Zion.

Elephant Butte has 672' of prominence.

RT Mileage: 2
RT Elevation Gain: 700'
Time Required: 1-2 hours
Latitude: +37.0682
Longitude: -112.8416
FA: Unknown
Etymology: In his *Utah's Canyon Country Place Names, Volume 1*, Steve Allen comments that this large sandstone butte looks somewhat like an elephant. I suppose it does.
Star Rating: **

Getting to the Trailhead:

Follow the directions given for Shunesburg Mountain to the point where the dirt road meets a side road heading east at Kane Spring. This junction is northwest of Elephant Butte and southwest of Sandstone Butte. Proceed up this side road to the area of the saddle between the two peaks and park.

Route: Northwest Aspect (class 1-2)

Hike cross-country toward the cliffs in the butte. Find then follow a good game trail that conveniently works through a break in the cliffs leading to the summit.

Sandstone Butte (6,508)

Sandstone Butte, which has a prominence of 328', is just north of Elephant Butte. It's a short scramble, and the views are nice.

Since the road passes right near the base of the peak, it makes a logical bonus peak for those committed to the sandy obscurity of Shunes Hollow.

RT Mileage: 1
RT Elevation Gain: 300'
Time Required: 1 hour
Latitude: +37.0855
Longitude: -112.8452
FA: Unknown
Etymology: The butte is made of sandstone.
Star Rating: ***

Tracy Foutz on the summit of Sandstone Butte

Getting to the Trailhead:
Follow the driving directions given for Elephant Butte. Drive north from the area of the saddle on a lesser dirt road that leads directly toward Sandstone Butte and terminates 100 feet from the slickrock at the base of the mountain. Park along (or before) the narrow ridge at road's end.

Route: Southwest Face (class 3)
Scramble up steep slickrock, weaving around as necessary to find ledges and slabs that keep the scrambling class 3. Be mindful of some exposure. Near the top, wander north to the highpoint.

Amidst a sprawling landscape of flattish pinyon-juniper plateaus and valleys practically as far as the eye can see, this rugged sandstone crag is somewhat unique to the area.

Eagle Crags – Ten Cent Peak (6,300)
Eagle Crags is the inspiring cluster of aesthetic crags one sees south of Springdale from the vicinity of the park's main entrance on UT-9. Ten Cent Peak is the name for the highpoint of the massif's eastern half. Ten Cent Peak and the actual highpoint of Eagle Crags are separated by a distinct saddle that can be readily made out from Springdale.

Although the final bit of scrambling to the highpoint of this narrow, exposed and awesome summit is high-quality, the awful bushwhack approach makes Ten Cent Peak a one-timer (for me).

DB on the small summit of Ten Cent Peak

RT Mileage: 7
RT Elevation Gain: 2,000'
Time Required: 5-7 hours
Latitude: +37.1288
Longitude: -113.0097
FA: Unknown
Etymology: On May 9, 2007, Ben Appleby (Athens, OH) and Nicholas Yaskoff (SLC, UT) climbed a route on the crag's east face and found a 1970 dime on a ledge. They dubbed the crag 'Ten Cent Peak'.
Star Rating: **

Getting There:
From the south end of Springdale, take UT-9 south to Bridge Road in Rockville. Turn south on Bridge Road and follow it 0.3 mile to the signed intersection of Bridge Road and Grafton Road. Here, the main road bends right while a lesser road continues straight and soon turns to dirt. Continue straight for 0.7 mile to a 3-way junction. Go straight at the 3-way (a high clearance vehicle is recommended beyond this point) and continue for 0.4 mile to a Y-junction. At the Y-junction, go straight and drive another 0.4 mile

to a parking area on your right. The unmarked trailhead is at the south end of the parking area.

Route: Southwest Ridge (class 3)

From the trailhead, follow the unmarked Eagle Crags Trail for about two miles to a point below the northern slopes of Eagle Crags. Noting the prominent saddle between the highpoint (right) and Ten Cent Peak (left), leave the trail and pick your way to the saddle. Be prepared to look for the 'best' route through some awful brush along the way.

Upon reaching the saddle angle left and work around blocks until you can gain the southwest ridge of Ten Cent Peak. A number of variations are possible. As you near the top, the route steepens. Getting within 40 feet of the summit, gain an exposed ledge on your left and walk 30 feet until you can scramble up to a small tree. From there, climb class 2-3 ledges to the tiny summit.

"Dalton Point" (4,892)

This unassuming peak near the Zion National Park boundary is the highpoint of the plateau above Dalton Wash, west of Crater Hill. It is a basalt peak with an interesting field of lava boulders atop the summit plateau.

Dalton Point has 352' of prominence.

RT Mileage: 2
RT Elevation Gain: 800'
Time Required: 2-3 hours
Latitude: +37.2172
Longitude: -113.1498
FA: Unknown
Etymology: N/A
Star Rating: **

Getting to the Trailhead:

Follow the directions given for Guacamole Trailhead to Dalton Wash Road. Follow the good dirt road for a mile or two to a point east of the summit. Park.

Route: East Face (class 3-4)

From Dalton Wash Road, hike west up steepening, rubbly slopes to the base of the basalt cliff band above. You may have to look around to find one of a handful of class 3-4 breaches in the cliffs. The breaches tend to require short sequences through small, steep problems.

Above the cliffs, continue up easier terrain (class 1-2) and then cross the jumbled, convoluted lava field just before the top.

The exposed traverse on the route to Smithsonian Butte

Smithsonian Butte (6,780)

Smithsonian Butte is the gorgeous red butte one's eyes are drawn to on the south side of the highway when approaching Zion National Park near Virgin, Utah. Well-protected by tall cliffs on all sides, one needs to look closely for a weakness, one that allows a mortal person to achieve the summit and its terrific views into nearby Zion Canyon.

RT Mileage: 5
RT Elevation Gain: 1,700'
Time Required: 5-7 hours
Latitude: +37.1140
Longitude: -113.0800
FA: Unknown
Etymology: Edward Dutton, the geologist on John Wesley Powell's expedition through Zion, named the peak after the Smithsonian Institute, which was sponsoring the expedition.
Star Rating: ****

Smithsonian Butte (right) and Smithsonian Butte-West (center) from the south. The route up the west summit essentially follows the left skyline. A traverse from the main summit to the west summit has certainly been accomplished, though I'm not sure of its difficulty.

Getting to the Trailhead:
From I-15 in St. George, Utah, follow signage north toward Zion National Park. Getting off I-15 at exit 16 (UT-9), follow UT-9 east toward the park. In Hurricane, Utah (9.8 miles from I-15), turn right onto Main Street. After 0.1 mile, turn left onto UT-59 and follow it about 13.9 miles to a good dirt road angling sharply off to the left. Follow the dirt road north for 1.4 miles to a dirt road paralleling a fence line on your right. Turn onto this decent dirt road and follow it for 1.1 miles to a fork. Veer left, then immediately left again, and continue for 0.6 mile to a turn-around at the end of the road. You'll be just west of a small drainage coming down from the southeast corner of Smithsonian Butte, though you may not see it through all the pinyon pines and junipers. High clearance vehicles should be able to make it to road's end.

Alternatively, from Rockville, Utah, one can turn onto Bridge Road and follow the paved road 1.6 miles to a dirt road on the left. The dirt road can be driven 6.0 miles to the fence line road you take on the final approach to the mountain.

Route: Southeast Ridge (YDS 5.3)
From the end of the dirt road, hike northeast for 0.75 mile to gain the crest of Smithsonian Butte's southeast ridge. Follow the ridge northwest until forced by steepening terrain and cliffs to drop east below the crest. Continuing along, parallel the ridge below the cliffs until you come to a large right-facing corner just before the cliffs become noticeably higher. Scramble up 30 feet of loose class 3-4 terrain to reach the bottom of a broken face 10 feet to the left (east) of the large corner. A 40-foot pitch of YDS 5.3 climbing takes you to a large boulder than can be used as a belay.

From the boulder, step around the corner, where you'll find an exposed narrow ledge with a small tree at its far end. Beyond the ledge, scramble up a short face/chimney and then wander to the summit a couple hundred feet above. Mostly class 2-3, the occasional short class 4-5 section (including a 12-foot crack with minimal exposure) should be expected.

To descend, retrace your steps. A boulder anchor can be used to rappel a 30-foot face to avoid the short face/chimney section adjacent to the narrow ledge. Additionally, upon reaching the boulder used to belay the YDS 5.3 pitch, one can continue down the ridge a bit to the east then do a short but attention-getting down-climb leading shortly thereafter to a final 50-foot rappel off a good tree.

A 60m rope is recommended for the route.

Smithsonian Butte-West (6,632)
This is a fine scramble to a great summit with outstanding views. The peak has 292' of prominence.

RT Mileage: 2
RT Elevation Gain: 1,600'
Time Required: 3-4 hours
Latitude: +37.1141
Longitude: -113.0859
FA: Unknown
Etymology: This is the west summit of Smithsonian Butte, which according to Steve Allen's *Utah's Canyon Country Place Names, Volume 2*, was named by Clarence Dutton of the Powell Survey in honor of the institution that funded the survey.
Star Rating: ****

Smithsonian Butte-West from the summit of Smithsonian Butte

Getting to the Trailhead:
Follow the directions given for Smithsonian Butte to the dirt road paralleling a fence line on your right. Rather than turn onto this lesser dirt road, continue on the main dirt road until another dirt road leading directly toward the base of our peak's west ridge comes in on the right. Turn onto this lesser dirt road and follow it 0.25 mile, bearing right at a fork, and park in a turn-around at road's end.

Route: West Ridge (YDS 5.0)

From the turn-around, follow a good trail that heads toward the base of the mountain. The trail will eventually peter out but you will continue up the steepening slope then scramble through cliff bands (class 3) to reach the rubbly slopes leading to the narrowing west ridge itself. Once on the ridge, scramble over and around obstacles toward the summit. The route-finding is interesting and not terribly difficult. Near the top, the crux is encountered: a steep, nasty chimney, which fortunately, is bypassed via an awkward (YDS 5.0) and squeezy crack 20 feet left of the chimney. Scramble on to the summit.

Climbing Zion Butte while Smithsonian Butte looks on in the distance

"Zion Butte" (7,259)

Zion Butte is a beautiful mountain located near the northwestern spur of Canaan Mountain. Infrequently climbed, the peak's northwest ridge is a delight. Climbing it one spring afternoon, I was fortunate enough to find a condor feather just below the summit!

RT Mileage: 4
RT Elevation Gain: 2,400'
Time Required: 6-8 hours

Latitude: +37.0708
Longitude: -113.0580
FA: Unknown
Etymology: We dubbed it Zion Butte for the phenomenal and unusual views one gets of the mouth of Zion Canyon from the summit.
Star Rating: ***

Getting to the Trailhead:

Follow the directions given for Smithsonian Butte to the good dirt road heading off from UT-59. Follow the dirt road north for 0.5 mile to a dirt road paralleling a fence line on the left. Turn onto this decent dirt road and follow it for 1.0 mile to a junction at an old fence line. Veering left then immediately right again, continue about 1.0 mile to a point near the toe of Zion Butte's northwest ridge. Look for a spot to park. High clearance vehicles can easily make it to the suggested parking area.

Alternatively, from Rockville, Utah, one can turn onto Bridge Road and follow the paved road 1.6 miles to a dirt road on the left. The dirt road can be driven 6.9 miles to the fence line road you take on the final approach to the mountain.

Zion Butte from the northwest

Route: Northwest Ridge (class 3+)

From near the toe of the northwest ridge, hike to a break in the cliffs near the eastern edge of the toe. A very short bit of class 3-4 scrambling should get you through it. Once through the cliffs, gain the crest of the ridge and start up. Although the going is initially elementary, eventually steeper, more craggy terrain will be encountered and route-finding becomes more interesting. With a bit of looking around, one can stay on or near the crest of the ridge all the way to the summit with scrambling no harder than class 3-4 in a few spots. It's typically much easier than that. About 2/3 way up, one will need to traverse right on a narrow ledge to avoid a significant cliffy crag lying along the crest. Just beyond the ledge, one gets into a sandy chute that leads back to the crest. The final summit crag can best be climbed via class 2-3 terrain under a large pine on its northeast side or an exposed traverse around its south side.

The view to Zion Butte from the summit of Canaan Mountain

Canaan Mountain (7,363)

Canaan Mountain is the sprawling, monstrous flat-topped mountain one sees just south of Zion National Park beyond UT-9. With a variety of stunning approaches, most notably the approach from Water Canyon (which is described here), the long, meandering stroll across the summit plateau to the highpoint takes one through lovely ponderosa forests, across acres of slickrock, past funky hoodoos, a striking notch in the mountainside known to locals as "The Box," and even past an old windlass. Back in the day, the windlass was used to lower timber from the plateau down to the "flatlands" below.

RT Mileage: 18
RT Elevation Gain: 3,000'
Time Required: 7-10 hours
Latitude: +37.0740
Longitude: -113.0375
FA: Unknown
Etymology: Like many named features found around Zion National Park, Canaan Mountain's name is Biblical in origin. Canaan was an early name for Israel.
Star Rating: ****

The mood is surreal and sublime at "The Box" on Canaan Mountain. The highly varied scenery and sweet spots like The Box make the Canaan Mountain hike a classic. If I didn't mention it before, during the right season the raspberries near the Water Canyon trailhead are a must-do pit stop along the route. You'll commonly see the local families harvesting the berries as the children wander about and play in the water.

Getting to the Trailhead:
Follow the directions given for Smithsonian Butte to the good dirt road heading off from UT-59. Instead of turning onto the dirt road, follow UT-59 another 7.8 miles to the town of Hildale. Turn onto Utah Avenue and follow it north for 2.9 miles (going straight at a stop sign at 1.9 miles) to the signed Water Canyon Road on the right. Turn onto the graded dirt Water Canyon Road and at 0.1 mile bend right to stay on the main road. At 0.7 mile, continue straight as the road branches off to the left. At 0.9 mile, go right at a fork; and after 1.1 miles, go left at a fork. After two miles from the pavement, the road ends at a parking area next to a small reservoir on the left. Water Canyon Road is generally in good condition, though winter and spring could make it challenging (or even impassable) at times.

Route: Via Water Canyon (class 2)
From the parking area, pick up the good use trail leading into Water Canyon. Soon entering the beautiful canyon, you'll bypass a couple of waterfalls on their left sides and eventually enter a lightly forested, vegetated area where the trail will begin to switchback steeply up to the rim above the canyon.

Once on the rim, the route-finding efforts pick up as the good trail disappears. Looking toward the northwest, note White Domes—a cluster of striking white hoodoos that stand out from the red and orange rock that is typical in the area—about a mile away. Hike toward White Domes then soon drop into a significant wash. Cut through the wash then either pick up the subsidiary drainage that runs directly up to White Domes or simply head up the slickrock slabs east of the drainage. Either way will work. From White Domes, pick up an old cattle trail (now used exclusively by hikers and ORV enthusiasts, apparently) and follow it generally west-northwest toward the highpoint, which is out of sight. Although you may lose the trail on occasion as you pass over slickrock areas, rest assured that it can be found again on the other side.

A bit beyond White Domes, you'll come to an area known as Black Rocks, where the rocks are darkly colored, in contrast to the lovely reds, oranges, and occasional whites you've been seeing. A short distance beyond Black Rocks is a prominent slickrock notch (known to some locals as "The Box"). The views here are terrific.

Beyond The Box, you'll soon come to the Windlass—the old cable works once used to lower timber from the mountain. Shortly beyond the Windlass, the trail starts to head more northerly toward Sawmill Spring. Instead of continuing to the spring, leave the trail and head cross-country to the northwest. The highpoint, though still not yet visible, is a hoodoo on the northwest edge of the mountain, right at the top of the mountain's skinny northwest ridge. The views from the summit are stupendous, far-reaching, and inspiring.

The Beehive (6,476)

This very nice, colorful dome near Hildale, Utah, allows for a wonderful traverse up its south side and down its north side.

The Beehive has 536' of prominence.

RT Mileage: 6-8
RT Elevation Gain: 1,800'
Time Required: 4-6 hours
Latitude: +37.0511
Longitude: -112.9408
FA: Unknown
Etymology: I suppose the peak looks a bit like a beehive—a little bit, not a lotta bit.
Star Rating: ***

Double-A nearing the summit of The Beehive along the south face route

Getting to the Trailhead:

Follow the directions given for Canaan Mountain to a parking area near the confluence of Water Canyon and Short Creek. The parking area is a surprisingly spacious dirt lot big enough for about 10 cars.

It's not uncommon to see the local Hildale/Colorado City families hiking around or riding horses in the area.

Route: South Face (class 3-4)

From the parking area, follow an old jeep track into Short Creek then wander that drainage north until Squirrel Creek comes in on the left, near the south toe of The Beehive. Hike up the left side of Squirrel Creek for a couple hundred yards until you can cross the drainage and scramble through the cliff bands above to reach the awesome slabby terrain of which the upper dome is comprised. Once above the initial cliff bands, wander beautiful slickrock slabs northward around obstacles to the summit. A fun, scrambling problem greets you at the summit block.

Route: North Face (class 4)

I'll describe this route as a descent option, since that's the only way I've done it.

From the summit, walk north down the slabs, keeping your eyes open for a groove in the ever-steepening terrain. Utilizing the groove and a handy network of adjacent narrow ledges, the base of the dome can be reached by class 3 scrambling (with just a class 4 move or two).

From the base of the dome, hike easy terrain north and then northwest toward the head of Squirrel Canyon, entering the canyon via the tongue of land that cuts between the canyon's two primary (north) forks. An old track can be followed down the canyon from here.

The Beehive from near the summit of Squirrel Peak

"Squirrel Peak" (6,310)

This easily overlooked but enjoyable peak rises above the confluence of Short Creek and Water Canyon, outside of Hildale. After a short, mostly harmless slog to the ridge crest, the remainder of the ascent offers neat scrambling in a sublime environment. In spring, the cactus flowers are exceptional. Keep your eyes peeled for the "Happy Face" rock during your ascent of the ridge. The views from the summit are extraordinary.

Squirrel Peak has 410' of prominence.

RT Mileage: 5
RT Elevation Gain: 1,300'
Time Required: 3-5 hours
Latitude: +37.0392
Longitude: -112.9472
Etymology: This surprisingly nice peak sits closely south of the head of Squirrel Canyon.
Star Rating: ***

Water Peak from near the summit of Squirrel Peak

Getting to the Mountain:
Follow the driving directions given for The Beehive.

Route: South Ridge (class 3)

From the parking area walk the road up Water Canyon to a point below the northern of two obvious rubble slopes leading up to the crest south of Squirrel Peak's summit. Leave the road, cross the creek at a suitable spot and wander up the rubble slope (class 2) to the crest. From here, scramble north along the remarkably nice ridge to the class 3 summit block.

"Water Peak" (6,860)

This peak (400' of prominence) forms the divide between Water Canyon and Squirrel Canyon. The peak is slightly southwest of The Beehive. Wander a bit southwest from the summit to get a close-up view of the eye-popping Water Canyon Arch, on the peak's upper southwest face above Water Canyon.

RT Mileage: 7-9
RT Elevation Gain: 2,200'
Time Required: 5-7 hours
Latitude: +37.0479
Longitude: -112.9537
FA: Unknown
Etymology: The peak is named for the super-impressive arch on its upper southwest face.
Star Rating: **

With friends at Water Canyon Arch

Route: North Slopes (class 2)

Follow the directions given for The Beehive to the head of Squirrel Canyon. Here, hike west a few hundred yards then angle left up mellow terrain that meanders south toward the summit. The summit block is class 3-4.

The cliffs of Zion

Appendix

Tales from the Backcountry

While heading to Mount Allgood, The West Temple dominates the backdrop

The Lost Lunch

One of the first significant peaks I climbed in Zion was The West Temple. With no published information to be found on routes to the summit (that were viable for me), I was lucky one day to stumble across a curious story a man had written about his ascent of the peak a decade earlier via a moderate technical route.

So one warm morning, armed with nothing more than some rope, water, food and three printed pages of the man's story for beta, a friend and I set out to climb what I felt to be the most impressive peak in all of Zion.

A few years later I told Ram how his story had been the catalyst for me to get up this noble, iconic peak. He enjoyed a good laugh then asked if I'd like to share it with others in my book.

Of course I would. So here it is:

Some recent talk about Zion peaks brought to mind an experience of mine, from years past. It was May of the year of the landslide that closed the main canyon road. 1995? Not being allowed to come down canyons into the Virgin, led to getting around to some projects on the back burner. We had seen the South Ridge of West Temple from many angles and we were very uncertain as to whether we could find a way up to the summit, but were willing to invest a day and take a peek.

We were a group of 4 on the trip, but Vladman had injured his foot badly enough that he felt a doctor needed to take a look. Ian, the Brit National who had been picked up hitchhiking and landed with us for the whole 9 day trip, agreed to be his driver. That left Steve "Cheeks" Levine and I.

We slept up on the Smith Butte and awoke at 3 AM and drove down into town to, I believe it is called Kinesava Estates now, and started hiking up, right out of town, at 3:45 AM with headlamps. Why such an early start you ask? Well, it had been awfully hot. Mid 90's every day and our approach route to the ridge was easterly exposed, so we thought it prudent to get as far as we could before our star started to melt us into the Kayenta slopes.

The total ascent, with minor ups and downs, is over 4,000 feet. A little "meat on the bone" on this hike. The sun came brilliantly over the Watchman as we approached the notch between West Temple and Mt. Kinesava. Really beautiful. We could look down at the tiny ants, ahhhh, I mean cars in Springdale as the early crowd started their day. We carried 5 quarts of water (not enough) and one of the good things about this route, is you come back the way you came, at least on the ridge you do. So, one can cache water on the way, lightening the load.

Once on the ridge, the climbing became interesting. The ridge has a little bit of everything. Slabs, towers to turn, knife edges, chimneys, spicy downclimbs, loose traverses, a climb down a tree, by a vertical wall, among other noteworthy spots and all on mediocre to poor rock. It is not sustained in its difficulty, but has everything from class 2 to easy 5th class climbing, all the way to the final pitch of Navajo rock, leading up to the high plateau. The ridge is double exposed, often with 1700 vertical feet of air on both sides. The good news is that the "drop" is not right upon you. There is usually 20-30 feet of angled slope, on each side before the world ends. A little easier on the mind. What is harder on the mind, is that the ridge appears to get harder and harder as you go. It does get harder, but not near as tough as it looks.

The final pitch loomed. Nervous. My stomach turned. The air smelled bad. I lightened my load. The smell of fear. On with the rock shoes. No rope brought and up we edged. Two parallel open corners were climbed. Up the first one half way, step right into the second, up some more and voila, the difficulties are over. Maybe 5.6 in difficulty. A stroll over the sandy manzanita flats and up the cap stone via a talus gully to the summit register. Lord, protect us on descent.

After the tough initial downclimb, the descent went uneventfully until just minutes from the notch. On the east side of the ridge top, I looked to climb down a sizable, slabby boulder and slip around the corner. Another of many exposed spots. Facing out, I crab walked down the boulder...The boulder slid several inches on the slab below it. Gulp! Double Gulp! I try and descend a bit more. Almost immediately, I feel the rock slip down once more. I stop. It stops. What to do? I have that calm adrenaline thing going. If the boulder goes, I take a ride steeply down 20 feet and off into the abyss. I note a ledge to my left. I make up my mind. As stealthily as I can, I launch the few feet out to the side and come to rest, standing and facing in on the ledge. The boulder slides and off the side it goes. What a racket...and the smell of rock turning to dust. Relief.

The step up, to the ridge is easy, so I...Something has a hold of me. I look down and see a small branch of a small juniper tree has entered my leg right along side the shin. It has slid along between the shin and my skin and out the other side just beyond the other side of my shin bone. Distance between entry and exit wounds is about one and a half inches. The branch is still attached to the tree. The bark is piled up against the entry wound. The branch is sticking out the exit wound about 3 inches. Sucker has got a hold of me. I try to slide it out. No go. Next, I reach down and snap the branch. Then I climb up and show Cheeks the "arrow" through my leg. He has a look of bemusement. On safer ground, I slide the branch out, pour some disinfectant on it and proceed. Not a problem. Feels a bit like a minor bruise.

Down, down, down we go. Try a different route down. It takes us to the cemetery and down to the Pizza Noodle restaurant. We get there at 12:45 PM. Ahhh, those early starts. Cheeks and I, on the patio, under the umbrellas, sipping a couple of beers, for an hour or so. Vlad and Ian return from Hurricane and join us.

Naturally the tale gets told, to the enjoyment of my pals. Upon describing the snapping of the branch and showing my battle scars, we all hear a retching sound from behind us. I turn and stare fully into the eyes of an attractive middle aged woman, sitting alone with her lunch. The look on her face, I took for horror. Time stood still for a second, as we all looked at her and she at me. Then she retched hard and her jowls puffed out hugely. Her look changed to one of panic, as tears came down her face. Her jowls deflated and she gulped. Closed her eyes. Paused for a second....grabbed her tray and ran for the door, retching all the way. We stared after her in silence for what felt like a long time.............. and then burst into laughter. We really did feel badly for the poor lady, but, you know, it was way too funny.

After lunch, more beers and an afternoon of swim and sun at the Pine Creek swimming hole. Do hope she got a doggy bag for her lunch.

~Ram

Mountain of Mystery

My friend and outstanding Zion backcountry partner Sarah Meiser (www.13ergirl.com) joined me on the second ascent of Mountain of Mystery (after my earlier failed attempt with another highly talented crew in June 2009). Sarah was kind enough to share her write-up of our November 2010 outing:

Mountain of Mystery (6,565 ft)
Descent via Orderville Canyon
Zion National Park
Partners: CP & Kevin

Mountain of Mystery...the name alone is enough to capture the attention of any respectable peakbagger. How could one's curiosity not be thoroughly piqued? For me the draw is intensified by the fact that the Mountain of Mystery is situated in the heart of my beloved and already innately mysterious Zion National Park. I'd eagerly listened to CP speculate about this enchanting summit on hikes in the past and when he recently told me he was ready to pull the trigger on another attempt I just couldn't help myself. A last-minute emergency trip to Zion was devised and Kevin quickly signed on board.

The history of the Mountain of Mystery is almost as good as its name. According to local Zion gurus only a single party has ever reached the summit and they had quite an epic adventure. Very long ropes were used to do a 300 foot rappel on the approach and bolts were installed on the descent to rappel 700 nearly vertical feet in a previously unexplored canyon. The party of two was forced to bivy for a night during the undertaking.

CP's done plenty of poking around and has reason to believe that there may be an alternative approach that does not require absurdly long ropes or a bolt kit. His proposed route will put us in five different canyons, involve a lengthy car shuttle, and require wetsuits. This time of year daylight hours are somewhat scarce so speed and efficiency will factor heavily into the equation. Furthermore, our success is contingent on the existence and climbability of a dead tree which, if it's still there, has been wedged almost vertically in the narrow canyon for more than 30 years! Without it upward progress is hopeless and it's game over. A report from the late seventies by a party who did not reach the summit references using this tree. Would you believe CP verified it was still there less than two years ago?!

Kevin and I pay a visit to Zion Adventure Company to rent wetsuits; neither of us have worn one before. The girl fitting us clearly instructs us that the zipper goes in the back but being sleep deprived from driving all night through a snowstorm I screw it up regardless... and upon walking out of the dressing room with the suit on backwards who do I run in to? Tom Jones: employee, master canyoneer, guidebook author, father of Imlay Canyon Gear...and incidentally one of two men who have stood atop the Mountain of Mystery. "Zipper goes in the back," he says. I play the role of dumb noob, pretend I don't know who he is, and retreat back to the changing area.

After our wetsuits are sorted out Tom seems slightly disturbed that we can't give him a straight answer about what canyon we plan on doing. The fact is we're not sure ourselves! Kevin finally lets it out of the bag that we are conspiring with CP to climb the Mountain of Mystery. Tom's reaction is a little hard to read; he seems surprised and a bit concerned. We chat for a few minutes but Kevin and I know so little about our intended route at this point that we can't satiate his curiosity.

Thanks to DB's help the car shuttle is greatly simplified. She drops CP, Kevin and I off in darkness at the eastern edge of the park boundary and we cruise the standard approach to popular Mystery Canyon by headlamp. Two miles of flat trail fly by and then the terrain roughens dramatically as we begin descending into Mystery Canyon. It feels good to be making such progress before the daylight clock has even started ticking.

Near the point of non-reversibility of Mystery Canyon our route exits via a bushwhack and makes a long and convoluted excursion in an attempt to avoid the 300 foot rappel executed by the first ascent party. We descend some obscure, mossy, aptly-named canyon known as "Not Worth It" in its entirety and find ourselves in famous Orderville Canyon. No time to gawk now though. Strolling around the corner into "Monolith Canyon," another small, mossy slot that parallels "Not Worth It" and also drains into Orderville, we stash our wetsuits and finally begin to gain elevation instead of losing it.

"Monolith Canyon" presents several interesting obstacles. At one point we find ourselves climbing a steep class 4+ dirt and pine needle slope and welcome the security of the rope. At another point I squeeze and thrash my way up through a very tight slot and belay/haul CP and Kevin up through a wider but more difficult one nearby.

The key dead tree is indeed still in position and it's in relatively good condition to boot! A 5th class climb up this log is the key to overcoming a 30 foot overhung drop in the canyon. It's intimidating to say the least. CP takes up the lead, protecting the pitch in true Zion form. He ties some webbing tightly above a knob in the trunk and then slings a little bush up high. The nubby knobs here and there along its length, although small, make surprisingly secure footholds. High up the walls of the slot start to offer some help.

Happy to have nailed the approach we take a snack break in upper Monolith Canyon and then turn our focus to solving the next part of the puzzle: finding the start of a ledge system that reportedly leads out of the canyon and toward the mountain's north ridge. With seemingly vertical walls towering overhead such a well placed ramp seems highly unlikely but we explore around and find what seems to be the only possibility. The ledge starts out wide and full of trees and pine needles. Life is good.

The fuzzy feelings subside however when the friendly ramp peters out and leaves us on an extremely dirty face of sorts below the north ridge. Extreme care is in order; the slope is steep and I don't think scrambling can get much dirtier than this. I pick my way onward behind CP thinking to myself that the angle has got to relent soon but the opposite keeps happening. The exposure below combined with the dirtiness of the scrambling is getting pretty intense. I reach my threshold and ask CP for a belay up one short section. Kevin's more than ready for one as well.

Soon we're more or less on the north ridge but we find it's actually not much of a ridge at all really. For the most part we pick the brushiest line upward because the bushes and trees offer the best protection against certain death in the void below. We belay ourselves on branches as we bash our way through the middle of little thickets. CP and I are enjoying the sicko scramble and are delighted with the unfolding of this highly implausible route. Kevin on the other hand doesn't seem nearly as amused and is ready for this craziness to end.

A short, dirty low 5th class pitch is eventually all that remains between us and the summit plateau. CP tosses the rope around a tree above for protection and then announces a few moves later that he's off belay. The pitch is easy but it's part dirt, part tree, part poor rock.

There are two summits on the summit plateau. We've topped out near the northern one but the true summit is still more than a quarter mile to the south. We begin casually strolling between manzanita bushes on the wide plateau but near the saddle it pinches in to form a fairly narrow ridge and a highly exposed traverse gets our full attention.

The final summit area looks difficult and the first ascent party reported roping up for some 5th class climbing here but CP thinks he's spied an easy weakness on the south side during his recon work. We circle the base of the summit cliffs and eventually find a short, low 5th class slab made easier by aiding up through a sturdy bush. At last, the top!

The views from the summit aren't anything special but that doesn't matter because we can't stick around anyway. We're on a tight schedule and still have our work cut out for us. We rap down from the summit plateau as well as the spiciest spot of the dirty face below. Various rope and partner assist tactics are used to overcome a few obstacles on the way back down "Monolith Canyon." Decent anchors aren't readily available or obvious but we manage.

The canyon spits us back into Orderville and the three of us change into wetsuits and prepare for the wet canyon ahead. I'm really excited to be in my first canyon with flowing water despite the fact that it's mid November and the air temperature is in the mid to upper forties. The canyon is beautiful and mellow. A handline is in place at the most difficult drop. Some pools are avoidable and others are not. The water is never more than chest deep. We move at a quick pace to stay as warm as possible and soon we're brushing arms with tourists in down jackets on the paved path back to the parking lot where DB awaits our arrival.

Groovy, man!

South Guardian Angel

The Year of the Angels

Although I've only once crossed paths with Bob Sihler (on a glorious outing into the Zion backcountry), I've observed in this man a passion for climbing rugged, inaccessible mountains. I asked Bob, who has made clear his love of Zion, if he'd be interested in composing an essay on some of his time in the park. He was delighted to put this together:

On a warm, bright afternoon in April 2008, while my wife hung out with a book in the sun, I set out to climb Tabernacle Dome with no beta other than a topo map on which I had noted some possible nontechnical routes.

I failed.

Lingering ice and snow on some of those routes, and difficult rock, left me unprepared and unable. Making matters worse, I at one point slipped on a patch of ice in a drainage and fell on my shoulder so hard that I could barely lift my arm for the next 24 hours. In fact, the pain lasted for several days.

As I walked back to the car that day, beaten and sore, I knew that I would have to return and find the right way up. And I also knew I needed to climb the South Guardian Angel.

Undoubtedly, I had seen South Guardian Angel many times before during the drive between St. George and Springdale, but until that day, I had not looked upon it knowing its name. but as I explored multiple ways to try accessing Tabernacle Dome's summit ridge, there was a moment when I struggled up an icy slope to reach a saddle that, disappointingly, proved to be another dead end but at the same time gave me a stunning view north to an isolated, spectacular peak that, after a quick check of my map, I realized was South Guardian Angel.

"What's in a name?" Shakespeare famously put those words into the mouth of one of his doomed tragic heroes. Sometimes, in the climbing world, a name can be reason enough to climb a peak, even to become obsessed with it. When the peak itself is elusive and spectacular, the obsession becomes deeper. Thus it was for me with South Guardian Angel and its sibling North Guardian Angel, which is technically harder but quite a bit easier to reach.

Zion's Kolob Terrace country lacks the sheer grandeur that comes from the narrowness, colors, and big walls of Zion Canyon. For most people who even know of it, it probably is little more than the gateway to the Subway. Much higher and a good bit cooler than the canyon, the Kolob Terrace area has a montane feel, and, while lacking the mob-drawing power of Zion Canyon, it boasts what the canyon lacks for the most part: stand-alone peaks that rise from the earth like sharp teeth.

And out in Kolob Terrace world, the two that stand out the most are the Guardian Angels. True to the name, they loom as sentinels over a vast complex mostly devoid of trails and other marks of human usage.

Four years—that is how long it took for me to get to those summits. Actually, I had my first shot in 2011. My wife and I hiked to the overlook at trail's end of the Northgate Peaks, and then I climbed both peaks while she waited. North Guardian Angel was so close, and I wanted to climb it so much, but I knew that was asking more of her patience than I had earned.

A year later, in April 2012, we were back, and that time I climbed the standard northeast ridge route on North Guardian Angel. Accounts of the quality of the route were not inaccurate; although it was easier than I thought it would be, there was still a lot of scrambling and some interesting exposure and route-finding choices. Further, the summit register was a minor gem. In it I found entries by several people I knew. Cool!

Despite all that, it was only bittersweet, for the best was also the worst: the incredible view of South Guardian Angel across the dark, deep defile of the Left Fork. A taunt was what it was.

Anecdotal evidence suggests that South Guardian Angel is one of those peaks that engenders more failures than successes. While it is only a Class 3 peak, the getting there seems to be the problem because the approach can involve three or more of the following: swimming, a Class 5 downclimb (and upclimb on the return), hours of exposure to the sun on rock radiating the heat, a dirty and awkward Class 4 section, and the need to spot an exact landmark or completely miss the crucial key to the route.

Regardless, I made it out there one July morning, against all advice, and became almost drunk on the excitement of seeing the summit within view and soon afterward actually standing upon one of Zion's, if not most difficult, at least most complicated and elusive summits.

Up there, I read the sparsely signed register. I looked north and saw a view of North Guardian Angel that only a handful of people see in any given year.

Not wanting to leave but knowing that I had to, I began the return journey.

My heart is split among two peaks in the Zion backcountry.

And I will keep going back to find those pieces and put them together again or to climb so many other peaks that my Guardian Angels become wispy memories.

Let it be the latter.

For it is in that endeavor that I plan my next trip to Zion even as I write this.

Climbing North Guardian Angel

The mighty Sentinel

Twice the Spice on The Sentinel

Here's a little story I wrote for the first edition of this book from an April 28, 2007 attempt on The Sentinel:

An Internet acquaintance of mine named Dow Williams, a man who'd had the pleasure of enjoying the last however-many years climbing in the beauty of the Canadian Rockies, was moving to St. George and wanted to get out and explore a bit of Zion. A self-proclaimed Zion guru, I was to be his host one day.

(But, geez! Does this guy even know what I'm about?!? This isn't Yosemite; this is Zion—a land of choss, a land of heavy brush; a maze of choss and heavy brush.)

Okay, brother, let's do it!

Meeting up one fine spring morning, I tell him that I want to climb The Sentinel. There'd been rumors of a class 3 summit route that had been found back in the 1930s but apparently no one had since been able to piece it together...or taken the time to try. Dow was all for it. Apparently he didn't know any better.

Welcome to Zion!

We started out on the Sand Bench Trail, but soon left and started working up a loose slope to the mouth of a chute that dumps out near the base of the mountain's east face. Gaining the chute, we climbed through a couple of short 4th and low 5th class problems. Before we knew it, we were covered in cactus spines and filthy red dirt, but at a sort of saddle high on the mountain. On the other side of the saddle was a small hanging valley,

Dropping into the valley, we climbed into a nasty, horribly loose and dirty chute that took us to easier ground leading to the base of a few-hundred-foot cliff just below the summit. Out came the rope, for we needed to work through a few minor problems that led us to...

...We were a hundred feet below the summit and staring up at three options. The leftmost was a flaring crack/chimney problem that required large gear, something we didn't have with us. The middle option was a stunning crack that appeared to take multiple pieces of small-to-medium gear, something we didn't have with us. The right option was the easiest—a short, crumbly wall of white sandstone next to a huge ponderosa that was perched over a monstrous abyss. The wall was more or less unprotectable, and would require a ton of nerve—something we definitely *didn't have with us.*

And so we collected ourselves, gave up, and started back down the mountain. Humbled.

A class 3 route up? Nope. It eroded away years ago.

On the descent, Dow shared with me that he'd climbed hundreds of fabulous (and often frightening) crumbly alpine routes in the Canadian Rockies, and rarely (if ever) turned around below the top. But he wasn't up to the challenge of this one. Too loose, too brushy, too cactus-choked. Too filthy, rotten dirty...

I say again, Welcome to Zion!

Since, Dow, a man who's let me dirty the sheets of his spare bedroom on many occasions, a man who's helped me through at least one terrifying jam in the mountains (including one just up the road on The Organ), a man who's inspired me, a man with whom I've broken bread, has become a good friend.

In spring 2008, a friend of mine and his partner took 30 hours to complete a new route on The Sentinel. From the top of their route, they traversed and gained the point where Dow and I had turned around just below the top. Confronted with sketchy climbing, they installed a couple of bolts and aided through the final difficulties that led to easy scrambling through the final cliff in the summit cap. In light of this information, my trusty and insanely fit partner Rick Kent and I headed out in September 2008 for another go at the mountain. Yet again, the summit proved elusive. I don't have a good excuse for our failure, but I'll say that it had everything to do with nerve and choss.

En Route

Jeff Branin, whom I met on G2 and have since enjoyed many hours in the slickrock backcountry of Red Rock Canyon, has always wowed me with his knack for language. He has a gift for storytelling, not unlike my pal Ram, but with a different flavor. Hailing from North Carolina, he gets to the Park once or twice a year to explore and climb mountains, to get off the beaten track. When he's not in Zion, he's dreaming of slickrock and obscure peaks, swell views, and generating sweet memories. And writing stories like this:

"The Doorskeepers of Zion,
They do not always stand
In helmet and whole armour,
With halberds in their hand."

--Rudyard Kipling

Mr. Kipling actually passed thru Utah on a train, but as far as I know he never visited what would become Zion National Park. Nonetheless with four lines of verse he assays the mounts that draw our gaze as we, the oh so many, roll thru Springdale. Kinesava, The West Temple, Mountain of the Sun, The Sentinel, The Watchman, G2, all on guard, all resolute, all so...wait a minute. G2? Where'd that come from? Hardly a lofty name and yet G2 defends in place and in line with Bridge, Watchman, and the rest.

G2, climbed it with CP and DB. Like I stepped into a Star Wars setting. Climbed it with bomabro and luvs_to_hike. Handles right out of a Google forum. Climbed it with James. No AKA for him. Our sextet was an ad hoc group having assembled in the parking lot at the end of the Zion tunnel, some of us meeting each other for the first time. G2 was new to most of us as well. Only one account of a prior ascent was known. Beta was slim. We sought the back door to this doorkeeper and the front door to adventure. We headed south and west and headed south and west again. Up and down and across. Zigs and zags. Frictioning up slickrock chutes and dancing across sandy landslide-y slopes. Summiting was sweaty and sweet.

Lot of laughs on the way. Mostly on the way back down. Courtney wore a ram's discarded crown. I found a balloon and gave it to Tanya. Anniversary or birthday, I'm afraid I forget. I remember a conversation we collectively had while resting right before Hepworth. We were about to cache some water. Courtney recalled a previous exploration not all that long ago that included a stashed canteen or two above nearby Gifford Canyon. Unfortunately, when they got back they discovered their stores had been stolen. Imagine that, rustling water.

"The first step ... shall be to lose the way."

--Galway Kinnell

Eagle Crags reign across the street from Zion. Just a short drive across the Bridge Street bridge in Rockville and up a dirt road hill gets you to the BLM trailhead. Three miles later on a well-constructed trail you arrive at the base of the Crags and find yourself looking onward following the alluring line of side slopes and cliffs and wondering why the trail itself doesn't go on.

That's how it went with me the first time. Years went by and I went back and this time a faint trail seemed to continue on. I followed, but it soon petered out. More years went by and eventually I read about a traverse between Hildale and the Crags. For a third time I rocketed thru the official Crags trail and then ratcheted my way thru the sideways trials of endless gullies and ravines before reaching a stock trail that ascended to the lower rim lands of Canaan Mountain.

These old stock trails always amaze me. All the backbreaking work that had to be expended to make that route go. There's one over by Cave Knoll that's been hewn into slickrock slopes. One time in the Swell I hiked up to the top of Horse Thief Trail in time to watch three planes take off from the airstrip below. Horsepower on display.

When you get to the top of the stock trail, it's trail's end. Until you get to Sawmill Springs and the old logging roads, it's just you and dead reckoning. There are features, drainages and high points, but close your eyes, turn around a time or two, and the view can be disorienting. Or still inviting. "Extend the limits," my ol' Professor Mitchell once said in Lit class. I think he was extolling Picasso (or more likely life itself). Which leaves the rest of the day to summit Canaan and/or explore the kaleidoscope landscapes en route. And the end of the day with canteens and gumption near empty, there's the search for that sole escape, the stock trail down thru cliffs, and the question that hovers when the exit is lost, "Now what?"

"The universe is made of stories, not of atoms."

--Muriel Rukeyser

First mountain I scrambled up was Cadillac in Acadia National Park. You can drive to the top, but my brothers and I took the trail from the campground. We were young and found the trek to offer uncivilness which was to our liking. Climbing the ledges high on the ridge we waved across to a solo hiker on Dorr. He waved back. Half century passes and I still feel that rush of camaraderie.

The hike to Cougar Mountain in Zion starts off civilized. From the trailhead a good route leads all the way to the start up Trail Canyon. No trails in Trail, just trials. Actually, just avoid the quicksand. The drainage eventually turns to slickrock and above that the plateau is wide open before you. Cougar Mountain is wide and long and you can wander and wonder with audacious views to all those doorkeepers. Arches and hoodoos also compete for attention. Miles from the start the summit is gained with a cairn marking the spot. I like summit cairns. There's that companionship of sharing a long trek with those who preceded who also took the time to mark the occasion.

The occasion of my first hike in Zion was after a fight with my brother Jon over a skillet of fried potatoes. I chose for some reason to hike the Sand Bench Trail. In June. Hot, yes, and the trail reeked of urine and worse. Final indignity: wrangler leading tourists on horseback asked if I was lost.

Later in the cool of the evening my brother and I hiked to the Emerald Pools and the next day drove on to the Grand Canyon where we got drunk and forgot about the fight. I didn't forget Zion. I came back the next year and the year after that. And I come back again and again like this past spring. And in the fall I hope to be once again en route.

To Dispel a Myth

In the course of preparing this edition, I began an e-mail correspondence with Dan Stih about his many and varied impressive accomplishments in Zion. Since the late 1990s, Dan and his various partners have quietly wandered about Zion, boldly and skillfully climbing some of the hardest and most remote mountains in the park. Dan's impressive resume of Zion first ascents includes The Sundial, Altar of Sacrifice, Meridian Tower, The Bishopric, Inclined Temple, Ivins Mountain, and others. And so in the course of chatting him up about his eventual traverse of the Towers of the Virgin, I asked about the persistent rumor that a French party had been the first to not only climb The Sundial and Altar of Sacrifice but to traverse the Towers of the Virgin from The West Temple to Altar of Sacrifice. In reply, Dan gave his thoughts on the rumor then shared a fascinating glimpse into the world of super-sketchy big peak climbing. Dig.

From: Daniel Stih
To: Courtney Purcell

Re: Zion summits
May 10, 2015

Hi CP,

That's funny about the French party thing. Maybe because my partner's last name was Raimonde? But I think that's Italian. I've heard the same thing. Our traverse, as far as I can gather, has never been repeated, nor the ascent of the Altar of Sacrifice by any other means (besides our second ascent). From what the locals tell me, a few years ago someone climbed the Three Marys in order to get a look at the rappel off The West Temple into the area near The Sundial—quite a climbing effort just to take a look at a rappel. They told me, "No way," meaning that there was no way they were going to attempt the rappel—smart lads. I'm not sure it will take bolts if you get into trouble. We didn't drill any. I used to think it was pretty easy but those were the days when a summit was worth that kind of risk. I guess it makes sense now why someone didn't do the traverse earlier or at least use that as access to the Altar. Then again, the concept of "traverse" is not something American climbers tend to think about. Maybe that's the French connection? The locals figured only Europeans would do something like that. The Brits, for sure.

There was a party that attempted the Altar by climbing up the back side of the area between The Sundial and The West Temple—it took them six days. "Hampered by lack of water" is what the note they left near The Sundial read—they did this in the late 80s. Back when we were getting permits for the original line on the Altar, the ranger told us a Japanese team with a film crew spent a month back there and didn't get anything done.

John Middendorf put a route up to the plateau called The Mountaineers' Route at least a year or two before we climbed the Altar. Why he didn't climb the Altar (or any of the other formations up there) was a mystery to me, except that maybe they were running low on water too and going extremely fast, so fast that they had to turn around as soon as they reached the top of the plateau. Middendorf was climbing with that ice climbing buddy of his from Alaska, doing speed tactics. We ran across evidence of their passage when we linked up with the last pitch or two of The Mountaineers' Route on our first ascent of the Altar. Instead of bolts they had placed a bunch of fixed bird beaks into the holes they drilled, creating a beak ladder instead of a bolt ladder. We tried not to use it.

Similarly, you can find in the records an ascent by Brad Quinn. Brad put an incredible aid line straight up from the ground just left of the Altar, also terminating on top of the plateau. I had wondered why Brad didn't go to the summit of the Altar. Perhaps he too was low on water. I think they were all exploration missions.

I will say that once Ron [Raimonde] and I got to the final summit formation of the Altar (in March 1997), things looked improbable. Middendorf and Quinn may have simply given it up as not possible. Ron and I, on the other hand, didn't understand that term. We knew we could climb anything. It was just a matter of time and to keep coming back for another try. We just had this belief, so we started climbing this crazy crack system and a huge, lose, bombay chimney that looked like it went nowhere…with huge loose rocks—it's not something you would go up unless that was the only way to go. What else were we to do? And as it turned out several pitches later we were on the top, much sooner than anticipated.

Ron has on the topo (at the visitor center) the "Couloir of Death" for the 5.9+ chimney section I lead. Near the top, the cracks were choked with ice and snow. I don't know how I climbed them. Loose snow, loose rock, no pro. I don't think I could do it today. I'm not the same climber, plus I want to live. Placing more bolts for pro will only get future parties so far. To get up the Altar, you have to want to get up the Altar more than anything else. Kind of like how you get up your first wall on El Capitan in Yosemite—lots of reasons to go down; you really have to want to go up.

A year after we did the first ascent of the Altar, I was in Zion with my parents, showing them the Altar (and the cairn we built on top of it) using the spotting scope outside the old visitor center. And the ranger kept telling my mom, "Yeah, but it's not as hard as El Cap, and no one will ever climb it [Altar of Sacrifice] again because it's all choss." My mom, of course, laid into him, asking why he didn't climb it. I told the ranger that you just can't compare the two. The magnitude of these formations—they are massive, loose, and not very forgiving.

Anyhow, this got me to thinking—which would be harder: to get up or get down? The difference is that on the Altar you can't haul; the clock is ticking. And you're on your own in regards to finding the way (up and down). Most people climbing El Capitan will study the topo to death and download the details to their phone. It's just not the same experience.

Dan

He e-mailed again a short time later:

From: Daniel Stih
To: Courtney Purcell

Re: Zion summits
May 10, 2015

I just realized why people think the first party was French—do you have copies of the original topos my partner Ron Raimonde drew of both the original ascent of the Altar and the traverse? He graded the whole thing using the ED system used in the Alps. We did this because of the mixed, alpine nature of everything. We had been visiting the Alps a bit, especially Ron. He would go over there every summer, dirt-broke, and just hang out trying to do odd jobs until I could come and we would go climbing. He soaked it all in. With the European way of grading routes, a final grade is not just a measure of the hardest move (like an American 5.10a, for example) but rather it's based on a combination of the hardest moves, sustainability, and the severity of the route. I am not proficient in the grading system. But all of our routes are graded that way. So if someone came across that in the visitor center you would certainly think the party was from Europe.

Just to clarify: the traverse was done after we did the first ascent of the same formations, ground up. The traverse was Ron's idea (again, he was the Alps man) and the brain behind that. It was me that pushed it, though. When we got to the top of The West Temple, I charged ahead and downward where it gets dicey to rappel. Before he could argue about the rappel I was setting up, I had the rope stacked and was throwing it. I was bent on going down. I chose the best bush possible and just did it. If he would have blatantly told me no, I would have probably said okay. We had safety checks built into our method by which if we both thought something impossible or too risky, we would probably not do it. But if one half of us did not object too much then the other thought it must not be too crazy, and we kept going

Ron and I were a good team. I was used to climbing with many different partners everywhere I could climb, from El Cap to the local sport crags. Ron, on the other hand, had kind of kept to himself, putting up new aid lines, always wearing his ice climbing boots; never his free boots. We would argue greatly about the way to climb something. I would bring in all the known and traditional methods; he would come up with new ones he thought of or got from the Alps. It was a combination of the two ideologies that got us up so many things. When one way didn't work, we were forced to consider something different. An example is the traverse, which we did in three days, just carrying what was on our backs. When we did the first ascent of the Altar, we fixed every rope we had. I was quite angry about fixing so much. Ron convinced me that that was how Everest was originally climbed—fixing rope—and that, after many attempts by us trying to climb it without fixed rope, fixing was the only way. I eventually gave in and let him have his way. So we fixed some rope on the first ascent. We cleaned up after ourselves quite well, though. You won't find a shred of anything left behind. And with the traverse I think we redeemed ourselves.

Dan

Patriarchs Traverse

A small group of highly-skilled and absurdly fast adventurers comprised of Buzz Burrell, Jared Campbell, and others, have quietly spent the last many years pushing the limits of endurance and creativity with such astounding projects as Zironman and Trifecta.

At blog.ultimatedirection.com, Buzz described Zironman as "an ingenious route, going from the west boundary of Zion National Park to past the east boundary via the most 'interesting' terrain. 'Zironman' was a fun way of saying the route involved climbing, running, and canyoneering, and it consisted of some iconic technical canyons as well as virgin country where apparently no one had been before." Over the course of the route, the group would descend Icebox Canyon, ascend North Guardian Angel and South Guardian Angel, descend Imlay Canyon, and then ascend Orderville Canyon to finish. Buzz, Jared and Ryan McDermott completed Zironman in 28 hours and two minutes.

Trifecta was the completion of the three sweetest Zion canyons—Imlay, Heaps and Kolob—in a single push. Buzz, Jared and Ryan managed to do the Trifecta in a day.

Buzz was kind enough to share his write-up of him and Jared's initial effort at another inspired project—a full traverse of the Court of the Patriarchs, from Mount Moroni to The Sentinel. Great, good stuff.

Jared [Campbell] conceived the idea of the Patriarch Traverse after our last trip there in October. The idea was to link all the summits in the cirque of the Patriarchs. Remarkably, while hundreds of great, good, and pointless link-ups have been done in mountain ranges all over the world, relatively little has been done in Zion NP. If completed, this would constitute a major alpine traverse, comparable in difficulty to some of the classics in the Sierra's and Alps. And rather than being obscure, the route is less than a mile from the main road, in full view of every tourist riding every shuttle bus. At the same time, this route is totally unknown, including if it could be done at all.

The initial ascent up Mt. Moroni went as expected. Some route finding, slow moving on shrubby, loose, cliff faces, and a rewarding view from the top (all summits in Zion could be described the same way). Jared had done a great job scouting with Google Earth, but that was just to gauge feasibility. From Moroni we surveyed the towering South Ridge of Jacob, our next objective in the Traverse, looming up in front of us. It looked like a real classic.

It wasn't. With Jared way out front, we scrambled unroped, making sketchy moves up dirty ramps, clutching bristly bushes in an attempt to stay in the crack systems, moving carefully over un-cemented white sandstone 'dinner plates' perched on smooth sandy slabs ready to slide off into the oblivion. I considered naming it "Choss Ridge." Maybe this ridge is a classic, but not in the sense one would prefer.

Summiting Jacob was nonetheless rewarding...more people climb Mt. Everest in one year than have ever climbed Jacob...and we walked across the characteristic flat summit plateau toward our next objective, Lady Mountain. Lady has a fabulous route up it—an unbelievably steep and exposed "trail" that was constructed by Zion Lodge to take tourists to the top—and then abandoned by the Park Service. This construction-abandonment combination creates the optimal type of route for the aspiring adventurer. We did one rap to get off Jacob, then joined the regular route/trail to the summit of Lady Mountain, 3,200' above the Valley floor.

We then walked across the completely flat Lady Mountain summit plateau discussing this odd and unique aspect of Zion topography. The plateau is a layer of sandstone more resistant than the others, and since it is horizontal, visually it looks like a flat wooded plain covers this part of the Park high country. As we looked over at Plateau Mountain [aka Cliff Dwelling Mountain], West Temple, and others, it seemed one could just jog over there in 30 minutes. The insanely steep, deep, and dark canyons that actually divide these summits from one another, and make passage between quite arduous, are completely invisible.

Until we intentionally enter them, which is what one does to accomplish a traverse. We got around the first problems, then rapped into the notch below Plateau Mt. Its East Face above us looked steep. We geared up, and Jared made an excellent lead up what turned out to be the nicest pitch of the day, a continuous 5.8 crack. Another pitch above that, and...it was 4:30 pm. A descent into Isaac Canyon was our objective for this initial foray, but it was on the other side of the mountain we were climbing, we had no idea how to drop into that canyon, had never heard of anyone ever doing it, the Google Earth images of that part of the route looked as smooth and steep as a toilet bowl, and the weather forecast called for 90% chance of rain that night and the next day.

I suggested we turn around. Jared is the best partner one could ever hope for; he is much stronger than I, but knows each person on the team must feel good about what's happening, so he transferred his prodigious positive energy and enthusiasm for finishing a goal into a reversal of direction that worked for me, and agreed.

I think that was a good thing. Taking a hot shower that evening and then sharing a bottle of wine his lady-friend Mindy had brought down was far more fun—at least for me; I'm not sure about Jared—than on-sight bolting a new rap route down a 300' blank face in the dark in the rain.

When conceived, we kept the Patriarch Traverse idea quiet. Didn't want the riffraff to go out there and nab it before we did, ya know? After our initial foray, we are unconcerned about this route being poached.

Bee Hive Peak

Although Bill Wright (co-author of *Speed Climbing!: How to Climb Faster and Better*) and I met only once (in spring 2008, on the upper west face of The East Temple, as I miraculously held back puke from an intense bout of nausea while simultaneously asking him about recent conditions on Great White Throne), for several years after we maintained a regular e-mail correspondence, as we share an illogical passion for climbing large, dirty mountains. I've always been inspired and humbled by Bill's casual approach to climbing stuff that terrifies me. For instance, I've twice failed on the filthy monster called The Sentinel, while Bill has soloed it.

Anyhow, Bill agreed to share the following excellent report on his climb of Bee Hive Peak, one of the very few objectives remaining on my Zion to-do list.

My trips to Zion have morphed away from pure rock climbing towards summit bagging, partly due to my own ambitions and partly due to my regular Zion partner, the Loobster's, waning desire for hard climbs, which encompasses most Zion climbing. But compelling summits have a strong pull on us, so this change in focus hasn't diminished my enthusiasm for Zion. One of the most striking is something called the Beehive, which lies above the Streaked Wall. The only listed climbs I could find went directly up the Streaked Wall and were A4 aid climbs. We had no interest in that—too scary and too technical for us—but it seemed like a route should go up the south ridge and we decided to take a look.

We started from the Zion History Museum and headed up steep, loose slopes toward a gully that split the Beehive massif from another blocky structure just to the east. We found a neat slot through the Red Band and then traversed over to the gully. The climbing up this gully was a mixture of scrambling, bushwhacking, and some low 5th class climbing, which we roped up for.

When we got to the saddle, we took a little break to eat and consolidate our gear into one pack. We found a fixed line hanging down off the wall here and we'd find others higher up, to what purpose, I don't know. Possibly for an easier descent for climbers topping out on the Streaked Wall. We roped up here and did an easy fifth class pitch. Above we scrambled up to a very steep headwall. The climbing here was too technical for us, though we saw another fixed line down a smooth dihedral.

We traversed to the left, to the edge of the wall, and around the south rib to the other side. We down climbed twenty feet there to a small ledge and found another partial fixed line and a more moderate angle with a reasonable crack. Getting to the start of the crack was probably the crux. Once at the crack, it accepted good gear and the climbing was no harder than 5.8. At the top of this pitch we found a fixed line leading hard to the left on a ledge system and then more fixed lines leading to the top of the steep climbing. We didn't use any of these old, super stiff lines, but followed their path.

Once atop this steep section we unroped and it was scrambling the rest of the way. First we climbed up 3rd class terrain to an intermediate bump on the ridge. This was equivalent to the top of the Streaked Wall. We still had to scamper up very cool, smooth, white slabs to the very summit. As always the case in Zion, the views were astounding. We hung out and ate lunch before starting down.

We reversed our route back to the top of the 5.8 pitch, but instead of rappelling down the wrong side of the rib, we traversed further around, following the fixed ropes, to where we found the bolted anchor that we had seen from below. We rappelled from this anchor, but couldn't pull our rope. I had to solo up 100 feet of 5.5, steep, semi-loose terrain to retrieve the rope. This was serious and scary and not recommended. I climbed up a big tree to the right (looking up) of the corner we rappelled down. There was a sling around this tree and now I know why. You need to rappel to this tree and then down, as it's the only way to get our rope to pull down.

The rest of the descent went smoothly. We spent 11 hours on the roundtrip, but never hurried and took our time finding the route. Our total ascent gained about 3000 feet, from 4000 feet to 7000 feet.

The bright and noble southeast face of The East Temple, which sits across Zion Canyon from Bee Hive Peak.

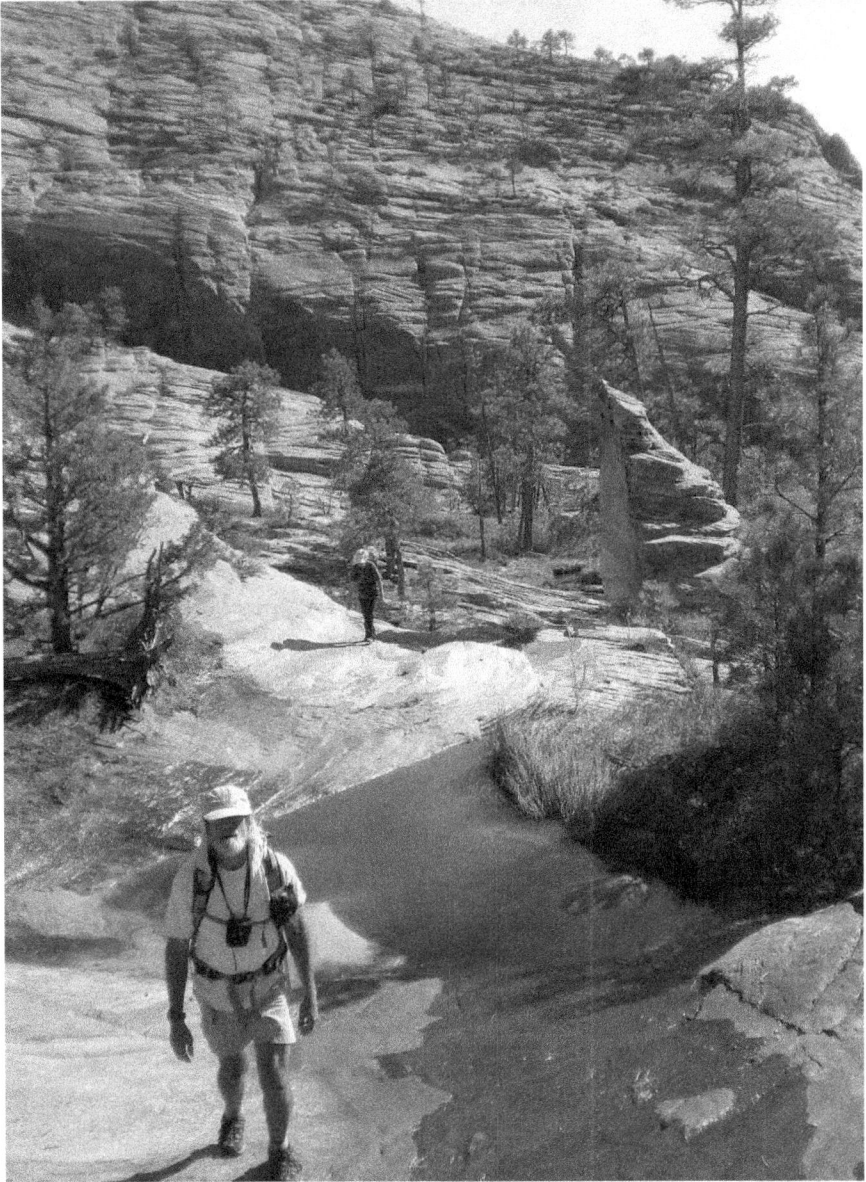

Wandering the backcountry of Zion National Park

Exploring Zion…and beyond.

Peaks Scattered about Southwest Utah

Snow Canyon State Park

Snow Canyon State Park is a small but charming and beautiful park in Ivins, Utah, near St. George. With solid rock climbing, good scrambling, lovely hiking (including to a lava tube), and nice camping, this is a must-visit place.

The aspiring Snow Canyon scrambler should be aware, though, that off-trail travel is generally prohibited or may require a permit. I suggest you inquire with park staff regarding the regulations concerning any of the routes described herein prior to doing them.

The peaks in this subsection are arranged from south-to-north.

"First Peak" (3,748)

This minor but enjoyable sandstone peak is south of Second Peak and southwest of Island in the Sky, above the main entrance to the park. Like most of the sandstone peaks around here, the route-finding is interesting.

-*Lat: +37.1844 Lon: -113.6508*
-*Class 3 via Southwest Face* ***

"Second Peak" (4,084)

This sandstone peak due west of Island in the Sky is a pleasant exercise in route-finding.

-*Lat: +37.1947 Lon: -113.6520*
-*Class 3 via East Face* **

"Island in the Sky" (3,820)

With 320' of prominence, Island in the Sky is a very interesting scramble on a neat feature. The summit area is sublime.

A north-to-south traverse of the mountain is easily one of the finest and most interesting scrambles in the region. Although the entire traverse is sometimes done without a rope, a 50m rope is recommended. Start the route at the northeastern toe of the mountain. Anticipate interesting route-finding, particular in the vast summit plateau maze, where people have gotten lost and required rescue.

-*Lat: +37.1940 Lon: -113.6429*
-*Class 4-5 via North Ridge* ****
-*YDS 5.2 via North-to-South Traverse* ****

"Balkan Dome" (3,616)

Balkan Dome is close to the highway, just east-southeast of Pictograph Mountain. It is a highly enjoyable exploratory scramble with neat views of the surrounding slickrock walls, slabs and domes.

It is an enjoyable exercise to meander to the top of this dome in the morning and then waste away an hour or two afterward watching climbers on the walls of Island in the Sky near Pioneer Names Trail.

-*Lat: +37.2032 Lon: -113.6463*
-*Class 2-3 from the highway* ***

"Pictograph Mountain" (4,217)

Pictograph Mountain is the next peak northwest of Second Peak. It is an outstanding exploratory route, with fascinating route-finding and interesting scrambling throughout the course of the route. With care, the canyon draining southeast from the summit can be used as a descent route.

Pictograph Mountain has 437' of prominence.
-*Lat: +37.2057 Lon: -113.6581*
-*Class 4 from the south-southeast* ****

"Cinder Cone" (4,875)

Cinder Cone has 375' of prominence. It is a short hike via a use trail from the highway.

-*Lat: +37.2422 Lon: -113.6288*
-*Class 1 from Highway 18* *

One of many interesting sections of the north-to-south traverse of Island in the Sky

Beaver Dam Mountains

The Beaver Dam Mountains is a 23-mile long range west of St. George, in the extreme southwestern corner of Utah, near the Arizona line. In addition to classic, rugged Mojave Desert ridges, peaks and canyons, the Beaver Dam

Mountains is home to Bloomington Cave. This cave is the fifth largest in Utah, mapped at a length of 1.3 miles and a depth of 240 feet.

(This cave chattering brings me back to my old spelunking days.)

The peaks in this subsection are arranged somewhat randomly.

Tabeau Peak (4,500)

Tabeau Peak sits near the Arizona-Utah-Nevada tri-border just outside of Mesquite, Nevada. Though some maps show the west summit as being higher, the east summit (where the summit register resides) appears to be a touch more prominent. The hike up the north ridge from the good dirt road at its base, while a bit of a slog most of the way, culminates in a fantastically aesthetic, steep class 4 scramble up the final face before the summit. The views from the top are immense.

From I-15 in far northwestern Arizona, leave the interstate at exit 8 (Littlefield/Beaver Dam) and head north for 9.7 miles. There, turn right onto a good dirt road (signed 'Woodbury Desert Study Area') that will take you to the base of the peak's north ridge.

-*Lat: +37.0123 Lon: -113.8726*
-*Class 4 via North Ridge* ***

Scrub Benchmark (6,786)

Scrub Benchmark is a high peak with stunning views. A 4WD service road picked up on the south side of the peak in Bulldog Canyon (southwest of Bulldog Pass) can be driven to a gate, where a pleasant hike leads to the highpoint.

Scrub Benchmark has 2,065' of prominence.
-*Lat: +37.0532 Lon: -113.8230*
-*Class 1 via service road* ***

"Zion View Peak" (6,835)

This is a short hike to a good viewpoint of distant Zion. The peak is approached from the service road leading to the top of West Mountain Peak.

Zion View Peak has 575' of prominence.
-*Lat: +37.1313 Lon: -113.8724*
-*Class 2 via Northeast Ridge from Hell Hole Pass* **

West Mountain Peak (7,680)

West Mountain Peak has astonishing views from its summit. A steep service road can be taken from the highway south-southeast of the summit and driven all the way to the top.

West Mountain Peak has 3,660' of prominence.
-*Lat: +37.1551 Lon: -113.8832*
-*Class 1 via service road* ***

Bulldog Knolls East (3,946)

Like its sister-peak to the northwest, this is a short hike from the car. Bolts encountered along the final summit ridge are from climbers coming directly up the vertical south face.

> The peak has 246' of prominence.
> *-Lat: +37.0287 Lon: -113.8640*
> *-Class 2-3 via North Face* **

Bulldog Knolls West (3,932)

This is a steep, short hike from the car, parking just south of the summit. Follow the driving directions given for Tabeau Peak to get to the vicinity of this peak.

> Bulldog Knolls West has 232' of prominence.
> *-Lat: +37.0312 Lon: -113.8687*
> *-Class 2 via East Slope* **

In the summit plateau maze of Island in the Sky

"Tahoari Peak" (6,295)

Tahoari Peak is northeast of Bulldog Knolls. It's a nice hike with great scenery.

> Tahoari Peak has 315' of prominence.
> *-Lat: +37.0370 Lon: -113.8297*

-Class 2 via South Slopes **

Pine Valley Mountains

The Pine Valley Mountains is the high, beautiful wall of mountains paralleling I-15 north of St. George.

The peaks in this subsection are arranged in descending order of elevation.

Signal Peak (10,365)

Signal Peak is the highpoint of the Pine Valley Mountain, a sprawling range that dominates the St. George area. A pleasant trail from Oak Grove (on the south side of the peak) can be followed to the crest, where you'll follow signage west toward (and beyond Further Water). The summit is southwest of Further Water. This is a very pretty area.

Signal Peak has 4,505' of prominence.

-Lat: +37.3195 Lon: -113.4922

-Class 1 via Oak Grove ***

Burger Peak (10,321)

From the north side of the peak, the Forsyth Canyon Trail can be followed to a point just south-southwest of the summit, where a short off-trail romp leads to the nice, craggy highpoint.

We once encountered a skunk on this trail—he casually wandered across the path in front of us, seemingly oblivious to our presence. Later, from the summit I ordered two tickets to BB King in Vegas for that night!

Burger Peak has 301' of prominence.

-Lat: +37.3254 Lon: -113.5011

-Class 2 via Forsyth Canyon Trail **

Peak 10,260 (10,260)

This minor peak is just northwest of where the trail to Signal Peak from Oak Grove reaches the crest of the range.

The peak has 320' of prominence.

-Lat: +37.3329 Lon: -113.4764

-Class 1-2 via Southwest Slope **

-Class 1-2 via East Slope **

Peak 10,194 (10,194)

This peak is west of Further Water and northeast of Signal Peak. It is a steep but pleasant side-trip from the trail to Signal Peak.

The peak has 294' of prominence.

-Lat: +37.3279 Lon: -113.4859

-Class 2 via East Slope **

Peak 10,177 (10,177)
This peak is closely northeast of where the trail to Signal Peak from Oak Grove reaches the crest of the range.

The peak has 397' of prominence.
-Lat: +37.3332 Lon: -113.4655
-Class 1-2 via North Slope **
-Class 2 via Southwest Slope *

DB on the summit of Mollies Nipple

Metropolitan St. George Area

St. George is the largest city in southwestern Utah. The greater metropolitan area has a population that exceeds 150,000. It was once the second-fastest growing area in the United States. As such, access to certain peaks within this quickly growing, heavily populated area is likely changed. It is possible that an approach or route I utilized years ago is no longer open to public access. Consult a map or other reliable resource to determine current access. Please stay off of private property.

(By the way, in a city with regrettably little good food, Benja Thai is an exception.)

The peaks in this subsection, which cover the immediate St. George area to Apple Valley, are arranged alphabetically.

"East Cinder Knoll" (3,700)

This small peak just northwest of downtown Hurricane is a short, pleasant hike.

The peak has 440' of prominence.
-*Lat: +37.1940 Lon: -113.3010*
-*Class 1 via South Slope* **

Gray Knoll (5,511)

This small cinder cone is close to Highway 59 near Apple Valley. Good dirt road lead to the base of the cone.

Gray Knoll has 331' of prominence.
-*Lat: +37.0775 Lon: -113.1444*
-*Class 1-2 from area roads* *

Harrisburg Bench (3,607)

This is a short, steep scramble from the road through Quail Lake State Park.

The peak has 387' of prominence.
-*Lat: +37.1790 Lon: -113.4000*
-*Class 3 via East Face* *

Hurricane Hill (3,620)

This is a 1-minute jaunt (literally) from Highway 59, just northeast of Hurricane.

-*Lat: +37.1814 Lon: -113.2750*
-*Class 1 from the highway* *

Mollies Nipple (4,650)

This eye-catching nipple near Hurricane has a nice use trail leading to its summit from near the mouth of Frog Canyon.

-*Lat: +37.1284 Lon: -113.2980*
-*Class 2 via North Ridge* **

Peak 3,180 (3,180)

This is a 10-minute roundtrip hike from near the police station and jail just off UT-9 outside of Hurricane.

The peak has 280' of prominence.
-*Lat: +37.1564 Lon: -113.4071*
-*Class 2 via Northeast Ridge* *

Price City Hills (3,090)

This is a very short hike from a short dirt road behind an industrial park.

The peak has 360' of prominence.
-*Lat: +37.0395 Lon: -113.5719*

*-Class 2 via gully southwest of summit ***

Red Hills (3,310)
A trail from the road leads right up and over the top of this little overlook near Pioneer Park. It's only a short jaunt, but a pleasant one with decent views.

-Lat: +37.1226 Lon: -113.5868
*-Class 1 via trail ****

Shinob Kibe (3,306)
A nice trail can be quickly hiked to the top from its beginning near the northwestern base of the mountain. I can't recall exactly what it was, but there's something sort of interesting on the top—perhaps some sort of aircraft signaling device?

The mountain has 576' of prominence.
-Lat: +37.1175 Lon: -113.4874
*-Class 1-2 via Northwest Face ****

"Sugarloaf" (3,068)
This is the sandstone crag everyone rappels from in Pioneer Park.

-Lat: +37.1154 Lon: -113.5794
*-Class 2 via trail ***

Sullivan Knoll (4,016)
This is the eye-catching cinder cone on the southwestern outskirts of Hurricane. It is also known as Volcano Mountain.

Sullivan Knoll has 648' of prominence.
-Lat: +37.1628 Lon: -113.3338
*-Class 1 via Northeast Slope ****

Washington Black Ridge (3,300)
The minor summit of this feature can be reached via a pleasant, nearly level hike from the local park to the southeast. Follow easy mountain bike trails toward the summit.

-Lat: +37.1583 Lon: -113.4729
*-Class 1 via trail ***

Washington Dome (3,300)
This is a short and easy peak with decent views of the St. George area.

Washington Dome has 404' of prominence.
-Lat: +37.1033 Lon: -113.4745
*-Class 1-2 from the north ***

Webb Hill (3,140)

This is an easy hike via the service road from the northeast. There are neat mountain bike trails all over this mountain.

The peak has 450' of prominence.
-Lat: +37.0636 Lon: -113.5727
-Class 1 via service road **

"West Cinder Knoll" (3,477)

This can be a quick bonus peak after East Cinder Knoll.
-Lat: +37.1867 Lon: -113.3190
-Class 1 via East Slope *

White Dome (2,850)

This very minor bump is just off River Road near the Arizona border.
-Lat: +37.37.0074 Lon: -113.5601
-Class 1 from the road *

Veyo Area

The tiny community of Veyo (population about 500) is north of St. George along Highway 18, on the edge of Dixie National Forest.

The peaks in this subsection are arranged north-to-south.

Veyo Volcano (5,239)

This old volcano lies just off Highway 18 south of Veyo. The peak has 619' of prominence.
-Lat: +37.3164 Lon: -113.6961
-Class 1 via South Slope *

"Veyo Peak" (4,900)

This obscure peak is a few miles south-southwest of Veyo Volcano. It has 320' of prominence.
-Lat: +37.2663 Lon: -113.7134
-Class 2 via North Ridge *

Leeds/Silver Reef Area

The tiny communities of Leeds and Silver Reef are located just off I-15 at exit 21, outside of St. George. A remarkably tasty ma-and-pa restaurant called Silver Reef Café, whose owner makes excellent, vegan-friendly salads for folks like me with plant-based diets, is a spot not to be missed—unfortunately, they're only open for breakfast and lunch. They're on the main drag in "downtown" Silver Reef.

The peaks in this subsection are arranged somewhat randomly.

Sandstone Mountain (3,860)

Sandstone Mountain is close to the Virgin River, southeast of Leeds. I've utilized a couple of different routes, both of which were approached from the dirt road to the northwest of the summit. The route-finding is fun and not particularly challenging.

Sandstone Mountain has 400' of prominence.

-*Lat: +37.2107 Lon: -113.3227*

-*Class 2 from the northwest* **

Peak 3,980 (3,980)

This is a pleasant hike across desert to a minor summit. The peak, which has 280' of prominence, is closely east of Leeds.

-*Lat: +37.2481 Lon: -113.3263*

-*Class 1-2 via Southwest Slope* **

White Reef (3,767)

This is a pretty peak above Leeds. The hike is short.

-*Lat: +37.2372 Lon: -113.3800*

-*Class 2 via East Face* *

Leeds Reef (3,620)

This small peak just off I-15 in Leeds has a residential road leading to its summit.

-*Lat: +37.2332 Lon: -113.3735*

-*Class 1 via road* *

Big Hill (3,820)

This minor peak is a trivial hike from the saddle it shares with Tecumseh Hill.

-*Lat: +37.2431 Lon: -113.3624*

-*Class 1 via West Slope* *

Tecumseh Hill (3,820)

Big Hill and Tecumseh Hill are minor summits along Buckeye Reef.

-*Lat: +37.2449 Lon: -113.3679*

-*Class 1 via East Slope* *

Leeds Benchmark (5,173)

This is a decent hike with nice views of the area. It's easily approached from the graded dirt road running along the base of the peak's north ridge.

The peak has 486' of prominence.

-*Lat: +37.2580 Lon: -113.3983*

-*Class 2 via North Ridge* **

"Point Marcus" (5,256)

This is a very pleasant hike to a summit with great views. It takes less than an hour for quicker types to make the roundtrip. The peak is accessed directly from the good dirt road heading to Oak Grove.

Point Marcus has 356' of prominence.
-*Lat: +37.2839 Lon: -113.3795*
-*Class 2 via lower West Face to Southwest Ridge* ***

Virgin Area

The peaks in this subsection are accessed from a paved road heading north from UT-9, a mile or two west of Virgin. The good road proceeds to the crest of the mesa above then becomes a graded dirt road that eventually leads out to Kolob Terrace Road near Left Fork Trailhead.

Hurricane Mesa (5,220)

Hurricane Mesa is the sprawling mesa towering over La Verkin. It has a large tower visible at the top. Like nearby Smith Mesa, the true summit of this mesa is off-limits (and inside a fenced, restricted area) but a good paved road takes you as close as you can legally get.

-*Lat: +37.2334 Lon: -113.2304*
-*Class 1 via road* *

Smith Mesa (5,900)

Smith Mesa is a massive, mellow mesa stretching from Kolob Terrace Road (on the east) virtually to I-15 on the west. Although the true summit is on private property, a graded dirt road gets one to within a short distance of the barely discernible highpoint. Please stay off private land.

-*Lat: +37.2904 Lon: -113.2171*
-*Class 1 via road* *

Grafton Area

The Grafton area is accessed from Rockville and UT-9, just outside the main entrance to Zion National Park. It seems somewhat absurd to include such cheesy summits when you consider their proximity to world-class greatness, but here you go.

The peaks in this subsection are arranged somewhat randomly.

Wire Valley Knoll (4,549)

This minor, north summit of Wire Mesa overlooks Grafton, Rockville and the Virgin River.

-*Lat: +37.1515 Lon: -113.0695*
-*Class 1 via South Slope* *

Wire Mesa (4,550)

The summit of this mellow mesa is easily reached from the Backcountry Byway running along its south side.

-*Lat: +37.1429 Lon: -113.0772*
-*Class 1 via Southeast Slope* *

Grafton Mesa (4,767)

Grafton Mesa is the first mesa west of Wire Mesa. The two are separated by deep South Wash. A mountain bike trail goes to the summit.

-*Lat: +37.1443 Lon: -113.0934*
-*Class 1 via South Slope* *

Mount Carmel Junction Area

Mount Carmel Junction, which sits at the junction of UT-9 and highway 89, is the first community one comes to when departing Zion's east entrance for Bryce Canyon National Park.

The peaks in this subsection are arranged somewhat randomly.

Peak 6,418 (6,418)

This peak lies south of UT-9, between the park's east entrance and Mount Carmel Junction. Peak 6,700 is to the northeast.

The peak, which has 318' of prominence, has a nice summit area with views toward Zion.

-*Lat: +37.2570 Lon: -112.7780*
-*Class 1-2 via Northeast Ridge* **

Peak 6,700 (6,700)

This is a pleasant hike to a nice, if somewhat forested, viewpoint. Remnants of the old highway (and a benchmark) are passed along the route to the summit.

-*Lat: +37.2725 Lon: -112.7597*
-*Class 2 via Southwest Ridge* **

Red Knoll (6,580)

This eye-catching summit, with 440' of prominence, is south of highway 89 and southeast of Mount Carmel Junction. A good dirt road leads south from the highway to within a short scramble of the top.

Although the north face is steep if tackled directly, it's easy enough to explore around its fringes to find a reasonable way to the top. Expect some loose rock.

-*Lat: +37.1555 Lon: -112.6353*
-*Class 2-3 via North Face* **

Kanab Area

Kanab is an interesting, little town along Kanab Creek near the Arizona border.

Crescent Butte (5,588)

This named peak is just north of the highway outside of Kanab. It can be easily combined with the feature's highpoint, Dishopan Hill.

-*Lat: +37.0434 Lon: -112.3478*
-*Class 2 via East Slopes* *

Dishopan Hill (5,626)

Dishopan Hill is the highpoint of the Crescent Butte massif. It has 334' of prominence.

-*Lat: +37.0449 Lon: -112.3414*
-*Class 2 via Northeast Aspect* **

"Cruiseliner Peak" (6,045)

Since I climbed this peak in a white-out, I have little concept of the route, other than that I approached it from the area between it and Crescent Butte. The route-finding (at least in the storm) was interesting and engaging.

Cruiseliner Peak has 551' of prominence.
-*Lat: +37.0523 Lon: -112.3259*
-*Class 3 from the southwest* **

Chronology of First Known Ascents

Since the topic of FAs and FKAs seems to get people uptight, I'll repeat what I said in the "Using this Guide" section of this book:

FA and FKA information is given based on available information. It is not necessarily presuming a peak was previously unclimbed; it is recognized that unrecorded ascents by Native Americans, early explorers, and/or other elusive souls who managed to climb these heinous summits without leaving a trace or record are possible. In an area with so little documented *peak* climbing history, I've tried to document what little we *do* know. It hasn't been easy; such information is hard to come by, and often ambiguous, as in the case of Zion's many big-walled peaks, where a first ascent of a wall does not necessarily mean that the party continued to the summit of the peak (which is my interest here). As such, the list below is heavy with error. If I failed to give credit to someone who came first (or otherwise completely overlooked someone's efforts), it's not because I intended to steal their thunder—it's because I didn't know about it.

In the spirit of preserving history, I have compiled the following chronological list of *known-to-me* first known ascents in Zion National Park. I have intentionally omitted information on summits in closed areas (or summits that cannot be reached without crossing closed areas), with the exception of certain peaks with mesa-top closures. I have also omitted many summits that have been climbed or would seem very likely to have been climbed though information on the first ascent was not available.

I encourage anyone with new or conflicting information to contact me so that the record can be updated.

A quick few words on first known ascents of named vs. unnamed summits: Unnamed summits have always been ignored; for some reason they're considered boring or unworthy. An official name legitimizes a peak, somehow making its profile more striking and its routes more classic.

Many of the park's named summits saw first ascents during the 20th century, though many more were not climbed until the early years of this century. Perhaps one or two are still waiting for an initial ascent. Perhaps.

Unnamed summits, on the other hand, have historically received very little attention, thus giving me and a few others free reign over the last decade to grab first known ascents of these unloved stepchildren. Like that rare parent who dotes over his fat, ugly kid to the dismay of his prettier siblings, unnamed summits get the lion's share of my attention in Zion and elsewhere; I've always rooted for the underdog and loved the kid who got picked last for the team. And yes, some of these ugly children remain unclimbed. For certain.

-Lady Mountain *(unknown party: 1924)*
-Angels Landing *(unknown party: 1924-25)*
-Great White Throne *(William Evans: June 27, 1927)*
-Cathedral Mountain *(Walter Becker, Fritz Becker & Rudolph Weidner: August 31, 1931)*
-The West Temple *(Normal Crawford, Newell Crawford and six others: 1933)*
-The East Temple *(Glen Dawson, Dick Jones, Homer Fuller, Wayland Gilbert & Jo Momyer: 1937)*
-The Sentinel *(Bob Brinton & Glen Dawson: 1938)*
-North Guardian Angel *(Arkel Erb: 1960s)*
-South Guardian Angel *(Arkel Erb: 1960s)*
-Bridge Mountain *(unknown party: 1965)*
-Twin Brothers *(unknown party: 1968)*
-The Pulpit *(+37.2843 -112.9470; Fred Beckey, Pat Callis, Galen Rowell, Eric Bjornstad & Hal Woodworth: April 15, 1968)*
-Mount Spry *(unknown party: 1970)*
-Lady Mountain-East Spur *(Curt Haire & Wes Hall: July 1975)*
-Church Mesa *(Steve Patehett, Phil Warrender & Dave Wilman: May 28, 1976)*
-Three Marys-Middle Mary *(Dave Anderson: May 1977)*
-The Organ *(Jim Beyer & Courtney Simpkins: 1978)*
-Timber Top Mountain *(William Forrest & William March: June 1980)*
-Red Arch Mountain *(Steve Chardon & Dave Jones: September 23, 1980)*
-Shuntavi Butte *(William Forrest & William March: October 24, 1980)*
-The Watchman *(Stacy Allison-Austin & Mark Austin: 1984)*
-Mount Moroni *(Brian Smoot & Les Ellison: April 1984)*
-Abraham *(John Middendorf & Walt Shipley: February 1990)*
-Isaac *(John Middendorf, Brad Quinn & Bill Hatcher: 1993)*
-"The Triplets" *(Steve Ramras: May 1996)*
-Altar of Sacrifice *(Dan Stih & Ron Raimonde: March 8, 1997)*
-"The Rotten Tooth" *(+37.2236 -113.0202; Dan Stih & Ron Raimonde: March 1997)*
-"The Broken Tooth" *(+37.2219 -113.0201; Dan Stih & Ron Raimonde: March 1997)*
-"The Witch Head" *(aka Batman; +37.2198 -113.0190; Dan Stih & Ron Raimonde: March 1997)*
-The Sundial *(Dan Stih & Ron Raimonde: March 1997)*
-"Rams Peak" *(Steve Ramras: October 1998)*
-"Cliff Dwelling Mountain" *(+37.2530 -112.9747; Dan Stih & Ron Raimonde: March 27, 1999)*
-Nagunt Mesa *(Kathy Dicker & Scott Cosgrove: October 2000)*
-Mountain of Mystery *(Brian Cabe & Tom Jones: 2001)*
-"Mount Allgood" *(Joe French & Bryan Bird: 2002)*
-"G1" *(Brody & Jared Greer: Spring 2005)*
-"Aires Butte" *(Dave Littman & Jeffery Herrick: Summer 2005)*
-"The Sanctuary" *(+37.2713 -113.0077; Joe French & Dave Littman: November 2005)*

-"The Fin" *(Courtney Purcell & Mark Beauchamp: May 27, 2006)*
-The Bishopric *(Dan Stih & David Everett: April 10, 2007)*
-"Gifford Peak" *(Dow Williams, Mike Cressman, Courtney Purcell & DB: September 22, 2007)*
-"Moqui Peak" *(Courtney Purcell & DB: 2008)*
-"G2" *(Joe French & Zach Lee: February 2008)*
-"Stevensworth Peak" *(Courtney Purcell & DB: March 29, 2008)*
-Meridian Tower *(Dan Stih & Dave Everett: April 29, 2008)*
-"The Hourglass" *(Courtney Purcell & Randi Poer: May 9, 2008)*
-"North Sentinel" *(Courtney Purcell & Rick Kent: September 20, 2008)*
-"No Mans Mountain" *(Courtney Purcell: October 25, 2008)*
-"The Hamster" *(Courtney Purcell: November 2008)*
-"Flagpole Mountain" *(Andy Archibald, Courtney Purcell & DB: November 15, 2008)*
-Jobs Head *(Courtney Purcell, DB & Andy Archibald: November 16, 2008)*
-"The Bodhisattva" *(Courtney Purcell & DB: November 24, 2008)*
-"Sneak Peak" *(DB & Courtney Purcell: January 19, 2009)*
-"Lady of the Cliff" *(Jared Campbell & Buzz Burrell: April 10, 2009)*
-"The Timeless Spire" *(Courtney Purcell: May 2009)*
-"Twin Peak" *(Courtney Purcell: November 9, 2009)*
-"Coalpits Peak" *(Courtney Purcell, DB, Sarah Meiser & Kevin Baker: November 15, 2009)*
-"Explorers Knoll" *(Courtney Purcell: April 11, 2010)*
-The Bishopric-West *(Courtney Purcell: April 17, 2010)*
-"Hop Valley Peak-South" *(Courtney Purcell, DB & Bryan Long: May 9, 2010)*
-"Beartrap Peak" *(Courtney Purcell: October 9, 2010)*
-Long Point *(Courtney Purcell: October 9, 2010)*
-"Jumbled Knoll" *(Harlan Stockman, Courtney Purcell & DB: October 16, 2010)*
-"Red Cone" *(Courtney Purcell, DB & Harlan Stockman: October 16, 2010)*
-"Little Northgate" *(Courtney Purcell: October 17, 2010)*
-"Stevens Peak" *(Reed McCoy, Courtney Purcell & Bryan Long: October 24, 2010)*
-"Arch Peak" *(Courtney Purcell & DB: October 29, 2010)*
-"Aeolian Point" *(Courtney Purcell: October 31, 2010)*
-Stapley Point *(Courtney Purcell: November 11, 2010)*
-"Das Peak" *(Courtney Purcell: November 12, 2010)*
-"Subway Peak" *(Courtney Purcell: November 12, 2010)*
-"Whale Peak" *(Courtney Purcell, Bob Sihler & Sarah and Dominic Meiser: April 20, 2011)*
-"East Neagle" *(Courtney Purcell: May 8, 2011)*
-Neagle Ridge *(DB & Courtney Purcell: May 8, 2011)*
-"Dennett Mountain" *(Courtney Purcell: June 4, 2011)*
-"Icebox Knoll" *(DB & Courtney Purcell: October 2, 2011)*
-"Bulloch Peak" *(DB, Courtney Purcell & Andy Archibald: October 28, 2011)*
-"Freezer Point" *(Courtney Purcell, DB & Andy Archibald: October 29, 2011)*

-"Turkey Peak" *(Andy Archibald, Courtney Purcell, DB & Sarah and Dominic Meiser: November 24, 2011)*

-"Consolation Peak" *(Courtney Purcell: November 26, 2011)*

-"Kolob Guardian East" *(RJ Hooper: 2012-ish)*

-"Emerald Peak" *(Bryan Long, James Hiebert, Courtney Purcell & Sarah and Dominic Meiser: November 19, 2012)*

-"Inclivins Point" *(Courtney Purcell, Bryan Long, James Hiebert & Sarah and Dominic Meiser: November 19, 2012)*

-"Elkhorn Peak" *(Courtney Purcell, James Hiebert, Bryan Long & Sarah and Dominic Meiser: November 23, 2012)*

-"Dead Tree Peak" *(James Hiebert, Courtney Purcell, Bryan Long & Sarah and Dominic Meiser: November 23, 2012)*

-"Imlay Point" *(Courtney Purcell: October 12, 2013)*

-Inclined Temple *(Dan Stih & Mike Schasch: November 2013)*

-"Peak Inaccessible" *(Dow Williams, Courtney Purcell & Andy Archibald: November 6, 2013)*

-"North Cougar Point" *(Courtney Purcell: November 9, 2013)*

-"Rabbit Ears" *(Sarah and Dominic Meiser & Courtney Purcell: November 29, 2013)*

-Upsilon Temple *(Courtney Purcell, Giles Wallace & Sarah and Dominic Meiser: November 30, 2013)*

-"Elephants Head" *(aka The Red Triangle; +37.2484 -113.0451; Garrett Weaver & Andrew Shipley: April 20, 2014)*

-"Artifact Arch Peak" *(Courtney Purcell: April 3, 2015)*

-Ivins Mountain *(Dan Stih & Matt Mower: April 4, 2015)*

-"Stevenson Peak" *(+37.3031 -113.0078; Owen Lunz & Darin Berdinka: April 17, 2015)*

-"Great White Dome" *(+37.2952 -113.0087; Owen Lunz & Darin Berdinka: April 17, 2015)*

-"Iron Lion" *(+37.2880 -113.0214; Owen Lunz & Darin Berdinka: April 19, 2015)*

-"Avalokiteshvara Temple" *(Courtney Purcell: May 1, 2015)*

-"Corral Hollow Peak" *(Andy Archibald & Courtney Purcell: May 13, 2015)*

-"Imsleepy Peak" *(Andy Archibald & Courtney Purcell: May 20, 2015)*

Heading into the backcountry after a spring snow storm

Acknowledgements

I'd like to thank some people:

-*My Zion peak partners*: Andy Archibald, Kevin Baker, Mark Beauchamp, Bo Beck, Jenn Beuchat, Mike Blackeye, Terence Bolden, Jeff Branin, Kristen Bridges, Donnie B, Michael Cressman, Lori Curry, Brett Dawson, DB, Dimples, Nga Do, Ed Forkos, Ron Graham, Carsten Habenicht, James Hiebert, Matthew Holliman (the first person to dayhike each of the 249 peaks on the Sierra Club's *Sierra Peaks Section* list—a notable endeavor once believed to be impossible), Rob Hooper, Walt Hutton, Jeff Jackson, Tom Jones, Rick "Iron Man" Kent, Luba Leef, Bryan Long, Andy Mac, Julie Marple, Kip Marshall, Rob Marshall, Reed McCoy, Sarah & Dominic Meiser, Mike with the Camera, Military Devon, Tanya Milligan, Steve Newell, Tom O'Brien, "Parks Pass" Patrick, Stan Pitcher, Randi Poer, Aron Ralston, Ram, Aaron Ramras, Michele Reyes, Ryan from Provo, Jared Seaquist, Mike Schasch, Rosie Sheppard, Bob Sihler, Matt Smith, Spidey & company, Harlan Stockman, Dwight Sunwall, Carrie Toelle, Giles Wallace, Jenny West, Dow Williams and all the other people I'm overlooking, for the company, conversations, contributions, accommodations, knowledge, expertise, enthusiasm, talent, assistance and tolerance;

-My beta providers: Steve Ramras (aka Ram) deserves thanks more than any other for the early info, vision and passion that eventually helped me up many of my favorite and most sought-after Zion peaks;

-For their technical assistance, unselfish donating of terrific photography, many hours of map-creating, guidance, suggestions, visions and inspirations, permissions, constructive criticism, comments and requests, time spent editing, proofreading and formatting, or general support of this project: Andy Archibald, Bo Beck (Zion Search and Rescue veteran; co-author of *Favorite Hikes In and Around Zion National Park*), Jeff Branin, Joe Braun (Joe Braun Photography at www.citrusmilo.com), DB, Buzz Burrell (blog.ultimatedirection.com), Shane Burrows (www.climb-utah.com), Jared Campbell (door5.com), Hazel Clark (Vishnu Temple Press), Michael Cressman, Rob Hooper (rjhooperphotography.blogspot.com), Tom Jones (www.CanyoneeringUSA.com), Rick Kent, John Kirk (for his addictive website: www.listsofjohn.com), Bryan Long (peakaestheticproductions.com), Tom Martin (Vishnu Temple Press), Sarah Meiser (www.13ergirl.com), Tanya Milligan (co-author of *Favorite Hikes In and Around Zion National Park*), Aron Ralston (author of *Between a Rock and a Hard Place*), Ram, Mike Schasch, Bob Sihler, Dan Stih, Harlan Stockman (hwstock.org), Dow Williams (www.dowclimbing.com), Bill Wright (co-author of *Speed Climbing!: How to Climb Faster and Better*), and Zion National Park (specifically, Ray O'Neil and Annette Werderich). Thanks to Steve Allen for the sheer awesomeness of his two-volume mega-fascinating *Utah's Canyon Country Place Names*. I'd also like to acknowledge the resources that are www.bigwalls.net and the American Alpine Club, for assistance with my research of various projects;

-& Dean Molen for the idea.

Index

www.ingramcontent.com/pod-product-compliance
Lightning Source LLC
Chambersburg PA
CBHW061559110426
42742CB00038B/1538